# Peaceful Islamist Mobilization in the Muslim World

# Peaceful Islamist Mobilization in the Muslim World

## What Went Right

Julie Chernov Hwang

First published in hardcover in 2009 by
PALGRAVE MACMILLAN® in the
United States - a division of St. Martin's Press LLC,
175 Fifth Avenue, New York, NY 10010.

Where this book is distributed in the UK, Europe and the
rest of the world, this is by Palgrave Macmillan, a division
of Macmillan Publishers Limited, registered in England,
company number 785998, of Houndmills, Basingstoke,
Hampshire RG21 6XS.

Palgrave Macmillan is the global academic imprint of the above
companies and has companies and representatives throughout the
world.

Palgrave® and Macmillan® are registered trademarks in the United States,
the United Kingdom, Europe and other countries.

ISBN: 978-0-230-12070-9

The Library of Congress has cataloged the hardcover edition as follows:

Chernov Hwang, Julie.
    Peaceful Islamist mobilization in the Muslim world: what went right / Julie
Chernov Hwang.
        p. cm.
    Includes bibliographical references and index.
    ISBN-13: 978-0-230-61767-4 (alk. paper)
    ISBN-10: 0-230-61767-0 (alk. paper)
        1. Political participation—Islamic countries. 2. Islam and politics.
    3. Political parties—Islamic countries. 4. Islamic countries—Politics
    and government. I. Title.

    JQ1852.A91C44 2009
    323'.042091767—dc22                                        2008055873

A catalogue record of the book is available from the British Library.

Design by Macmillan Publishing Solutions

First PALGRAVE MACMILLAN paperback edition: December 2011

10 9 8 7 6 5 4 3 2 1

Transferred to Digital Printing in 2011

*For Dae*

# Contents

# List of Figures

# List of Tables

# Acknowledgments

I have benefited greatly from the input and sagely advice of scholars in the United States, Indonesia, Singapore, Malaysia, and Turkey. Most notably, I wish to express my profound gratitude and deep respect for Dr. William Safran, my dissertation chair and advisor at the University of Colorado-Boulder. Thank you for taking me on, as your last graduate student, and working with me through the nuts and bolts of this project. Your insight and input have been invaluable to me over the years. You have taught me what it means to be a good scholar, colleague, and mentor, not only through your advice, good humor, and subtle criticism, but also by your example.

I am also indebted to my dissertation committee: Sumit Ganguly, Fred Denny, Sven Steinmo, and Peter Gries, whose constructive comments had a profound impact on the development of this project. I am deeply grateful to Greg Barton for his advice on case selection and for his insights on radical Islam in Indonesia and progressive Islam in Indonesia and Turkey and to Steve Chan, Colin Dueck, Sam Fitch, and Kim Niles for their advice while this project was being conceptualized. I also want to thank Jenny Kehl for her suggestions on how to improve the introduction as well as Ihsan Ali Fauzi and Badrus Sholeh for their feedback on the Indonesia chapters. I am indebted to the anonymous reviewers at Palgrave, *International Political Science Review, Indonesia*, and *Asian Security* for their rigorous critiques on the Indonesia and Turkey chapters. I would also like to express my deep appreciation to Farideh Koohi-Kamali and Asa Johnson at Palgrave Press for their hard work on this project. Their advice, support, and knowledge of the market have been invaluable. Erin Ivy and the editorial teams at Palgrave Macmillan and Macmillan Publishing Solutions did a great job of sharpening the language.

In Indonesia, I wish to thank those who provided comments, who discussed their views with me, who let me interview them, and who assisted in the research and data-gathering process. This work would not have been possible without the assistance of the Freedom Institute for Democracy, xiv • Acknowledgments

Nationalism and Market Studies in Jakarta and the scholars who reside there: Dr. Rizal Mallarangeng, Dr. Saiful Mujani, Hamid Basyaib, Nong Darol Mahmada, Dr. Luthfi Assyaukanie, and Aan Sugianto Tandra. I want to express my gratitude to Kyai Hj Abdurrahman Wahid, Kyai Hj Hasyim Muzadi, Dr. Din Syamsuddin, Syafi'i Ma'arif, Azyumardi Azra, Abdul Mukti, Mutammimul Ula, Yoyoh Yusroh, Zulkieflimansyah, Zuhairi Misrawi, Mas'dar Masudi, Mariah Ulfah, Dr. Bahtiar Effendy, Badrus Sholeh, I.G. Wilakuda, Dr. Irwan Abdullah, Dr. Mochtar Mas'oed, Syafi Anwar, Dr. Mochtar Buchori, Kevin O'Rourke, Ichsan Ali Fauzi as well as numerous other leaders of Nahdlatul Ulama, Young NU, Fatayat Welfare Foundation, Muhammadiyah, Young Muhammadiyah, Jaringan Islam Liberal, the International Center for Islam and Pluralism, Lembaga Dakwah Kampus at UIN Syarif Hidayatullah, Hizbut Tahrir, Front Pembela Islam, Majelis Mujihideen Indonesia, Partai Keadilan Sejahtera, Partai Kebangkitan Bangsa, Partai Bulan Bintang, and Partai Persatuan Pembangunan and so many others, who took time from their schedules to meet with me and discuss their organizations and their views on the role of Islam in politics, the democratic transition, and the Indonesian state. Thank you also to Jennifer Epley, who was a sounding board, a friend, and a guide through Indonesian bureaucracy. I also want to express my deep appreciation to my two research assistants, A'an Suryana in Jakarta and Imam Malik Ridwan in Yogyakarta, for being such extraordinary fixers and friends. The Indonesia portion of this project is stronger for their hard work, input, and assistance. I'd also like to thank the US-Indonesia Society for giving me a travel grant to support the hiring of these two research assistants.

In Malaysia, this work would not have been possible without the help of the University of Malaya and the Center for Civilizational Dialogue. Specifically, I wish to express my sincere gratitude to Dr. Azizan Baharuddin, who made me feel welcome and gave me access to the center's contacts and provided me with a workspace and facilities. There are so many scholars, NGO leaders, and political figures who let me interview them and who shared with me their impressions of their country and why mobilization there had remained so peaceful for so long. These include former prime minister Mahathir Muhammad, Dr. Syed Ali Tawfik Al Attas, Dr. Patricia Martinez, Dato Dr. Khoo Kay Kim, Dato Dr. Shamsul Amri Baharuddin, Dr. Osman Bakar, Dr. Zainah Anwar, Dr. Noraini Othman, Dr. Clive Kessler, Dr. Rosnani Hashim, Dr. Chandra Muzaffar, Dato Shahrir Abdul Samad, Zaid Kamaruddin, Tan Sri Dato Seri Dr. Ahmad Sarji Bin Abdul Hamid, Shahran Kasim, Rita Sim, Dr. Mohammad Hazim Shah, and many others. I would like to extend sincere appreciation to those from the University of Malaya branch in Kelantan who arranged my stay in that province and those from PAS and from the state government ministries who met with me during my time in Kota Bahru. Finally, I'd also express my gratitude to Dr. Abdi Omar, his wife, Salmi, and their children, Shafiqah and Abdu, who welcomed me into their home and treated me as a member of the family.

In Turkey, I wish to thank those scholars, NGO leaders, and politicians who permitted me to interview them and gave me insight into this complex and unique nation. These include Dr. Ilter Turan, Dr. Tufan Buzpinar, Dr.Ihsan Dagi, Dr.Nuri Tinaz, politicians from the AKP, and members of Fetullah Gulen. I would also like to thank Ali Bardakoglu, the president of the Diyanet Isleri Baskanligi, the Directorate of Religious Affairs, for agreeing to meet with me and discuss the role and responsibilities of this ministry. In addition, I would like to extend thanks to my dear colleagues, Ozge Celik, who arranged my stay in Ankara, and Murat Ozkaleli, who provided me with key contacts and important insights about Turkish politics and culture.

Finally, I wish to express my deepest and most profound gratitude, love, and respect for my family. To my parents, thank you for your unwavering support. To the Hwangs and the Kims, thank you for your understanding. To Dae, thank you for inspiring me, for knowing when to push me and when to help me relax, and above all for not being a political scientist. Thank you for bearing all of this with me.

# Abbreviations and Acronyms

| | |
|---|---|
| ABIM | Angkatan Belia Islam Malaysia (Malaysian Islamic Youth Movement) |
| AKP | Adalet ve Kalkinma Partisi (Justice and Development Party) |
| AL | Awami League |
| BA | Barisan Alternatif |
| BN | Barisan Nasional |
| BNP | Bangladesh National Party |
| DAP | Democratic Action Party |
| DDII | Dewan Dakwah Islamiyah Indonesia (Indonesian Islamic Propagation Council) |
| FP | Fazilet Partisi (Virtue Party) |
| FPI | Front Pembela Islam (Islamic Defenders Front) |
| Golkar | Golongan Karya (Functional Groups) |
| HuJI | Harkat ul-Jihad-al-Islami (Movement of the Islamic Holy War) |
| HT | Hizbut Tahrir |
| ICM | Islamic Constitution Movement |
| ICMI | Ikatan Cendekiawan Muslim Se-Indonesia (Association of Indonesian Muslim Scholars) |
| IKIM | Institut Kefahamaman Islam Malaysia (Malaysian Institute for Islamic Understanding) |
| IOJ | Islami Oikya Jote (Islamic Unity Front) |
| ISTAC | International Institute of Islamic Thought and Civilization |
| JAKIM | Jabatan Kemajuan Islam Malaysia (Department for the Advancement of Islam) |
| JI | Jemaah Islamiyah (Islamic Community) |
| JIL | Jaringan Islam Liberal (Liberal Islam Network) |
| JIM | Jamaah Islah Malaysia (Society for Islamic Reform) |
| JMB | Jordanian Muslim Brotherhood |

| | |
|---|---|
| JMB | Jama'atul Mujihideen Bangladesh (Community of the Mujihideen of Bangladesh) |
| JMJB | Jagrata Muslim Janata Bangladesh (Awakened Muslim Masses of Bangladesh) |
| LJ | Laskar Jihad (Holy War Militia) |
| Masyumi | Majelis Syura Muslimin Indonesia (Consultative Council on Indonesian Muslims) |
| MDI | Majelis Dakwah Indonesia (Indonesia Dawkah Council) |
| MMI | Majelis Mujihideen Indonesia (Indonesian Holy Warriors Council) |
| MSP | Milli Selamet Partisi (National Salvation Party) |
| MUI | Majelis Ulama Indonesia (Indonesian Ulama Council) |
| NU | Nahdlatul Ulama (Awakening of the Scholars) |
| PAN | Partai Amanat Nasional (National Mandate Party) |
| PAS | Partai Islam se-Malaysia (Malaysian Islamic Party) |
| PDI-P | Partai Demokrat Indonesia-Perjuangan (Indonesian Democratic Party-Struggle) |
| PBB | Partai Bulan Bintang (Crescent and Star Party) |
| PK | Partai Keadilan (Justice Party) now PKS |
| PKB | Partai Kebangkitan Bangsa (National Awakening Party) |
| PKS | Partai Keadilan Sejahtera (Prosperous Justice Party) |
| PKR | Partai Keadilan Rakyat (People's Justice Party) |
| PPP | Partai Persatuan Pembangunan (United Development Party) |
| RP | Refah Partisi (Welfare Party) |
| SARA | Suku, Agama, Ras, Antar-Golongan (Tribe, Religion, Race, Inter-Communal Relations) |
| THB | Turkish Hizballah |
| UMNO | United Malays National Organization |
| YIP | Yemeni Islah Party |

# CHAPTER 1

# Introduction

The central message of this book is that the state matters. Muslim states are often characterized as dictatorial and repressive or overwhelmed and powerless in the face of mushrooming Islamist movements, which will take over if the states initiate political liberalization. However, such views represent gross exaggerations. Muslim states can and do influence—through their policies, the institutions for participation they permit, and their capacity to function effectively—the mobilization strategies that Islamist groups choose. They can be positive actors by providing political access and public goods. This book illuminates these powers of the state.

This book begins with the Islamic revival in the early 1970s and continues through 2006. That 35-year period witnessed a proliferation of new Islamist movements throughout the Middle East, Muslim Asia, and Africa. Many of these revivalists believed that Islam provided a comprehensive political, economic, and social system with the potential to succeed where the foreign ideologies of capitalism, socialism, and nationalism had failed. With the onset of the Islamic revolution in Iran, they began to see the power that Islam held for effecting a change of status-quo authoritarian, corrupt, and, all too often, Western-supported governments. Some of these movements advocated the reestablishment of the caliphate or the development of Iranian-style Islamic states. Others had more modest goals, persuading Muslims to become more pious or improving the quality of Islamic education.

Depending on the country, Islamic revivalists adopted different strategies. In Turkey, after the political liberalization of the mid-1980s, Islamist groups began to mobilize through newfound political openings. Sufi brotherhoods grew more active, and sympathetic newspapers were launched. When the Refah Party (Welfare Party, RP) came into existence in 1983, it developed intricate networks for garnering support, often on the basis of the social services it offered. After its victory in the national elections in 1995, it formed a coalition government with the center-right Dogru Yol Partisi (True Path Party, DYP). In Malaysia, after the state adopted a more favorable stance toward the Islamization of society, leaders of the influential Angkatan Belia Islam Malaysia (Muslim Youth Movement of Malaysia, ABIM) agreed to a co-optation and an alliance with the state. Co-opted leaders proceeded to take active roles in promoting Islamic banking, establishing an Islamic university and limiting gambling. In contrast, in Indonesia, during the 1970s and 1980s the New Order government was highly suspicious of resurgent Islam. Therefore, much of early revivalism in Indonesia was quietist, tending to focus more on enhancing personal piety, improving Islamic education, and providing an outlet for sociocultural expression than on formal Islamist politics.

Numerous revivalist movements initially took root on college campuses. Malaysia's ABIM was an indigenous *dakwah* (Islamic propagation) movement that fused Islamic revivalism with Malay nationalism. The Islamic Representative Council, in contrast, was established by Malays who had studied in Great Britain and were influenced by the revivalist ideologies of the Middle East. In Indonesia, Gerakan Tarbiyah (education movement) took root in public university campuses, inspired by the teachings of Hasan al Bana and the Egyptian Muslim Brotherhood. In Egypt, the militant al Gamma al Islamiyah set up summer camps for Muslim youths to learn how to live Islamically. Throughout the Muslim world, revivalists formed study circles, grassroots organizations, madrasas, social welfare organizations, camps, and charities to achieve the goals of greater Islamization of society and often the state.

Other Islamist groups attempted to effect change through violent strategies. In Algeria, in the 1990s, the Armee Islamique du Salut (AIS) and the Armed Islamic Group (GIA) waged a civil war against each other. Bangladesh has seen a proliferation of radical movements, particularly in the Southeast, near the Burma border. In 2005, Jamaatul Mujihideen Bangladesh (JMB) and Jagrata Muslim Janata Bangladesh (JMJB) coordinated the explosion of 450 bombs in cities throughout the country in an hour. In Indonesia, the Front Pembela Islam (FPI) employs intimidation and destruction of property in its drive for the enforcement of anti-vice laws. Weak states often face problems with violent Islamist mobilization, most notably countries with lawless regions where state authority is not dominant. It has been a challenge for these states to muster sufficient capacity to end the violence.

The study of Islamist mobilization is important due to its timeliness. With the ongoing politicization of Islam and increased terrorism by radical

Muslim groups over the past decade, the attention of policy makers, scholars, and media outlets has been drawn more acutely to the Muslim world. However, inaccurate generalizations are often made about the character of Islamist movements and of political Islam itself. Much as certain sects of Judaism and Christianity push their adherents to improve personal piety, many Islamic revivalist movements encourage Muslims to become more observant. Islamic revivalists cannot be simply categorized as orthodox, traditionalist, or fundamentalist. They may subscribe to any one of the numerous Islamic sects, movements, or organizations from politicized Salafi groups to mystic Sufi *tarikats* (brotherhoods) to quietist missionaries like the Tablighis to syncretist Sunni traditionalists from Nahdlatul Ulama (NU). It is important to note that among the many groups that seek a greater role for Islam in society and politics, only a fraction endorses an Islamic state based on the Iranian or Taliban model, and of those, a limited number employs violent strategies. In Pakistan, which is often assumed to be a hotbed of Islamist radicalism, only an estimated 10–15 percent of all madrasas espouse radical sectarian ideologies.[1] The majority of Islamist groups consistently take advantage of new opportunities for political participation. It is important that scholars and policy makers see Islamist radicalism in context.

This book departs from many other studies on political Islam in two main ways. First, it proposes a new framework for examining state-Islamist group relations and the variation in Islamist mobilization. Numerous studies today focus on collective violence and rebellion. They highlight the role of external forces in fostering violent Islamist mobilization, the nexus between exclusion and indiscriminate repression, and the way in which anomie and identity crises can lead young Muslims to join radical movements.[2] These studies tend to view the state as a negative actor that coerces, represses, and manipulates. However, few studies to date have highlighted the potential positive powers of the state. This book demonstrates the power that the state possesses for limiting violence in the name of Islam, not through brute force but rather by providing public goods and opportunities for participation.

Second, numerous studies on political Islam today are single-country case studies often focusing on a single social movement or conflict.[3] These books are invaluable contributions to an understanding of Islamism in the countries they, respectively, cover. However, their theoretical ramifications often do not extend beyond the case at hand. They illuminate the behavior of Hamas in Gaza, the evolution of collective violence in Indonesia, or the reasons for the rise of Islamist militancy in Bangladesh, but they do not put forth theories that have the potential for generalization across countries and regions. The goal of this book is to posit a framework for analyzing state-Islamist group relations that can be applicable to states both in Muslim Asia and the larger Islamic world.

## The Importance of Political Participation

While some scholars contend that Islam is incompatible with democracy, this assumption is false.[4] The results of the 1995–1996 and 2000–2002 World Values Surveys indicate that between 92 and 99 percent of Muslims living in Albania, Egypt, Bangladesh, Azerbaijan, Indonesia, Morocco, and Turkey support democratic institutions.[5] John Esposito and James Piscatori highlight the willingness of Islamist movements in Algeria, Egypt, Jordan, Pakistan, and Tunisia to form political parties, contest elections, and work through parliamentary processes.[6] The Koran requires only that governments be consultative, just, and non-oppressive, making no mention of an obligation to provide an "Islamic state."[7] The problem is not that Islam is somehow antithetical to democracy. Instead, the question is whether Muslim states provide Islamist groups with opportunities for political participation through institutionalized channels.

Numerous scholars have noted the benefits that institutional inclusion has on social movements.[8] Samuel Huntington and Giovanni Sartori highlighted the importance of institutionalized channels for political participation as a hedge against instability and violence.[9] Huntington argued that countries become unstable when the rates of social mobilization exceed the development of political institutions and their capacity to channel popular discontent.[10] Most often, this situation occurs in transitional regimes with a diverse array of social forces or in authoritarian regimes that lack channels for political participation. Without proper institutions, there is no way to communicate popular interests to decision makers. More recently, Jack Snyder posed a similar argument highlighting the necessity of capable democratic political institutions as a precursor to any democratic transition to prevent elites from utilizing exclusionary nationalism to foster instability and conflict.[11]

The application to Islamist movements is clear. Ali Abootalebi notes that while an institutionalized opposition may be successfully incorporated or co-opted into the political system, the chances for a crisis based on political exclusion increase when an opposition exists but lacks an institutional way to pressure the state.[12] Najib Ghadbian concurs, noting that in countries where Islamists have legal political parties or faux-party political movements, such as Jordan, Yemen, and Kuwait, Islamist violence is much rarer than in those countries that refuse to grant Islamist groups legal political status—Syria, Egypt, and Algeria.[13] Anwar Ibrahim argued that lack of political access and opportunities for participation play a significant role in the formation of violent groups.

> Bin Laden and his protégés... come from countries where political struggle through peaceful means is futile. In many Muslim countries, political dissent is simply illegal... These people need space to express their political and social concerns. But state control is total, leaving no room for civil society to grow.[14]

Ibrahim notes the importance of political openness in providing opportunities for political inclusion as a hedge against violent mobilization.

By these arguments, we should see less violence in Malaysia, Turkey, Morocco, and Jordan, where clear institutions exist, and more violence in Algeria, Egypt, and Syria, where those institutions are poorly developed, restricted, or nonexistent. Indeed this is true. However, participation alone is not sufficient. There are institutionalized channels for political participation in Yemen, Bangladesh, and Pakistan; yet, these countries have experienced high levels of Islamist violence. In Indonesia, even as the vast majority of Islamist groups use institutionalized political channels to work toward their goals, radical Islamist militias attack demonstrators who oppose their policy goals and target religious minorities. Thus, there must be other factors at work.

Social movement theorists studying collective violence and revolution often see political inclusion or exclusion operating in tandem with levels of repression. In his examination of revolutionary movements, Jeff Goodwin contends that revolutions are most likely to occur in exclusionary, indiscriminately repressive, and infrastructurally weak states.[15] In his study of Islamist rebellions, Mohammed Hafez largely concurs with Goodwin, noting that Islamist movements are most likely to turn violent when

> they encounter exclusionary states that deny them meaningful access to political institutions and employ indiscriminate repressive policies against their citizens during periods of mass mobilization. Political exclusion and state repression unleash a dynamic of radicalization characterized by exclusive rebel [groups] that isolate Islamist from the broader society and foster anti-system ideologies.[16]

While Goodwin and Hafez's arguments provide a compelling answer to the question of rebellion, their arguments are less convincing when applied to communal violence that stops short of revolt. There are numerous cases of states having experienced high levels of internal violence, although they have not repressed indiscriminately. In Pakistan and Bangladesh, there has been no indiscriminate repression; yet, there are frequent outbursts of violence by radical Islamist groups. Between 1998 and 2002, when violence by radical Islamist (and radical Christian) militias was at its height in Indonesia, repression by security services was at its nadir. In Indonesia, youth clashes between Christian and Muslim gangs often spiraled into riots in the years following the collapse of the New Order, while incidents of perceived insult to religious faith sparked violence during the Suharto period.[17] Thus, other elements must be at play.

### The Evil Is External: Laying the Blame at the Feet of External Forces

Some scholars attribute increasing militancy to various external forces. In some Muslim circles, radical Islam is seen as a backlash against the West—its foreign policy, culture, and values. Some Muslim activists fear that the increasing influence of Western culture will lead to the erosion of Muslim culture, political power, and military defense, culminating in the eventual domination of Muslim countries by Western powers.[18] The "Western attack" on Islam has become a rallying cry for drawing Muslims to radical organizations and for inflaming their fears of domination by Western powers. Another "external forces" argument underscores the destabilizing influence of international extremist networks. Since September 11, 2001, scholars such as Zachary Abuza and Stephen Schwartz have highlighted the role of Afghan veterans and the export of Wahabi ideology, respectively, in fomenting violent Islamist mobilization. Schwartz cautions against a global Wahabi campaign to dominate the Islamic discourse.[19] According to his argument, the Wahabi export movement seeks out recruits in countries where Muslims are mired in war and poverty, such as Tajikistan, Afghanistan, Chechnya, and Lebanon, in the hope of fostering support among Muslims for a Wahabi-modeled state in the conflict-ridden countries.[20]

These external forces arguments tend to oversimplify the issue at hand. Many Islamist groups may be concerned about undue Western influence, but few take violent action against the West or symbols of it. The contention that external forces are a key causal agent obscures more proximate domestic causes of violence such as elite manipulation, political exclusion, economic marginalization, or indiscriminate repression. In Indonesia, the conflicts in Maluku and Central Sulawesi between 1998 and 2002 were rooted in economic grievances. The ongoing Indo-Pak conflict has its roots in a land dispute over Kashmir, as did the Azerbaijani-Armenian conflict in the 1990s over Nagorno-Karabakh. While funding from external forces often aids domestic radical groups in continuing violence, they are rarely the primary cause.

## A Backlash of a Different Sort: Grievances Due to Modernization

Other scholars have explained the rise of radical Islam as a response to Muslims nations' failed attempts at modernization.[21] Peasants flock to the cities and are unable to find satisfactory employment. They live in disease-infested slums, where the government provides them with little, if anything, in terms of education, social services, and sanitation. The benefits of modernization do not sufficiently reach them, which engenders anomie.[22] Some socio-psychological scholars argue that radical Islamism is a result of regimes breaking the bargain they had made with their populations in the 1950s and 1960s, where "the subjects relinquished their claims to basic civil rights in return for the state providing them with education and health care, employment, subsidies for necessities such as staples, cooking gas and transportation."[23] Thus, by this argument, it was this weakening of the state, its inability to provide services to the urbanizing population that led some disgruntled youths to join radical organizations.[24]

If we are looking for a generalizable theory to explain the variation in Islamist mobilization strategies, the backlash against modernization does not accomplish this goal. Although many radical Islamist movements emerged from the socioeconomic dislocation that characterized the 1960s and 1970s, so too did numerous organizations that utilized peaceful strategies and rejected violence.[25] These theories address why people joined Islamist organizations but not why some organizations eschewed violence while others embraced it. In addition, since these theories tend to be rooted in the socioeconomic dislocations of the 1960s, 1970s, and 1980s, many do not take into account the political liberalization taking place in many Muslim states today, which has increased opportunities for political participation, and as a result, state legitimacy.

## Defining Concepts

Since this book highlights the variation in Islamist mobilization, it is necessary to define both peaceful and violent Islamist mobilization. Peaceful Islamist mobilization implies a group dynamic. It may include forming political parties, contesting elections, establishing alliances, developing state-civil society partnerships, and starting civil society organizations. It may consist of working with government agencies to propose and adopt more policies rooted in Islamic values. It often involves formation of alliances at the state and local levels among parties, between Islamist organizations and like-minded parties, and among Islamist organizations to pursue common systemic goals.

Violent mobilization also implies a group dynamic. A violent act may be committed by an individual or a group. Violent mobilization, however, includes targeting individuals or groups that oppose a movement's goals or strategic choices, minority religious sects, and certain segments of the population as well as rioting, collective violence, or revolt. Attacks on property would also fall into this category as would acts of intimidation. It is not one Muslim individual killing one Christian individual, for such an event could occur for a variety of reasons that have little to do with religion.

Another term utilized throughout this book is "state capacity." In its simplest form, effective state capacity implies the ability to provide specific public goods, most notably law and order, education, social welfare, and poverty relief. In so doing, the state has a positive presence in the lives of its citizens. While a state's capacity can also refer to bureaucratic ability to "make the trains run on time" or to wider "environmental capacities," this book utilizes a more narrow definition, focusing on the tangible products that point to the presence or absence of the state.

Scholars, politicians, and journalists use various terms in discussing Islamist politics. The term "Islamism" is frequently used for the ideology of political Islam. Islamism seeks a greater role for Islam in the government, economy, and society of Muslim countries. The practitioners of Islamism are Islamists, and while some may seek an Islamic state based on sharia, others may simply want a greater role for Islam in Muslim society. The policies they advocate are often classified as Islamization and shariatization, meaning they aim to make the country more reflective of "Islamic values" and, in many instances, sharia, often through the legislative process. Another related concept is *dakwah* or Islamic propagation. *Dakwah* organizations focus on grassroots efforts to encourage Muslims to become more pious. They seek to transform society from the ground upward, beginning with Muslim individuals. Some are politically Islamist, while others are apolitical.

Some scholars use the term "Islamist" to denote Muslims who utilize strategies of violence. However, most Islamists work to increase the influence of Islam in the public sphere employing nonviolent methods, and as such, this book uses "Islamist" to denote groups that utilize peaceful strategies. I prefer to use the term "radical Islamist" to refer to groups that utilize violent strategies because they advocate drastic social transformation and are willing to use violence, intimidation, and destruction of property to achieve their end. Radicals reject the possibility of engagement with the state and participation in the political system. On occasion, I may use the term "militant Islamist" interchangeably with radical Islamist. These terms are not always black and white. Some movements may use a combination of peaceful and violent strategies, lobbying and petitioning on the one hand and destroying property on the other. Some groups use nonviolent methods in their own activities, but tacitly endorse violence by other domestic actors. Still others may employ peaceful strategies but advocate revolutionary change, for example, the establishment of a pan-Islamic caliphate. So long as those particular movements are specified as such, this is not problematic for the purposes of this book.

### The Variation in Islamist Mobilization Explained: The Importance of the Participation-Capacity Nexus

How are some states able to encourage Islamist groups to employ peaceful strategies and eschew violence, while other states are seemingly unable? The question posed here addresses variation in state behavior, and how this has an impact on the strategic responses of Islamist movements. The central argument put forth in this book is that states can influence Islamist mobilization strategies in three main ways: They can encourage Islamist groups to adopt peaceful strategies by providing opportunities for political participation. When states permit political participation through institutionalized channels, the vast majority of Islamist groups will react strategically and use those channels to pursue their goals. However, it is not sufficient for states to promote systemic strategies; they must also actively take steps to discourage violent, anti-systemic ones. Some Islamist groups are amenable to utilizing strategies of violence and intimidation, and it is not sufficient to provide them with channels for political participation. The state must go a step further and discourage radical groups from employing violence by ensuring (a) law and order within its borders and (b) a measure of education and social services. By providing these public goods, the state maintains a positive presence in the lives of its citizens and gains legitimacy as a result. Equally important, radical Islamist groups are thwarted from making inroads and popularity gains at the state's expense.

If the state fails to ensure either law and order or education and social welfare, Muslims often become more reliant on the Islamic social service sector for these public goods. While mainstream Islamist NGOs offer critical supplementary services, this also gives radical movements an opportunity to exploit the state's lapses for their own ends, providing security and protection in lieu of the state and gaining a measure of legitimacy in the process. In these instances, external forces (Afghan veterans, international terrorist groups, meddling revolutionary neighbors) exacerbate the violent mobilization already taking place, by funneling money, weapons, materials, and training to radical Islamist groups. In contrast, if the state can maintain law and order within its territories and provide a measure of education and social welfare, the influence of external forces will be far more limited.

## Variation in Participation: Institutionalized Channels for Participation versus Exclusion

An ideal participatory state would not merely hold elections, but create an atmosphere conducive for political parties and civil society organizations to emerge, develop, and operate. Elections would be largely free and fair, and the state would not curtail the right of the political parties to participate. These parties would have platforms and staying power and not simply function as personal electoral vehicles. They would seek to achieve their goals through the system, rather than through revolutionary or anti-systemic means. They would utilize elections and lawmaking as a means of changing policy. Islamist parties may try to make incremental gains by passing sharia-inspired laws on such issues as interest-free banking, personal modesty, Koran literacy, and the status and quality of Islamic education. They may form issue-based alliances within the legislature or local-level governing alliances. In countries with a dominant party, opposition parties may not prevail nationally, but they can win control of state and municipal governments and increase seats in the national legislature. In other words, the dominant party would not win at all levels.

NGOs from across the politico-religious spectrum would be able to form, conduct programs, and generally draw support to their causes through clear and institutionalized processes and channels. They can work with the state without being co-opted and join the bureaucracy or the government without becoming token figures. They can form umbrella coalitions to leverage their influence when they lobby the legislature, participate in hearings, and hold petition drives. They can act as watchdog organizations without being disbanded, and at least some public criticism of the state would be tolerated. The actual proscription of an organization would be rare, rather than a common feature of state-civil society relations.

## Variation in State Capacity

A state is considered to possess effective capacity when it fulfills two conditions. First, it maintains law and order within the territories within its borders so that there are no lawless regions where state authority either cannot penetrate or does not dominate. In other words, the state possesses a monopoly on the legitimate use of force and enforces the rule of law. Second, it plays a significant role in the social service sector. I am not contending that Muslim nations must adopt European-style welfare states. Ideally, the state would be engaged in the provision of education, social welfare and poverty relief as a major player with Islamist groups, mainstream Islamic mass organizations, and secular organizations playing supplemental roles. By providing the public with tangible goods and services, a state can improve perceptions of legitimacy. Through education, the state not only has an impact on the personal and material development of young people but also has the opportunity to impart its own secular, nationalist and/or Islamic values. An effective state also has the capacity to monitor Islamic schools and encourage them to work in an open manner. In some instances, the government may dictate the curriculum or set parameters for curricular development to ensure that portions of the religious school curriculum are devoted to secular studies such as mathematics, sciences, and language. In countries like Indonesia, which has an independent Islamic school tradition, it may mean that the state provides opportunities for Islamic schools to augment their curriculum, without abandoning their fundamental religious content.

By contrast, a state which lacks effective capacity, or an ineffective state, will be unable to stem outbreaks of communal violence or preserve law and order in certain regions. Vigilante militias may take the law into their own hands with impunity. In some instances, elements within the state's bureaucracy or military may arm certain radical Islamist groups to take action against other perceived enemies. Some states may be adept at maintaining law and order but they may fall short in their ability to ensure either education or social welfare, ceding one or more spheres of influence to the Islamist social service sector. This often allows radical Islamist groups to make inroads at the state's expense, particularly through the supplemental provision of education. If a country has an powerful civil society, including mainstream Islamic mass organizations, these shortcomings in social welfare or education may be less problematic, for radical organizations will make less headway. These Islamic mass organizations and other civil society organizations will also be engaged in supplemental efforts and gain support in the process. For example, one out of every three Indonesians belongs to either NU or Muhammadiyah; these organizations offer Islamic education, supplemental health care, and poverty relief to their members. During the transition period immediately following the Asian Financial Crisis, when the state retrenched significantly in providing social welfare, the continued activities of NU and Muhammadiyah limited the ability of new radical Islamist movements to gain supporters and sympathizers by providing these services in lieu of the state.

## External Forces

External forces tend to exacerbate violent mobilization, but they are rarely the sole cause of it. While an external force may be positive, such as Turkey's desire to join the European Union or Fetullah Gulen's worldwide Islamic education movement, in this book, I will primarily examine negative external influences including (a) spillover effects from wars, (b) revolutionary neighbors, (c) Afghan veterans, and (d) transnational terrorist organizations. I argue that these negative external influences will not significantly destabilize those countries that are both participatory and effective. An effective state can limit the influence of spillover effects from wars, as Malaysia has with the conflict in southern Thailand. It is not only exceedingly difficult but also impractical for international terrorist organizations to set up training camps and bases of operations undetected in countries with effective security apparatuses. Finally, while the literature on violent mobilization notes the role of Afghan veterans in the creation of major radical groups, they have been comparably less active and destabilizing in states that enable institutionalized participation, such as Malaysia, Turkey, and Kuwait.

Table 1.1 clearly illustrates the relationship between effective capacity and channels for political participation. On the basis of the four boxes shown below, we can say that there are four categories of states: (a) effective participatory, (b) effective authoritarian, (c) ineffective participatory, and (d) ineffective authoritarian. The link between capacity and participation in each category has important implications for state-Islamist group relations.

**Table 1.1**  State effectiveness versus participation

|  | *Political participation* | *Lacking political participation* |
| --- | --- | --- |
| Effective state | Peaceful mobilization dominates/violence is rare | Islamist groups go underground. Mobilization is limited |
| Ineffective state | Mixed mobilization. Majority of Islamist groups use peaceful strategies. Some use violence to push boundaries of acceptable behavior | Highly violent mobilization |

**Category 1.1** The Effective Participatory State.

An effective participatory state provides opportunities for Islamist groups to participate in the political system while maintaining effective capacity in both law and order and social services. Thus, there are no lawless regions. The state also provides a measure of education and poverty relief, which allows it to maintain legitimacy on multiple bases—performance as well as citizen consent. In this environment, Islamist groups from across the politico-religious spectrum react strategically. If they engage in politics through the channels available to them, they can make gains. If they utilize strategies of violence and intimidation, they are not only likely to be arrested but also are unlikely to win popular support. Moreover, as their members came of age, they too benefited from the state's provision of education and social services. As a result, they may be less hostile to the state.

The state's capacities in the above-mentioned domains limit the ability of external forces to intervene. It is unlikely that wars in neighboring states will spill over. Capable security services can stymie terrorist plots. Revolutionary neighbors will be less successful in their attempts to exploit the grievances of minority populations if those groups too reap the benefits of the state's social services. In this model, peaceful and systemic strategies will be the dominant means of mobilization. Rarely will violent strategies be adopted.

There is significant variation among effective participatory states. Perhaps the best example of this kind of state is Malaysia, where the state provides opportunities for participation while maintaining effective capacity in both law and order and education and social welfare. Since 2000 Turkey has also become an effective participatory state, after it improved its law and order capacity in the 1990s. Contemporary Kuwait would also fit into this category, despite the fact that it is far less open than either Turkey or Malaysia.

**Category 1.2** The Effective Authoritarian State.

Effective authoritarian states do not permit participation through institutionalized channels. However, they maintain law and order within their territories and provide a measure of education and social welfare. Although the states may co-opt certain Islamist leaders into their bureaucracies, they do not allow them to offer substantive policy input. While Islamist movements may exist in a nonpolitical capacity to offer supplemental social services or religious assistance, their political activities will be inhibited and potential opposition movements repressed. This increases the likelihood that politico-Islamist movements will respond by going underground, often restricting their scope of social interaction to like-minded members and planning for the day when the state is more receptive to their goals. Effective authoritarian states' legitimacy is largely based on their ability to deliver goods and services to their populations, which is a particularly tenuous form of legitimacy. These states are also more repressive than the effective participatory states, for they view politico-Islamist groups as potential threats, rather than as opposition movements or as parties among others. While the states will still be able to limit the ability of some external forces to intervene, they may face threats from others who prey on the frustration of particular aggrieved groups.

In the short term, the states may have the ability to discourage radical Islamist groups from mobilizing violently. However, should state capacity falter in times of crisis, effective authoritarian states are liable to see a significant increase in violence. Furthermore, they are more likely to face ongoing instances of violence by underground radical movements, who reject the state's legitimacy and refuse to abide by the rules of the game.

Indonesia in the New Order era and Bahrain fit well into this category, for both states capably provided education and social welfare and prevented the emergence of lawless regions. However, they limited participation, which drove oppositional groups underground. In Bahrain, this enabled revolutionary Iran to exploit the grievances of the disenfranchised Shiite majority and channel weapons and aid to radical Shiite groups.

**Category 1.3**   The Ineffective Participatory State.

An ineffective participatory state provides institutionalized channels for participation but falls short in its ability to maintain effective capacity either in law and order or education and social services or both. There may be lawless regions where the state authority cannot penetrate or does not dominate. In the best of circumstances, the state may capably offer some social services like education, while falling short in other areas like poverty relief. In some cases the state may offer education and social welfare, but the programs are poorly implemented and the benefits do not reach the people. At worst, the state may have altogether ceded the provision of public goods to the Islamic social service sector. There is likely to be a significant degree of intervention by external forces. An ineffective participatory state is likely to see mixed mobilization as the majority of Islamist groups take advantage of the opportunities to participate in the political system and work through systemic channels to achieve their goals. However, there is also likely to be a significant amount of violence by radical Islamist groups who exploit state weaknesses for their own ends.

There is tremendous diversity in the ineffective participatory state category, for it includes countries such as Indonesia, Bangladesh and Yemen. At one end is contemporary Indonesia, after the fall of Suharto, which arguably has the strongest institutionalized channels for participation in the Muslim world, but it struggles to improve the delivery mechanisms of social service programs and enforce the rule of law against local militias. At the other end, Yemen has fragile institutionalized channels for participation, and there are entire regions of the country where state authority does not dominate and the social service sphere has been ceded.

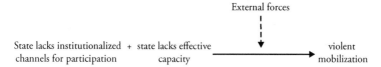

**Category 1.4** The Ineffective Authoritarian State.

An ineffective authoritarian state lacks both institutionalized channels for participation and sufficient capacity to provide public goods. There may be entire regions of territory where the state lacks a monopoly in the legitimate use of force. Intervention by external forces will be high. Radical movements will use strategies of violence and intimidation more frequently than in other types of states.

The variation among ineffective authoritarian states is also substantial. At one end, there are states such as Algeria, which severely retrenched public expenditure on education and social welfare and constrained the ability of Islamist groups to participate in politics; at the other end there are failed states such as Sudan. This category is beyond the scope of this book.

These four categories are not static or rigid. Some countries fit neatly and clearly into one, while others sit on the margins. Some states may even move between categories over time. For example, although opportunities for political participation have long existed in Turkey, it could not maintain law and order within its borders from the 1960s to the 1990s, particularly in the Southeast. In the late 1990s, it reasserted its control over the Southeast, which had been home to numerous radical movements, including the Kurdish Workers Party (PKK), Hizballah, and the Great East Islamic Raiders Front (IBDA-C). In doing so, it has moved from being an ineffective participatory state to an effective participatory state.

### Muslim Asian Cases

In this book, I examine four Asian Muslim cases: Indonesia under the New Order (1966–1998), Indonesia in the *reformasi* period (1998 to the present), Malaysia, and Turkey. I chose these cases to move away from the overemphasis on the Arab world. The majority of books written on Islam today highlight Arab cases; yet, the most democratic and prosperous countries in the Muslim world exist in Islamic Asia, where over 50 percent of Muslims live. Thus, I wanted to see, if I began with a different set of cases, would new factors emerge to explain the variation in Islamist mobilization strategies.

These cases vary significantly in terms of heterogeneity and regime type. Malaysia is 58 percent Muslim, and its political system is a hybrid of both democratic and authoritarian components, while Turkey is 99 percent Muslim and a democratic regime with an influential military. In Turkey and Malaysia, Islamists have long been able to form political parties and contest elections and work to achieve incremental goals from civil society. Indonesia, with an 88 percent Muslim majority, tells two very different stories. Indonesia was ruled by an authoritarian dictator, Suharto, from 1965 to 1998. During its early democratic transition period, from 1998 to 2003, it retained some authoritarian elements, most notably the military's continued role in politics and its territorial command structure. However, the country has made great strides toward democracy, eliminating seats for the military in the legislature, holding two free and fair elections, and the first direct elections for president in the nation's history in 2004. Thus, it is clear that these states vary in the opportunities they provide for political participation. In three cases, Indonesia post–New Order, Malaysia, and Turkey, the state has permitted Islamist groups to participate in the political system through various institutionalized channels. In contrast, New Order Indonesia severely limited the ability of Islamist groups to participate.

These states vary significantly in terms of their ability to maintain effective capacity. Of the four cases, Malaysia has been most successful in providing security, education, and social services. Turkey has been inconsistent in its ability to provide law and order while being quite competent in its provision of education and poverty relief. During the New Order era, Indonesia made great strides in improving the quality of education and social welfare for the general population but was unable to consistently ensure law and order within its territories, often being complicit in the disorder. Finally, contemporary Indonesia has struggled to provide public goods for its citizens. While it has developed programs for free education and a social safety net, there have been significant problems in implementation. While it has improved mightily since the early transition era, particularly in law and order, lingering challenges remain.

This book examines Indonesia as a microcosm of Islamist mobilization strategies, for it has experienced both extensive peaceful mobilization and episodic violent mobilization. On the one hand, the 1999 Indonesian elections constituted a victory for secular nationalist parties and moderate inclusive Islamist parties. On the other hand, during the same period, radical Islamist groups held violent demonstrations, ransacked bars and clubs, and bombed businesses of prominent government officials. This violent mobilization coexisted with the increasing proliferation of peaceful Islamist organizations and the institutionalization and consolidation of democratic political channels.

The Indonesian case illustrates many of the advances Muslim countries are making toward democratic development and the lingering impediments countries face in stemming violent mobilization. Throughout the Muslim world, in Jordan, Bahrain, Morocco, Turkey, and Malaysia, political systems are liberalizing. Some countries, such as Malaysia and Morocco, have a long history of peaceful activities and, for the foreseeable future, Islamist groups will continue to mobilize using the constructive channels available to them. However, for other countries, such as Pakistan, Yemen, and Bangladesh, the future remains bleak; these states have experienced increasing or consistently high levels of violent mobilization, which has destabilized entire regions or provinces.

## Methods and Field Research

In terms of research methodology, I utilized the comparative case study methodology to create structured-focused comparisons across the four cases: Malaysia, Indonesia during the New Order, Indonesia post–New Order, and Turkey. The primary period of focus of this book is 1970–2006, but I have updated the chapters on Indonesia, Malaysia, and Turkey in light of recent events, including the 2007 Turkish elections, the 2008 Malaysian elections, and the 2008 Indonesian joint ministerial statement on Ahmadiyah. The book will be in press at the time of the 2009 Indonesian elections.

I conducted field research for this book in Indonesia, Malaysia, Turkey, and Singapore in 2005, 2006, and 2008, which included over 100 elite interviews with key political actors, including scholars, bureaucrats from the education and religion ministries, members of parliament, party founders, leaders, and managers, Muslim activists, journalists, international NGO observers, heads of and teachers at Islamic boarding schools, and senior military officials. I attended demonstrations, party congresses, panel discussions, conferences, workshops, speeches, and meetings of NGOs on topics related to this book. I spent many hours researching in the libraries at the Institute for Southeast Asian Studies, Singapore; University of Malaya, Kuala Lumpur; and the Freedom Institute and the Center for Strategic and International Studies, Jakarta.

In Indonesia, I conducted research in three cities well known for Islamic activism: Jakarta, Yogyakarta, and Solo. While Yogyakarta has experienced mostly peaceful mobilization, Solo is known for being home to many radical Islamist movements. I interviewed academics at UIN Syarif Hidayatullah and Gadjah Mada University; party leaders from the National Awakening Party (PKB), Prosperous Justice Party (PKS), United Development Party (PPP), and Crescent and Star Party (PBB); and leaders from NU and Muhammadiyah as well as from Young NU, Young Muhammadiyah, and Fatayat NU Women's Wing subgroups. I met with leaders of the progressive Muslim communities at the Center for the Study of Islam and Society (LKIS), the Liberal Islam Network (JIL), and the International Center for Islam and Pluralism (ICIP) and ultraconservative Islamists from Hizbut Tahrir. In Yogyakarta and Solo, I interviewed leaders of radical Islamist movements, including the Front Pembela Islam (FPI) in Solo and the Majelis Mujihideen Indonesia (MMI) outside Yogyakarta.

I visited *pesantren* (Islamic boarding schools) run by Nahdlatul Ulama in Bogor and Yogyakarta in order to gain a greater understanding of the facilities available for these students and how they cooperate with the government in monitoring efforts. In addition, I interviewed headmasters and teachers from the radical Ngruki and Al-Mujihideen *pesantren* to learn their views on Indonesian politics, the legitimacy of the democratic system, and how they perceive state efforts to regulate them. I also met with officials from the Department of Religion to inquire about their assistance to the *pesantren* and the leaders of the Indonesian Society for Pesantren and Community Development (P3M) who discussed their efforts to aid the

Islamic boarding school community. I interviewed officials from the Ministry of Education and the Ministry of Statistics to better understand the post-New Order education reforms. Finally, I interviewed leaders from several international NGOs to gain their assessments of the strengths and weaknesses of the Indonesian political institutions, the challenges facing Indonesia in terms of law and order.

In Malaysia, time was divided between Kuala Lumpur and the state of Kelantan. In Kuala Lumpur, I interviewed leaders of the Malaysian Islamic Youth Movement (ABIM), Sisters in Islam, Perkim, the International Movement for a Just World (JUST), and Jemaah Islah Malaysia (JIM); members of parliament from the United Malays National Organization, the Malaysian Chinese Association, and Malaysian Islamic Party (PAS). The leaders and members of these organizations provided me great insight on how Islamist groups in Malaysia work for their goals. I met with bureaucrats from the Ministry of Education in the departments of Islamic education and curriculum development, who explained the various types of state-funded Islamic education, the component parts of the curriculum, and how the Malaysian government assists poor families in sending their kids to school. I spoke with numerous academics the University of Malaya, Malaysia National University, and the International Islamic University of Malaysia. We discussed the nature of state-Islamist group relations in Malaysia, why violent mobilization by Islamist groups is so rare in Malaysia, and how the Malaysian government provides social services.

Kelantan is a unique state in Malaysia, for it has been governed under sharia by the PAS since 1990. In Kota Bahru, capital of Kelantan, I interviewed state government ministers and officials from PAS. We discussed how PAS had changed its campaign strategy in the recent elections, how PAS governs Kelantan, and the programs through which PAS provides education and poverty relief to the residents of Kelantan. We also discussed the conflict in southern Thailand, and they informed me that it had not spilled over into Kelantan.

In Turkey, I conducted research in two cities: Istanbul and Ankara. I interviewed academics at Middle East Technical University, Ankara, and Fatih University, Istanbul, as well as think tank researchers at Islam Arastirmalari Merkezi (ISAM), Istanbul. These scholars provided me great insight into state-Islamist group relations in Turkey. I also met with members of parliament from the governing Adalet ve Kalkinma Partisi (Justice and Development Party, AKP) and a former member of the Refah women's wing. I also was fortunate to interview activists from Fetullah Gulen and the president of the Diyanet Isleri Baskanligi (Directorate of Religious Affairs).

## Structure of This Book

Chapter 2 analyzes the role of institutionalized participation and effective state capacity in Turkey, which is widely considered a secular state, but has a strong tradition of Islamist mobilization. First, it examines how alliances between Islamist organizations and political parties and between secular and religious-based political parties engendered greater engagement of Islamist groups in politics. Second, it identifies the reach of state authority and explains how inconsistent state control in the Southeast led to the emergence of radical Islamist groups, which used violence in the pursuit of their goals. It shows how violence decreased after the state reasserted its authority in the Southeast. Third, this chapter focuses on the dominance of the state in the provision of health care and education as well as the methods by which the state monitors and regulates Islamic *imam-hatip* schools. Finally, it examines the intervening role of external forces, most notably the influence of Iran, in funding and training Turkish radical Islamist groups, during those periods where the state lost control of the Southeast.

Chapter 3 examines Indonesia during Suharto's New Order and tests whether participation matters. It looks at the constraints that the Suharto regime put on participation and the three different reactions by Islamist groups: co-optation, depoliticization, and underground mobilization. Then, it analyzes the manner in which the Suharto regime maintained law and order, which was at once more repressive and also more inconsistent than in either Malaysia or Turkey. The chapter discusses the improvements the Suharto regime made in education and poverty reduction, with the supplemental assistance of NU and Muhammadiyah. Finally, it touches on the limited role played by external forces, arguing that the lack of influence by external forces (Afghan veterans, international terrorist networks) was largely a function of timing. For example, although Jemaah Islamiyah formed in 1993, it began to utilize terror-based strategies in late 1999, over a year after Suharto's resignation.

Chapter 4 examines Indonesia in the post–New Order period. First, it analyzes how sudden changes and new opportunities for political participation affected Islamist mobilization strategies. It highlights how Islamist groups have reacted strategically to these new channels. They have established political parties and contested elections, formed alliances within the legislature to work for their goals, made alliances between civil society and parties to act as effective pressure groups, and lobbied locally for the passage of legislation. Second, the chapter investigates how lapses in state authority may have encouraged certain Islamist organizations to utilize strategies of violence and intimidation in provinces experiencing communal conflict between 1999 and 2002 and thereafter in dealing with religious minorities. Third, it analyzes the well-meaning yet insufficient attempts by the state to provide education and poverty relief, which have contributed to the perception of state incompetence. Finally, it analyzes how the Jemaah Islamiyah terrorist organization exacerbated the violent mobilization.

Chapter 5 provides an interesting counterpoint to the Indonesia chapters, especially since Malaysia has a long history of peaceful Islamist mobilization; out of all the cases in this study, violent Islamist mobilization is most rare in Malaysia. This chapter examines how the development and institutionalization of political channels for participation has affected Islamist mobilization strategies. It analyzes the government's success in co-opting key Islamist leaders and ideas; the influence of the Malaysian Islamic Party (PAS) and oppositional Islamist organizations; PAS electoral victories at the state and local government levels; and how Islamist groups work around curbs on civil liberties. Second, it investigates how Malaysia's use of its security services ensure law and order and stability within its borders. Third, it examines the degree to which Malaysia has provided education and social welfare services to the population and their capacity to regulate and engage with Islamist organizations who supplement their efforts. Finally, this chapter studies how Malaysia has limited the influence of external forces, most notably the Afghan veterans and international terrorist groups.

Chapter 6 briefly examines four additional cases: Kuwait, Bangladesh, Bahrain, and Yemen. The results indicate that the theory holds in each case. Bahrain has important parallels to Suharto's Indonesia insofar as both states restricted political participation while maintaining effective capacity. Kuwait has similarities with the case of Malaysia, for both have provided certain opportunities for political participation, while maintaining effective capacity. In doing so, both have been able to limit the influence of external forces, most notably spillover effects from wars. Finally, Bangladesh and Yemen can be grouped with post–New Order Indonesia, although both states are in *far* worse straits. There are some basic similarities insofar as both states provide opportunities for participation while falling short in efforts to ensure effective capacity.

Chapter 7 highlights the patterns derived from the eight cases examined in this book. It then answers several questions the book itself has raised, including why participation is indeed necessary; how the state should be a positive presence; why the government should not just rely on brute force repression; why the state should avoid the practice of arming radical movements to take actions against other enemies; how mainstream Islamic mass organizations can assist the government in limiting the opportunities for radical Islamist groups to make inroads at the state's expense in times of crisis;

and why external forces do not act the same everywhere. Finally, it proposes four theoretical propositions to act as a framework for future research.

As scholars and policy makers attempt to understand the reasons for increased Islamist radicalism and terrorism, many have neglected a comparably thorough examination of countries where peaceful Islamist mobilization clearly dominates over violent mobilization. Some have sought to blame Islam. Others have focused too heavily on what went wrong. In doing so, they have given insufficient attention to what went right—the positive changes taking place in Muslim Asia, where the majority of Muslims live today. This has led some to have an incomplete picture of state-religious relations, Islamist groups, and Islamist mobilization strategies. This book seeks to complete that picture by investigating the variation in Islamist group mobilization strategies and highlighting the positive and negative means through which the state can affect those strategies. Subsequent chapters highlight Turkey, New Order Indonesia, Indonesia post New Order, and Malaysia in order to understand why some states are adept at encouraging peaceful mobilization, while others are plagued by violence in the name of Islam.

# CHAPTER 2

# Islamist Mobilization and Variation in the Turkish State

Turkey presents an extremely interesting and unique case for understanding the variation in Islamist mobilization. It has the historical legacy of the Ottoman Empire, where the caliphate was the center of Islam.[1] Yet, in 1923, it charted a new course when it underwent a radical secularizing revolution that severely limited the role of religion in the public sphere. In what some might call an Islamic counterrevolution, many of the most severe of these policies were eased in the 1950s. Now, Turkey seeks to become the first Muslim country to be admitted into the European Union. Throughout its history, Turkey has actively chartered courses, rather than passively responding to them.

Turkey has evolved over the past three decades from an ineffective participatory state to an effective participatory one. Since 1970, Islamist political parties have entered into coalitions with secular parties. Adalet ve Kalkinma Partisi (Justice and Development Party, AKP), a moderate Islamist party, currently governs Turkey, and Islamist civil society groups mobilize in an overwhelmingly peaceful manner. Yet, Turkey was buffeted by episodes of severe violent mobilization from leftists and ultranationalists in the 1960s and 1970s and from radical Islamist groups in the 1990s. The Turkish state has sought to effectively regulate the religious sphere. It maintains control over religion through institutions such as the Diyanet Isleri Baskanligi (Directorate of Religious Affairs), which employs all muftis and imams and writes and disseminates the Friday sermon for all Turkish mosques. The Turkish state also specifies the curriculum for both secular and Islamic schools. This degree of control makes it exceptional among the states being considered in this book.

This chapter will examine the variation in Turkish Islamist mobilization from the 1970s to the present. Thus, while this book may reference to the Ottoman era, the liberalizing 1950s, or the onset of radical politics in the

1960s, it will not examine those periods in great detail. The choice of 1970 is well advised because the first explicitly Islamist party formed in 1969. Prior to that, Islamist groups worked through center-right and right-wing political parties. This chapter first examines how changing opportunities for political participation impacted the variation in Islamist mobilization. Then, it turns to issues of effective state capacity: law and order and education and social services. Finally, it analyzes the role played by the intervention of external forces, most notably the influence of Iran in facilitating terrorism by radical Islamists.

## Participation

Islamist groups engage with the political system in three main ways: forming political parties and contesting elections, infiltrating the bureaucracy to attempt to pass favored policies, and creating and mobilizing through civil society groups. While Islamist organizations may work outside the political system to increase personal piety or to attract attention to Muslim causes, many also work within it, allying with political parties or with receptive government ministries. These allied civil society organizations have played key roles in developing a mass base for religious parties. This high level of engagement opportunity enables Islamist groups to actively mobilize through the state system. The heavy hand of the state ensures that they mobilize through established channels and in an acceptable manner. In Turkey, there are clear acceptable channels for popular participation and Islamist mobilization.

Turkey has a 58-year-old tradition of political parties in a variety of party systems. The system has metamorphosed from bipartyism (1950–1960) to moderate multipartyism (1960–1980) to moderate multipartyism with a dominant party (1983–1991) to extreme multipartyism with no dominant party (1991–2002) to multipartyism with one dominant party (2002–2009).[2] Political parties must abide by the Political Parties Law, which imposes a standard organizational model on all parties consisting of party conventions and elected executive committees at the national, provincial, and sub-provincial levels.[3] The smallest organizational unit is the sub-province; parties are prohibited from having village-level offices. Islamist parties have been active participants in all the multiparty periods, beginning with the short-lived Milli Nizam Partisi (National Order Party, MNP) in 1969. Prior to the emergence of religious parties, Islamist voters supported center-right parties such as the Justice Party and the Democrat Party, which subscribed to a more flexible interpretation of Kemalist secularism than the Cumhuriyetci Halk Partisi (Republican People's Party, CHP).

At the helm of every major Islamist party has been Necmettin Erbakan, who founded the MNP; the Milli Selamet Partisi (National Salvation Party,

MSP); and the Refah Partisi (Welfare Party) and was instrumental behind the scenes in the development of the Fazilet Partisi (Virtue Party). After the split following the closure of the Virtue Party, he sided with those who founded the Saadet Partisi (Felicity Party). In each of these cases, parties abided by the rules stipulated in the Political Party Law and other government regulations restricting their activities. For example, since parties are forbidden from using religious language in their platforms or Islamic symbols in their party labels, all Turkish Islamist parties allude to Islamic principles by using vague terms such as "traditional Turkish values" and "a just order." No party platform has ever called explicitly for the imposition of sharia.

The Turkish state has recognized the importance of policies to promote Islamist incorporation and the equal necessity of ensuring that parties continue to follow the rules of the game. Since the early 1980s, the state has pursued a dual-track policy of co-optation and containment by opening more channels for Islamist groups to participate in the political process in a regulated manner.[4] As a result, Islamist groups have been incorporated into the democratic process, and this institutional inclusion has in turn softened and altered Islamist goals and demands.[5]

### Turkish Islamist Parties

Erbakan founded the MNP in 1969, the first political party in contemporary Turkish history to have an explicit Islamist orientation. Not surprisingly, it was banned with the 1971 coup. Erbakan left Turkey for a year, following the coup, fearing the crackdown that would ensue. On return, he established the MSP in time for the 1973 elections. It would endure for seven years, until it too was banned in the 1980 coup.

The MSP saw Islam as a key base for social organization, liberally employed Islamic discourse, and pushed for the adoption of Islamist policy programs.[6] Its platform emphasized traditional values, closer ties with Muslim states, and a desire to reform education so as to focus on the teaching of morals and piety. The MSP was supported by the notable *tarikats* and organizations of the period: the Naksibendi, the Nurcu (for part of its tenure), the National Turkish Student Union (MTTB), and Erbakan's own Naksibendi-centered network, the Milli Gorus (National View).[7]

The emergence of the MSP coincided with a key point in Turkish history, where civil society organizations began to achieve considerable autonomy vis-à-vis the state.[8] The MSP was more militant than the MNP, due, in part, to the overall climate of radicalism that pervaded Turkish politics in the 1970s. Its rallies attacked both Ataturk and the Laic system.[9] Yet, it was willing to work through the political system to pursue its goals and take advantage of opportunities for alliances when they presented themselves. The MSP participated, as a junior partner, in three coalition governments with secular political parties and used the opportunity to infiltrate certain ministries, packing its members into the lower levels of the ministries of education and the interior.[10] This move also had the effect of giving Islamist cadres the impression that they were progressing toward their goals. The lion's share of violent mobilization in Turkey, during this period, was perpetrated by communist parties on the far left and ultranationalists on the far right. Thus, during the 1970s, when Turkish politics was increasingly polarized and violent, when parties like the ultranationalist Milliyetci Hareket Partisi (National Action Party, MHP) were forming their own militia, the MSP provided an important channel for Islamists to engage in the system, rather than take up arms against it.

With the military coup of 1980, all political parties were temporarily banned and then slowly permitted again. During this period, the military government, led by General Evren, constructed a policy prescription known as the Turkish-Islam synthesis, which was designed to incorporate a controlled and systemic Islam into the Turkish national consciousness to reduce the influence of the Marxist-Leninist left. Among the initial parties allowed was the center-right Anavatan Partisi (Motherland Party, ANAP) led by Turgut Ozal, a member of the Naksibendi order. Due to its pragmatic use of religion, ANAP attracted many former MSP voters as well as members of the Nurcu, Suleymanci, and Naksibendi religious orders.[11] The ANAP built places for worship in government ministries and in the Grand National Assembly, increased the number of *imam-hatip* religious schools, launched state-run Koran classes, and employed new imams. Other center-right parties like the Dogru Yol Partisi (True Path Party, DYP) also emerged in the late 1980s, and they also utilized religion pragmatically, endorsing the policies of the Turkish-Islam synthesis. Given the repressive military regime, the emergence of the ANAP and the True Path Party was important, for they provided mechanisms for Islamist integration into politics at a time when direct affiliation with an Islamist party was impossible.

By 1983, the political atmosphere had become more liberal, and Erbakan reconstituted the MSP, renaming it as the Refah Party. This party was less overtly Islamist in intent than the MSP, but this was more a matter of degree than a substantive ideological shift. Islamists left the ANAP and its policies of sympathetic accommodation and joined the Refah Party.[12] What is notable here is that pro-political Islam voters now had a choice—they could stay with the ANAP and encourage it to maintain its religious direction or they could join Refah, which clearly was an Islamist party with substantial religious goals. This led to the greater incorporation of Islamist groups, most notably through political party networks.

The Refah Party ran on a platform calling for a *saadet nizami* (just order), which rejected capitalism, yet accepted the free market; rejected membership in the EU; and advocated a foreign policy reorientation toward the Middle East.[13] It too was supported by Milli Gorus, some Naksibendi congregations, and the successor of the MTTB, the Birlik Vakfi.[14] The Refah Party's primary electoral strategy was to incorporate marginalized classes into the political system. Thus, not surprisingly, its most substantial gains were in the *gecekondus,* the squatter districts that surround all Turkish cities. It realized the potential base of the urban migrants from the Islam-oriented periphery, who had been neglected by the other parties.[15] Thus, to harness and incorporate these voters, the Refah Party combined traditional Islamist roles in the provision of education and social welfare with electoral canvassing.[16] Refah also developed interest clubs, and its network of teachers would engage men in discussions in coffee houses.[17] These policies resulted in networks that also incorporated conservative Muslims from marginalized regions into the political system.

The Refah Party's overall mobilization strategy relied heavily on interpersonal trust and was successful beyond all expectations. According to Jenny White,

> Refah presided over a network of independent, interlocking support groups, in addition to the party's formal representation at the provincial, municipal and neighborhood levels. Informally linked associations and groups of activists rooted the party in every block in every street. This organizational level was achieved in every province. All groups claimed autonomy from the municipality and party, while they may have worked for both. The groups organized fleets of volunteers into cells.[18]

A former member of the Refah Party's women's wing notes that the party also harnessed the power of women in developing women's branches. "Every neighborhood had a leader, a popular woman, who knew everyone—she would be in charge of finding out who needed food assistance, economic assistance, scholarships."[19] Around election time, these women would canvass, bringing out the vote for Refah. By these methodical strategies, the party incorporated conservative Muslim men and women from *gecekondus* and from marginalized regions such as the Southeast, and it increased opportunities in those areas for political influence and incorporation.

The Refah Party made slow gains throughout the 1980s and early 1990s, its influence reaching a zenith with the mid-1990s elections. In the 1994 municipal elections, the party won "28 mayoral races, six major metropolitan centers, and the leadership of 327 local governments."[20] In the 1995 national elections, it secured 21.4 percent of the votes, gaining 158 seats in parliament and the first prime ministership by an Islamist party in Turkish history.[21]

However, one can compare the party's time in power to tightrope walking. It incorporated Islamists into the political system, softening their demands. The government joined the European Custom's Union and improved military-to-military relations with Israel. Yet, as prime minister, Erbakan also attempted to reorient Turkey toward the Middle East through several symbolic gestures, including visiting Colonel Qadaffi in Libya and expanding ties with Iran. These moves were welcomed by Islamist sectors but they alarmed the pro-Western Kemalist-dominated military.

At the municipal level, the Refah Party pursued a combination of religious and pragmatic policies.[22] For example, while Istanbul mayor Recep Tayyip Erdogan banned alcohol at municipal functions and permitted firemen to wear beards, he also succeeded in removing "hills of garbage," solving water shortages, adding ferries to ease traffic, planting thousands of trees, and ending the city's dependency on poor quality coal by increasing the use of natural gas.[23] The Refah Party's mayors also implemented socially popular religious policies such as setting up tents during Ramadan with free food for the break-fast for the poor.[24] These policies had the effect of incorporating Islamist groups, formerly on the periphery of Turkish politics, into the political system.

After the Constitutional Court banned the Refah Party on charges of Islamic incitation, following inflammatory statements by several of its young leaders, the party reconstituted itself as the Virtue Party, under the leadership of Recai Kutan. Erbakan had been banned from politics for five years.[25] The Virtue Party represented a moderate shift from the Refah Party and formally abandoned many of its positions, including Refah's anti-Western stance, its opposition to EU membership, and its opposition to capitalism.[26] Virtue also couched its Islamic goals in the rhetoric of religious freedom, which included freedom of practice and dress.[27] While one might think that Virtue would have appealed to a larger segment of the population than the Refah Party, this indeed was not the case. Due to the ramifications of the February 28, 1997, "soft coup," it was widely believed that this party would not be allowed to assume power. Those on the left of the party turned to the ANAP and the True Path Party, while many Islamists on the right defected from the party.[28] Right-wingers in the party, especially those in central, eastern, and southeastern Anatolia, turned to the ultranationalist MHP.[29]

With a mere 15 percent of the votes in the 1999 election, Virtue too was banned. The period 1997–1999 witnessed state containment of Islamists—to set limits of what would be acceptable policy and rhetoric and what would result in further repression. This caused a major reconsideration among Turkish Islamists. A minority chose to withdraw from the political system. The remainder split into two parties: Saadet Partisi (Felicity Party), which followed in the Virtue tradition and continued to utilize religious rhetoric, and the conservative Justice and Development Party, (AKP), which was patterned on European Christian democratic parties. Felicity is led by Recai Kutan, since Erbakan is still banned from politics, and most of its leadership is over 75 years old.

The AKP calls itself a conservative party, which in Turkish political discourse implies a certain level of religiosity.[30] It works for its goals within the limits set by the Turkish state following the February 28th Process and utilizes those available channels to appeal to the widest array of voters. According to Dr. Tufan Buzpinar, roughly one-third of Saadet and AKP are similar in outlook.[31] Ismail Safi, vice president of the AKP, explained the party's conservatism in terms of three interrelated factors: (a) familial and social conservatism, (b) the synthesis of traditional Turkish values and democratic reform, and (c) the promotion of religious pluralism.[32] Its goals center on economic development, democratic reforms, and the expansion of human rights.[33] However, when one examines the AKP's foreign policy, it is evident that the party allies itself more closely with the Middle East and the Islamic *umma* in comparison with previous center-right government coalitions. In doing so, it is becoming a more active participant in Middle Eastern politics, establishing warm relations with Hamas and presiding over peace negotiations between Israel and Syria.

The AKP has incorporated other groups into Turkish Islamist politics in addition to the traditional urban and rural Refah Party loyalists. These include the Islamic middle class as well as a new urban class of horizontally connected groups with rural origins and shared Islamic mores.[34] This class was never part of the Kemalist elite, preferring to rely on Islamist networks for political inclusion.[35] Interestingly, unlike the Refah Party, the AKP never actively canvassed to win the support of these voters. Instead, these groups mobilized themselves to redefine the political center of Turkish politics in terms of their values and their conceptions of Turkish religious-tinged conservatism.[36] These Islamic solidarity networks were highly active in various forms of community service and outreach, and the AKP became their favored party.[37]

The 2002 elections highlighted this major realignment taking place in Turkish politics, with the AKP winning 34.2 percent of the vote and 363/550 seats in parliament.[38] The only other party to pass the 10 percent threshold was the left-leaning Republican People's Party. The ANAP and the True Path Party failed to do so; they had been discredited due to allegations of corruption, their inability to fix the battered economy, and the perception that they were out of touch with the needs of ordinary Turks.

The AKP's support has grown since taking power in 2002, for it has worked arduously to bring down inflation by 25 percent, to implement economic reform, and to fulfill the reform requirements set out for EU membership. This has attracted a wide array of center-right and centrist voters to its side. It appealed to the poor through social welfare programs, including the distribution of free coal to 1.2 million families; the allocation of food to 70,000 people per day; and the initiation of a $260 million program to send poor families on holiday.[39] It has sought to pass legislation to equalize the *imam-hatip* (Islamic school) diploma and the secular high school diploma so that *imam-hatip* graduates can attend university. These policy and programmatic successes were highlighted in 2007, when the AKP was reelected with 46.58 percent of the vote.[40] Since the CHP and the MHP also crossed the 10 percent electoral threshold, however, the percentage of seats allocated to the AKP decreased from 363 to 341.[41] Nevertheless, the margin of victory was sufficient for the AKP to form a single-party government.

In sum, Turkish Islamist and center-right political parties as well as the state have utilized religion to attract voters. This has had the effect of incorporating previously marginalized groups into the Turkish political system and enabling them to shape and influence policy and discourse. Parties such as Virtue and Refah have utilized strategies based on networks of interpersonal trust to attract voters in the *gecekondus* (slums), combining traditional Islamic charity work with electoral canvassing.[42] Although the AKP has not directly participated in these networks, the networks themselves have assisted it in achieving electoral victory. Interestingly, this engagement has led Turkish Islamist parties to become a proactive force in the democratic process and a contributor to Turkey's democratic deepening.[43]Since Turkish Islamists have the opportunity to work within the political system to achieve their goals, the vast majority do. However, Islamists have also utilized techniques other than forming political parties and voting. They have worked through the bureaucracy and as part of *tarikats*. The next section will examine these activities.

### Alliance Building

Some Turkish *tarikats* have a long tradition of allying with political parties on certain sides of the political spectrum. For example, the Nurcu order has tended to form alliances with the center-right parties, and the Naksibendi has generally allied with the Islamist parties headed by Necmettin Erbakan, a Naksibendi devotee of Sheikh Mehmet Kotku. This has been most notable in the case of the Iskender Pasa congregation, which has supported not only the MNP, but also the MSP, Refah Party, and Virtue Party.[44] However, it also briefly supported the ANAP, during the 1980s, when Erbakan was banned from politics and fellow Naksibendi Turgut Ozal was head of the party.[45]

Sheikh Mehmet Kotku spearheaded the Naksibendi policy of engagement with contemporary Islamic and center-right parties due to the Naksibendi goal of furthering Islamism in Turkey. He believed in an incremental approach, focusing on the moral and cultural reorientation of Turkish society prior to any attempt at establishing an Islamic state.[46] Thus, this made the Naksibendi willing to support those center-right or Islamist parties that might facilitate the achievement of those goals and any party that it could influence in a more Islamic direction.[47] While the Naksibendi order was the most politically active in Turkey, the level of political activity it engaged in varied somewhat by congregation. Iskender Pasa was among the most politicized of the Naksibendi congregations. It actively trained students to become influential in politics and the media and to spread Islamic values among the population.[48] Ismail Aga, Kibrisi, and Carsamba—other influential Naksibendi congregations—supported both the Refah Party and the Virtue Party.[49]

The Nurcu initially supported the MNP and the MSP, but broke away from the MSP due to the domination of Erbakan and the Naksibendi order.[50] With this move, the MSP lost a substantial number of votes. In subsequent elections, the Nurcu movement would support the center-right True Path Party, which was open to ideas of societal piety and was respectful of religion, although not explicitly an Islamist party.

*Tarikats* have a long tradition of providing assistance to the poor. The Nurcu, the Neo-Nurcu (Fetullah Gulen), and the Naksibendi also provide education services. The Iskender Pasa congregation offers services that appeal to middle-class Turks, including private high schools, hospitals, radio and television stations, commercial firms, summer camps, and business networks.[51] Fetullah Gulen is famous worldwide for its network of schools and universities. *Tarikats* also run unofficial Koran courses and dormitories. The services made available by the *tarikats* enable them to form networks of supporters and members that can be rallied to support a particular center-right or Islamist political party and thereby increase their level of engagement.

The interaction with political parties makes members of the politically active *tarikats* to feel that they are progressing toward their goals. If they seek gradual societal Islamization, their relations with conservative parties provide a channel toward attainment of that goal. The inclusion of groups such as the Naksibendi and the Nurcu fosters a sense of engagement—of being an actor in the Turkish nation-state and able to effect gradual change.

This makes it far more likely that *tarikats* will continue to mobilize through established channels. Likewise, there is less possibility that disillusioned members will splinter off to join radical groups.

Other Islamist organizations are also closely allied with Islamist parties. In particular, Milli Gorus, which was created by Erbakan himself, has formed the base of every Islamist party since the MSP. In the beginning, the core of the Milli Gorus was the Naksibendi order.[52] However, since that time, it has expanded to represent a coalition of various Islamist and politically conservative groups.[53] With the banning of Virtue, some Milli Gorus members joined Saadet to continue the struggle to push Turkey in a more Islamist direction. Other members came to the conclusion that they would never be permitted to run the country if they did not adopt a more integrationist line, abiding by the accepted parameters of the state establishment.[54] Many of these people now form the core of the AKP. In addition to Milli Gorus, student groups such as the MTTB and its successor organization, the Birlik Vakfi, built campus support networks for the MSP and, later, Refah. Formal alliances like Milli Gorus and more informal alliances with student groups serve to incorporate Islamists into the political process, which facilitates constructive political engagement.

Turkey has benefited from open and institutionalized channels for Islamist participation since the 1969. Islamist groups have formed political parties, contested elections, and secured victories. They have entered into alliances with secular political parties to form governments, both as junior and senior partners. They have utilized these opportunities to pack the education and interior ministries with their members, thus gaining another channel through which to influence policy. Sufi *tarikats,* Islamist NGOs, and student groups have entered into formal and informal alliances with Islamist political parties and with center-right parties to "get out the vote," and to work toward common policy goals. These policies of inclusion have encouraged peaceful mobilization strategies and discouraged violent ones. This sustained engagement is, in large part, responsible for the climate of systemic mobilization where radical Islamist organizations and terrorist organizations operate on the fringes of society, lacking any substantial popular support.

However, radical Islamist groups and terrorist groups have been active intermittently in Turkey from the 1970s to the present day. The following sections will seek to discern why, despite the clear predominance of peaceful mobilization, pockets of violent activity exist, particularly in southeastern Turkey. They will also explain why certain periods in contemporary Turkish history have experienced more Islamist violence than others, why certain regions face more violence than others, and how the state has contributed to these events.

## Effective State Capacity

Turkey has a long historical tradition of a strong and effective state.[55] However, the Turkish state has not remained constant. At various points, the state has failed to provide sufficient security to its citizens, prompting military intervention to restore law and order. This is particularly true with regard to its response to insurgencies and the rise of radical Islamist groups in the Southeast. It is important to state, however, that for the most part, Islamist groups have submitted to the state and respected its authority.[56]

*Provision of Security*

This section will examine two instances in which the state lost control of certain territories within its borders and the subsequent response by radical Islamist groups. First, it will analyze the state's lapses in the maintenance of law and order in various cities during the ideologically polarized 1970s. Then, it will examine the state's reach of authority in the Kurdish-dominated Southeast. While this may, at first glance, seem tautological, this chapter endeavors to show how specific Turkish state policies had a direct impact in permitting or even encouraging violent Islamist mobilization. Finally, it will examine how the state improved its level of effectiveness in this area and the subsequent decline in violence resulting from its new policies.

Militant Islamist groups have historically comprised a tiny minority of the overall Islamist mobilization occurring in Turkey. Yet, in times of diminishing state authority, one has seen a rise in violence. The 1970s was a period of intense ideological polarization, with communists on the left and ultranationalists on the right. Each faction had its own militant wing. Turkish communist parties were affiliated with militant leftist groups; the ultranationalist MHP had its own radical militia, the Grey Wolves; and a breakaway faction of the MSP formed the Islami Buyukdogu Akincilar Cephesi (Great East Islamic Raiders Front, IBDA-C). It is interesting to note, however, that unlike the direct connection between the MHP and the Grey Wolves or Kurdish leftist parties and their militant wings, the MSP did not formally or informally align with the IBDA-C. The MSP used this period of state weakness to voice its demands, rather than take up arms.

The majority of Islamist violence during that period was from young radicals in high schools and universities, fighting against secularist groups or leftist Kurdish groups.[57] It is interesting that these conflicts occurred so often on campuses, for one would think that it would be fairly easy to reestablish law and order there. At that time, the state authorities were too weak to do so. Additionally, the campus violence spilled over into rural areas and small towns where left-right conflicts engendered intra-religious tensions between radical Sunnis on the right and members of the Alevi Muslim minority on the left.[58] In December 1978 alone, 105 people, most of whom were Alevis, were killed in Kahramanmaras by Sunni militants.[59] For perhaps the first time in 30 years, young Muslim radicals knew they could resort to violence with impunity against their perceived enemies on the left. Following the military's 1980 coup and its subsequent crackdown, law and order was restored to the campuses and violence decreased. Furthermore, as the state has been able to maintain law and order since the early 1980s, there has not been another explosion of campus violence since.

Turkey's subsequent military interventions, most notably the February 28, 1997 "soft coup" by the Constitutional Court, are viewed with reference to this prior lawless period to justify the state enforcing law and order and setting boundaries around political debates so that violence does not recur. The February 28th Process, as it is called, alarmed Islamists, as well as secular democrats, because it resulted in the widespread closure and banning of Islamist media outlets and organizations as well as the arrest of key leaders for short prison sentences. However, it is also widely viewed by the Turks as the specifying and enforcement of limits for Islamist politics.

It is important to note that certain policies of the Turkish state also directly impacted the rise in violent Islamist mobilization. In the 1980s and the 1990s, elements within the Turkish security apparatus made a fundamental mistake: they permitted radical Islamist groups to flourish to help stem the leftist threat. This was particularly true in the Kurdish-dominated Southeast, where the Marxist terrorist organization, the Kurdish Workers Party (PKK) was active. The majority of Muslim militants who sought training in Pakistan, Afghanistan, Lebanon, and Iran were from the Kurdish areas.[60] While scholars currently dispute whether the elements of the Turkish security apparatus actually armed radical Islamist groups, the consensus is that they, at least, looked the other way and permitted these groups to conduct activities in the southeastern region. This policy course makes these elements complicit in the increase in violent mobilization that occurred during this period.

As a response to the PKK and militant leftist groups, radical Islamist movements formed, most notably Hizballah and the IBDA-C. Initially, there were cordial ties between Hizballah and the PKK, with Hizballah members receiving training in PKK camps, but the two groups soon became rivals.[61] While some elements within Hizballah and the IBDA-C were initially sympathetic to the Kurdish cause, the dominant wing of Hizballah, the Ilimciler, frequently attacked PKK targets throughout the 1990s. They contended the PKK was "murdering Muslims, cooperating with the Armenians, serving Communism, and seeking to divide the

Muslim community."[62] It is not surprising perhaps that security forces were tolerant of Hizballah, because it was perceived as playing an instrumental role in fighting PKK terrorism.[63] Bulent Aras and Gokhan Bacik, the foremost experts on Turkish Hizballah, maintain that strategic relations existed between Hizballah and certain factions of the state bureaucracy.[64] Among Turkish scholars and journalists, it is widely believed that certain groups within the state bureaucracy supported Hizballah for their own ends.[65] According to Ali Bulac, a well-known Islamist writer, "The state knew about the Hizballah and this was kept hidden by the 'deep layers' [derin tabakalar]. With the state's eventual triumph over the PKK, it became necessary to purge Hizballah."[66] The logic behind this theory notes that

"since the PKK is a Marxist organization, the formation of an enemy terrorist organization, based on Islamic ideology would have been a logical move on the state's part. From 1990–1995, the PKK gained control of a large social base in Southeastern Turkey. Having Hizballah as a tool during this time would've been very useful to the state. Hizballah killed more than 500 PKK members and other Kurds, including NGO members, journalists, intellectuals, and politicians. This was clearly in the state's interest."[67]

The important fact to glean from this relationship, be it implicit or explicit, between Turkish Hizballah and elements of the Turkish state is that Hizballah contributed to the atmosphere of lawlessness plaguing the Southeast with the tacit endorsement of the elements in the Turkish security apparatus. In permitting Hizballah to attack PKK members and supporters, they set the stage for the day when Hizballah would turn its attention to overthrowing the Kemalist state apparatus. Security services in other countries have made a similar Faustian bargain. In Indonesia, elements of the military trained the Laskar Jihad militia, and senior police officials supported the creation of the Islamic Defenders Front. In Pakistan, close relations have existed between members of the Inter-Services Intelligence (ISI) and members of radical Islamist militias fighting in Kashmir. In sum, the state's inability to maintain law and order in the Kurd-dominated areas of the Southeast led it to undertake unwise policies with regard to Hizballah, which perpetuated the climate of lawlessness in the region.

Just as the state had the capacity to encourage or permit violence through its policies, it also had the capacity to discourage it through targeted actions. In 1991, the Turkish state began to undertake careful investigations of Hizballah and the IBDA-C with the intent of putting a stop to their activities. However, the going was slow because both groups were exceedingly secretive; in the meantime, they also stepped up violence.[68] Yet, gradual progress was made in diffusing the threat posed by these groups. In 1994, security authorities arrested 659 Hizballah members;[69] violence dropped precipitously, with 86 incidents in 1995 compared with 464 in 1994.[70] By the mid-1990s, security officials claimed that "almost all" of the IBDA-C activists were in jail.[71] In the late 1990s, the Turkish authorities rooted out and arrested members of smaller militant Islamist groups, including the Vassat, led by Sahmerdan Sari, and the Islamic Movement Organization.[72]

Hizballah proved more difficult to root out. Throughout the 1990s, the national police and the Turkish National Intelligence Organization conducted a series of raids that led to numerous important arrests and the discovery of documentary evidence illustrating key aspects of the organization. According to John Nugent, the big break came when

> authorities in Istanbul launched a massive series of operations against the leadership, safe houses and nerve centers of THB [Turkish Hizballah]. These successful actions led to the killing of Huseyin Velioglu, the leader of THB, and two of his key lieutenants. It also unearthed a treasure trove of documentary, computer, video and forensic evidence. Upwards of 600,000 pages of secret THB documents were found, detailing the operations, safe houses and hierarchy of the organization.[73]

The subsequent raids in January 2000 on the houses of Hizballah cells unearthed the bodies of dozens of Hizballah victims, many of whom had been tortured on videotape.[74] This led to more arrests. By 2002, Turkish Hizballah was no longer a threat.

In sum, this section sought to show that radical Islamist mobilization will often increase, despite opportunities for participation, if the state cannot control the territories within its borders. When the state could not control state university campuses, radical youths from across the political spectrum took the opportunity to use violence against their ideological opponents. When the state could not control the Southeast, this region served as a breeding ground for radical organizations. When states cannot control certain territories within their borders, it may lead them to make unwise alliances to stem the destabilizing threat. In the Turkish case, the state permitted radical Islamist groups to remain active, if not encouraging them directly, so that they might take action against the PKK. Yet, this permissiveness eventually led Turkish radical groups to turn their actions against non-PKK affiliated Kurds and Turks—academics, journalists, secularists, and ordinary civilians. Although the state may have thought it wise to encourage Hizballah at the expense of the PKK, it turned out to be a Faustian bargain. In the long term it led to an increase in violent Islamist mobilization.

It is not the contention here that Islamist groups turn radical in lawless periods. However, radical groups may take up violence when the opportunity permits or when encouraged by organs of the state bureaucracy. In those instances, these groups are armed and will frequently take action against the larger society or the state. Then, it becomes far more difficult to root out these groups and discourage their violent activities. It took the Turkish authorities years to gather sufficient information to launch a concerted attack against Hizballah and the IBDA-C.

From analyzing Turkey over the past five years, one can see that opportunities for participation combined with the maintenance of law and order throughout the country has led to a significant decline in violent Islamist mobilization. While peaceful action was always the dominant mobilization strategy for Turkish Islamists, violent Islamist mobilization has become rare.

### Social Welfare

The Turkish state gains legitimacy from its provision of social services. However, within that sphere, there is an explicit division. The Turkish state dominates the provision of health care, but Islamist parties and organizations take the primary role in poverty relief. *Tarikats* have traditionally provided food, fuel, and shelter to the poor[75] Ali Bardakoglu, the president of the Directorate of Religious Affairs, acknowledges the strength of Islamist groups in these areas: "Islamist groups help the poor through *waqfs* [land endowments]. It is their tradition to provide food and services to the needy."[76] This role has not been ceded to *tarikats* and societal Islamist groups. Islamist political parties provide poverty assistance, especially around election time. For example, the Refah party worked as a social service agency for the poor, distributing clothing, food, and coal just prior to elections.[77] Local governments also maintain a strong presence among the poor.

The Turkish state is the primary provider of health care and education, which inhibits the ability of radical groups to make significant inroads. In addition, the competition among liberal, moderate, orthodox, and fundamentalist Islamist groups in this area enables the sphere of social welfare provision to be divided such that no party takes the lion's share of the gains.

### Education

While the Turkish state has slowly receded in its enforcement of strict Kemalist secularism with the adoption of the Turkish-Islam Synthesis, it has maintained control over all institutions of primary and secondary education.

In Turkey, the state has a long history of dominating the provision of education, by restricting the proliferation of Islamic schools and by stipulating the curriculum for all schools, both religious and secular. In the initial republican period of the 1920s and the 1930s, Islamic schools were banned. When they were again permitted, the state restricted the number of Islamic schools and allowed them to function only to train the clergy. With the relaxation of laws governing the establishment of *imam-hatip* schools in the 1970s, Islamic associations carried out a sustained campaign to build new schools through fundraising and building projects.[78] During this initial period, the state integrated *imam-hatip* schools into the regular school system, granting them the same accreditation as other state schools.[79] According to a Refah party booklet, "Between 1974 and 1978, we [Milli Gorus] opened 450 new *imam-hatip* schools; 10 Institutes of Higher Islamic Studies; [and] 3000 Koran vocational projects."[80] Koran schools often represented the first foray into formal Islamic education for the young, where children, five to six years old, learned to recite the Koran in Arabic. This proliferation led many Kemalists to view *imam-hatip* schools as a Trojan horse of Islamism.[81] In accordance with this view, it is not surprising that the state monitored these institutions of Islamic learning.

The state strictly controlled the curriculum of Islamic schools, regulating the percentage of core courses versus the percentage of religious courses that students were required to take. In middle school, religious courses were permitted to constitute only 20 percent of the curriculum, while the remaining 80 percent were the standard secular academic courses; this percentage increased in high school to 31 percent in the ninth and tenth grades, to 44 percent in the twelfth grade.[82] The state dictated the parameters of the curriculum and the courses that were to be taught within them, even if it did not directly operate or finance the schools. Even when Milli Gorus and Fetullah Gulen owned or ran schools, they abided by the state-mandated curriculum.[83] Today, students in *imam-hatip* schools study the standard core curriculum taught in all public schools in addition to religious studies. State-approved religious education is disseminated through the Directorate of Religious Affairs, which has offices at the province and sub-province level.[84] In addition to formulating the curriculum, designing the textbooks, and training the teachers, state officials carry out random checks on the schools, to ensure they are following the state approved-curriculum. The Directorate of Religious Affairs has sufficient capacity to regulate Islamic education, given its ample budget, which is larger than that of the Ministry of Foreign Affairs, and a staff of over 80,000 civil servants.[85] No other country studied in this book has an institution at par with the monitoring capabilities of the Directorate of Religious Affairs.

During the period of the Turkish-Islam synthesis, the state mandated the teaching of religion in public schools. This served to incorporate Islam within official parameters, which would restrict opportunities for political Islam to gain a foothold among future generations and also blunt the influence of communist ideologies.[86] The state went so far as to enshrine this right to religious education in the 1982 Constitution, Article 24 on Freedom of Religion and Conscience, which states, "Education and instruction in religion and ethnics shall be conducted under state supervision and control. Instruction in religious culture and moral education shall be compulsory in primary and secondary schools."[87] This action gave the state a measure of religious legitimacy and made devout Turks feel that the state was not opposed to Islam.[88] These policies served to increase feelings of national identification among religious Muslims. Yet, it was also a strategic action on the part of the Turkish state, for it enabled the state to ensure the provision, monitoring, and regulation of religious education to prevent the development of certain anti-system Islamist ideologies. While other states such as Bangladesh and Yemen struggled to avoid ceding the sphere, the Turkish state sought to dominate it.

In recent years, the state has used its authority to actively restrict the proliferation of *imam-hatip* schools, after seeing the rise of the Refah Party and the potential threat posed by its brand of political Islam. It sought to cut attendance in *imam-hatip* schools by half, after seeing their enrollment numbers rise 611 percent over 20 years.[89] This was largely done through administrative changes. After the Constitutional Court forced Erbakan from office in 1997, the National Security Council pushed for the introduction of compulsory eight-year public secular education, which effectively eliminated *imam-hatip* middle schools.[90] The state also barred private Koran courses and raised the age at which a child could learn the Koran from 8 years to 15.[91] Thus, one could only begin *imam-hatip* style religious education in high school. The Turkish state saw these actions as necessary for it feared that early religious indoctrination would lead to children rejecting Turkish secularism.[92]

The state also attempted to discourage application to *imam-hatip* high schools by restricting the number of *imam-hatip* graduates who could enter universities. It accomplished this in two ways. It set stricter requirements for their admission and restricted their choice of majors to theological fields.[93] This had the intended effect because many religious school students did not want to become imams, and the number of *imam-hatip* applicants declined from 34,000 in 1994 to 2,000 in 1997.[94] Yet, some argue that this move was a driving force behind the election of the AKP.[95] Since the AKP has come to power, it has sought to liberalize these regulations. In May

2004, the AKP-dominated parliament passed a law allowing *imam-hatip* graduates to compete on an equal footing with graduates of secular high schools for entry into universities and colleges.[96] Secular authorities, including members of the military, were alarmed by these actions, seeing them as proof of a hidden AKP agenda.[97] However, they have permitted the legislation to stand.

These actions show that the state has the capacity to monitor, regulate, and limit the influence of *imam-hatip* schools. First, the state provides a viable public school alternative. Second, it can control the curriculum taught within both secular and religious schools. Recent actions also indicate the state has the capacity to administratively limit the ability of *imam-hatip* schools to proliferate. The Turkish state's actions toward the *imam-hatip* schools following the banning of the Refah Party in 1997 are excessive. However, it is important to note the combined effects of opportunities for participation and effective state capacity. Since both have existed, the state has had the opportunity to attempt to limit the influence of *imam-hatip* schools, while Islamist groups have had the opportunity to mobilize behind their party of choice to work for the rescinding of the most egregious regulations. With the election of the AKP, it is clear that their efforts have paid off. This indicates how this potent combination can promote peaceful Islamist mobilization, and, by presenting this viable channel for grievance, discourage alienation and violent Islamist mobilization.

Islamist organizations and Sufi *tarikats* also play important supplementary roles in the state education system. First, as stated earlier, both run *imam-hatip* schools. Second, for approximately 20 years, *tarikats*, Islamic foundations, and Islamic organizations have also provided scholarships and dormitory facilities to students. A wide variety of groups have provided such services. Hizballah sought to attract members by providing boarding houses for students, yet the liberal Fetullah Gulen movement also maintains dorm facilities.[98] The Refah Party also provided these same services during its time. Secular organizations also provide these services. Thus, there is significant competition within civil society over this area. This is an important area of concern because the provision of student dormitories and scholarships by radical Islamist groups could potentially provide them with a goldmine of support. In Turkey, students, both secular and religious, have numerous choices regarding where they reside.

In sum, Turkey's effective state capacity in providing education and welfare services has limited the ability of radical Islamist groups to make gains in these areas. While Islamist groups participate in the provision of scholarships, poverty relief, and education, the Turkish state has not ceded any of these spheres. By enforcing a standard curriculum and keeping a watchful eye over educational institutions, the Turkish state works to limit the ability of radical groups to infiltrate these areas. Therefore, while the proliferation of radical Islamic schools has swelled the numbers of extremist groups in Pakistan, Morocco, Bangladesh, and Yemen, this has not been the case in Turkey. Furthermore, through the provision of educational services, including the provision of religious education in public schools, the state maintains a presence in society in the lives of ordinary Turkish families and gains legitimacy from that presence. In this regulation, the bureaucracy may go too far in the direction of discrimination, yet democratic institutional channels exist to channel mobilization in order to check excessive bureaucratic authority.

## External Forces

As a result of Turkey's lapses in law and order, the country has faced some negative external forces intervention from neighboring Iran. However, external forces in Turkey are not as destabilizing as in Pakistan, Bangladesh, or Indonesia. Turkey has not been home to major international terrorist groups like Jemaah Islamiyah. Turkey did not have high numbers of Afghan veterans like Algeria, Bangladesh, or Yemen. Thus, it did not have the problems facing these states about how to reintegrate the mujihideen into politics and society.

### Iranian Intervention

The locus of external forces intervention was in the Kurdish Southeast, where the state lost control of the territory until 2001. Iran was the main source of active external forces intervention, both utilizing peaceful techniques and supporting violent groups. Iran used the cultural centers it had opened throughout Turkey to rally support for its revolutionary Islamic model among Turks.[99] These actions alarmed Turkish secularists in no small measure. Yet, this alone would not be a substantial threat to Turkish security had it not been for Iran's intervention in the Turkish Southeast.

The inability of the Turkish state to control the Southeast gave Iran an opportunity to become involved with the militant movements operating in the area. Iran became a primary sponsor of Hizballah and IBDA-C terrorism and provided safe havens for PKK guerilla fighters during the 1990s.[100] The latter issue led to extremely chilly relations between the Turkish government and Iran, but the Turkish government could take no measures against it because it could not control the southeastern territory. The Iranian government's harboring of PKK fighters led to greater ease of mobility and activity, and, in turn, greater violent mobilization.

We find the same story with Iranian assistance to Hizballah and the IBDA-C. Iran's financing, training, and support for Hizballah contributed to its adeptness in utilizing violent strategies. Hizballah and IBDA-C terrorists who murdered investigative journalist Ugur Mumcu, an Iranian dissident, a Jewish businessman, and three Turkish intellectuals between 1990 and 1993 were connected with Iranian agents, including diplomats stationed in Turkey.[101] Thousands of Hizballah militants received military training in Iran, and, in return, Hizballah advocated the Iranian revolutionary Islamic model[102] Even if the Turkish state supported Hizballah, it did not train them. That came from Iran.

For a long time, the Turkish state turned a blind eye to Iranian support of Hizballah in the hopes of winning Iranian support for ending PKK terrorism on its soil.[103] Yet, when Refah initiated rapprochement with Iran in 1997, the Turkish military vociferously denounced Iran for sponsoring terrorist activities on Turkish soil.[104] The Iranian intervention was a direct result of the lack of state authority in the Southeast. Had Turkish authority in the Southeast been stronger in the 1990s, Iran would not have had the ability to make such strong inroads with the PKK, the IBDA-C, and Hizballah.

*Iraq War*

Another external force has been the negative spillover effects from the Iraq war. Until 2005, by all accounts, there had been few spillover effects from the Iraq war into southeastern Turkey. However, 2006 and 2007 saw an increase in attacks and cross-border raids by the PKK , this time, from bases in northern Iraq. The Turkish and Iranian governments say that rebels loyal to the PKK and its sister organization in Iran, the Kurdish Free Life Party (KFLP), have launched repeated cross-border attacks from their safe havens in northern Iraq, a predominately Kurdish region.[105] This has led the Turkish and Iranian governments to launch coordinated artillery attacks on the PKK areas, in an attempt to flush out the rebels and destroy their base camps.[106]

While the exact number of PKK fighters residing in Iraq is unclear, it is evident that PKK fighters are adopting the methods and weaponry of Iraqi insurgents.[107] According to the International Crisis Group, "Explosives from Iraq were used in the bombings. The PKK started imitating the road-side explosive techniques of Iraqi insurgents. The unilateral PKK ceasefire became increasingly ragged and casualties rose, including 64 Turkish soldiers in the upsurge of fighting from January to June 2007."[108] These attacks have included a roadside bombing, which killed six soldiers outside of Sirnak in May 2007; a series of bomb attacks, which killed three Turks and wounded dozens more in tourist areas across Turkey in August 2006; and a series of cross-border raids, in which soldiers were attacked throughout 2006 and 2007.[109] The sum total of these actions was to once again destabilize the Kurdish-dominated Southeast and increase the levels of violence taking place. This led some in the Turkish government and military to propose invading northern Iraq to destroy all PKK bases.

While the violence is certainly not a severe as it was during the 1980s and 1990s, the PKK attacks today are occurring in a different context. Iraqi Kurdistan is an autonomous region within Iraq and is far stronger and more independent than it was under Saddam Hussein. Therefore, it provides an attractive vision and model for both PKK fighters and Kurdish nationalists. While Iraqi Kurdish leaders do not support the PKK's actions on their soil, they refuse to expel them either, citing their preference for a negotiated solution.[110] Until such a solution can be devised, however, Iraqi Kurdistan continues to be a safe haven for the PKK, and the attacks against Turkish targets continue.

## Conclusion

Turkey presents a compelling case for understanding how variations in state capacity impact Islamist mobilization strategies. In Turkey, the state permits participation through acceptable institutionalized channels. The vast majority of Turkish Islamist movements use these channels to work toward their goals. They form political parties, contest elections, pass the 10 percent electoral threshold, form coalition governments, and lead the nation. As civil society groups, Islamic *tarikats*, foundations, and associations may make informal alliances with political parties to achieve mutual goals. This open political environment goes a long way toward encouraging Islamist groups to engage in the political system and eschew violent methods. Yet, for all the touting of participation by scholars as the antidote to jihadism, institutional inclusion is a necessary condition for peaceful Islamist mobilization, but not a sufficient one.

The capacity of the Turkish state to ensure law and order within its borders has varied significantly from highly ineffective to highly effective. Turkey has experienced high rates of violence carried out by communist and ultranationalist militias in the 1960s and the 1970s and by the Marxist PKK and the radical Islamist Hizballah and IBDA-C in the 1990s. This was a result of the inability of the Turkish state to consistently maintain law and order in its territories during these periods. In the 1990s, the inability of the Turkish state to provide for law and order within its borders provided radical Islamist groups like Hizballah and the IBDA-C opportunities to make inroads into society in Southeast, to gain recruits, and to make contacts with external forces like the Iranians, who trained and funded them. Worse still, the Turkish state, in its zeal to regain control over the Southeast, turned a blind eye to Hizballah activities and may have actually encouraged them, so long as any violence was directed against the PKK. Thus, the Turkish case highlights the necessity of ensuring security within state borders as a hedge against violent Islamist mobilization and the importance of undertaking smart policies when dealing with violent groups. Hizballah and the IBDA-C showed themselves to be pragmatic: they mobilized in the area where the state lacked control and were very effective in those areas. When the Turkish state re-exerted control over the Southeast and arrested leaders and members of Hizballah and the IBDA-C in sustained and targeted campaigns, violent mobilization decreased significantly.

The Turkish state has been quite effective in providing education and health care services for the public. The state has dominated the sphere of education, monitoring the curriculum, ensuring compliance with that curriculum, taking action against the unrestrained proliferation of *imam-hatip* schools, and providing religious education in public schools. All of this has impeded the ability of radical groups to make inroads into this area. While *imam-hatip* graduates may be more conservative than the national norm, they are certainly not anti-system or militant. When we look at the groups that have established Islamic schools, including Milli Gorus and Fetullah Gulen, they are the clearly systemic ones. Various elements of state and society share the provision of social welfare. The state, secular civil society, and *tarikats,* and Islamist organizations, offer dormitory facilities and scholarships. Local governments, secular civil society, Islamist political parties, and Islamic civil society all share in the provision of poverty relief. The presence of the state in this area shows that it has not retrenched in its provision of education and welfare services. This has limited the ability of radical groups to make inroads into these areas. Furthermore, the competition between the state, secular groups, and various Islamic and Islamist groups in these areas has meant that no one group dominates the social welfare sphere and obtains the majority of legitimacy gains.

In sum, we find a long-standing tradition of peaceful Islamist mobilization in Turkey, punctuated by episodic periods of instability. This peaceful Islamist mobilization was brought about by the opportunities the Turkish state provided for institutionalized mobilization as well as its refusal to cede the sphere in providing education and welfare to Islamist groups. Periods of violent Islamist mobilization largely resulted from the state's loss of the Southeast and its reaction to that loss. The unwise policies it undertook to regain control of the Southeast were largely responsible for the increased violent mobilization in that area and eventually nationwide. Likewise, the loss of control over the Southeast enabled external forces, most notably Iranian groups, to inflame the violent mobilization by training and funding Hizballah and the IBDA-C as well as by providing safe havens to the PKK. Today, we find that Turkey is a clear example of an effective participatory state. Peaceful Islamist mobilization dominates. Violent Islamist mobilization is becoming an increasingly rare occurrence.

# CHAPTER 3

## Does Participation Matter? Effective Authoritarianism in New Order Indonesia

Unlike the other cases in this book, Suharto's New Order regime severely restricted political participation while attempting to ensure law and order and providing a high level of education and poverty relief. Thus, this case presents an alternative strategy and begs the question of whether participation really matters. If states seek to positively influence Islamist group mobilization strategies, does effectiveness matter more than institutional inclusion? Are Islamist groups that eschew violence only responding to material and coercive incentives? This chapter highlights the shortcomings of the effective authoritarian model, the importance of political access, and the consequences of limiting political participation.

The Suharto regime did not necessarily distinguish between groups that utilized peaceful strategies and those that employed violent ones. For most of the New Order, all organizations that advocated an Islamic state or Islamic law were viewed as a political threat, and the state undertook efforts to depoliticize Islam. This drove many who advocated the implementation of some measure of Islamic law to the margins of civil society and to underground movements. The regime's supporters argued that limits on participation were necessary for stability. If this were true, we would find that violent mobilization was rare during the Suharto era. However, this is not the case; violent Islamist mobilization continued at a low hum throughout the New Order. At times, it was a reaction to Suharto's policies, while in other instances the state was complicit in the violence. Moreover, the seeds for much of the violence Indonesia experienced in the early years of the democratic transition were planted in the Suharto era.

The marginalization of political Islam did not begin under Suharto but instead under his predecessor, Sukarno. Both Sukarno and Suharto saw the threat to their rule posed by political Islam and sought to constrain and delegitimize it in the eyes of Indonesians as a viable political force. Neither leader accepted the threat of political opposition posed by such groups, so both sought to limit their ability to participate in formal politics.

Sukarno's most significant move toward marginalizing political Islam came in 1960, when he banned the Majelis Shura Muslimin Indonesia (Consultative Council on Indonesian Muslims, Masyumi) party, after it refused to endorse his decision to abandon democracy in favor of an authoritarian system he termed "Guided Democracy." Although the secular nationalist Partai Nasionalis Indonesia (Indonesian Nationalist Party, PNI); Partai Komunis Indonesia (Indonesian Communist Party, PKI); and Nahdlatul Ulama, (NU) endorsed Sukarno's decision, Masyumi refused to cooperate.

Prior to its banning, Masyumi played an important role in Indonesian Islamist politics because it provided an institutionalized political channel for those advocating the implementation of Islamic law in Indonesia. Although the party sought to establish an Islamic state, it was open to compromise on what character that state should take and how sharia should be implemented. Masyumi was never united in one singular vision of political Islam or sharia but represented many streams of thought in the modernist community from progressive to puritan, including those of Muhammadiyah, Persatuan Islam (Persis), al-Irsyad, the Indonesian Muslim Student Movement (GPII), the Indonesian [Tertiary] Students Association (HMI), and the Indonesian [secondary] Students Association (PII).[1]

Among the four major parties in the Indonesian political system, Masyumi was also the staunchest proponent of Western style democracy. Party president Mohammed Natsir explained that "the Masyumi party wishes to achieve its purpose through the democratic and parliamentarian way not with violence."[2] In other words, any establishment of an Islamic state or sharia had to be accomplished through democratic institutions and procedures. Although Sukarno banned Masyumi in 1960, it remained a political constituency, bound by a network of educational institutions, friendships, civil society organizations, and intermarriage.[3]

It is not altogether clear why Suharto refused to re-legalize Masyumi. However, one can argue that Masyumi's combination of democratic commitment, critical tradition, and Islamist program caused it to be viewed as an unmanageable participant in what would become a highly constrained political environment under Suharto's authoritarian New Order regime. At that time, Masyumi would have proved too difficult to co-opt without ceding ground on Islamic law. Suharto's refusal to re-legalize Masyumi or provide a credible alternative as an institutional outlet for those advocating the implementation of sharia had profound consequences. It drove those seeking a greater political role for Islam to underground movements. Abdullah Sungkar and Abu Bakar Basyir, the cofounders of Jemaah Islamiyah (JI) were leaders in the GPII, a student association with close ties to Masyumi, in their youth.[4] According to one Indonesianist, Abdullah Sungkar joined the radical Darul Islam movement in 1976 because he could not join Masyumi.[5]

The refusal to re-legalize Masyumi was but the first in a series of measures that the Suharto regime took to limit and ultimately curtail institutional and extra-institutional political participation by those groups advocating a role for political Islam in Indonesia. Harsh actions were taken against any Islamist organization with political intentions that ran counter to Suharto's vision for Indonesian society. The sum total of those policies effectively disempowered political Islam. The coming sections of this chapter will analyze these policies and the varied responses by Islamist movements.

## Institutional Limitations on Political Participation

Although Masyumi modernists had supported Suharto's assumption of power and subsequent brutal repression of the PKI, he did not re-legalize the party. Instead, he permitted the modernists to form a new party, Partai Muslim Indonesia (Indonesian Muslim Party, Parmusi) but refused to allow any senior Masyumi leaders to participate. Some Masyumi members took advantage of this opportunity and joined the new party. However, Suharto sought to keep Parmusi weak and divided by instigating leadership splits; rejecting the party's choice for chairman, Mohammed Roem, in favor of a more pliable alternative; and fostering quarrels among party factions.[6] This had the desired effect of delegitimizing Parmusi as the voice of the modernist community, as evidenced by the fact that while Masyumi gained 20.9 percent of the vote in 1955, Parmusi garnered only 5.4 percent in the 1971 elections. Suharto's personal vehicle, Golongan Karya (Functional Groups Party, Golkar), won a supra-majority in the 1971 elections, aided by widespread vote manipulation and intimidation in its favor. Although the four Islamist parties obtained only 27.2 percent of the vote, in contrast with Golkar's 62.8 percent, the regime recognized the potential threat posed by the 27.2 percent of the population that endorsed an Islamist alternative.[7]

Thus, following the 1971 elections, the New Order adopted a two-pronged strategy toward Islam. While the New Order regime promoted personal piety and cultural displays of Islam, it opposed any politicization of Islam.[8] This is the key point to understand at the outset—the New Order regime was not opposed to Islam per se but the politicization of Islam and the oppositional threat it could potentially pose. To that end, Suharto eliminated most Islamist figures from the cabinet and took the Ministry of Religious Affairs from NU. The ministry had long been an NU bastion. The most notable changes, however, concerned a drastic restructuring of the political party system to limit the ability of Islamist parties (and all other alternative ideologies) to effectively compete. The New Order regime enacted a series of policies, beginning with the fusion of the party system. The four Islamist parties (Parmusi, NU, Perti, and the PSII) were amalgamated into one political party, the Partai Persatuan Pembangunan (United Development Party, PPP), which was designated as the "Islamist party." However, the four parties represented different streams within Islam, and the party was wracked by infighting and struggles for power between the modernists, represented by Muhammadiyah and former Masyumi members in Parmusi and the PSII, and the traditionalists from Nahdlatul Ulama and Perti. The other sanctioned party, the Partai Demokrat Indonesia (Indonesian Democratic Party, PDI), was the amalgamation of all the nationalist and Christian parties. It also faced similar problems.

To ensure that the PPP could never gain sufficient grassroots support to mount a viable electoral challenge to Golkar, the New Order barred parties from opening offices at the subdistrict or village level and forbade them from holding rallies and recruitment drives until one month prior to the election. Furthermore, Suharto insisted that all civil servants must swear their loyalty exclusively to the state (*monoloyalitas*), and in so doing, vote consistently for Golkar. This policy was vigorously enforced. Government bureaucrats, soldiers, military officials, teachers, professors, and administrators at public schools and state universities were all required by law to vote for Golkar. According to Irwan Abdullah, director of the Graduate School at the Gadjah Mada University, "I felt forced to vote for Golkar. I felt fear of people spying on me."[9]

Together with the *monoloyalitas* policy, the Suharto regime also implemented what General Ali Moertopo termed "the Floating Mass Concept," which made political activity permissible only during election campaigns.[10] Thus, the state-sanctioned Islamist party was forbidden to hold recruitment drives. It could not consult with its supporters at the village level to discern their grievances and thus be an effective channel for Muslim interests. It was not allowed to hold office at the lower levels of government; all governors, mayors, and village heads came from Golkar. Moreover, the PPP could never win a majority in the elections. According to Dr. Husnan Bey, editor-in-chief of *Majalah Pakar*, the PPP magazine, "PPP was never a big party. We were always number two to Golkar. It was forbidden for us to exceed Golkar."[11]

The Suharto regime also sought to discredit the PPP by making loose allegations linking it with a shadowy, radical Islamist group, Kommando Jihad (Holy War Command), which allegedly aimed to overthrow the government. However, despite these efforts and the restrictions on political parties, and widespread violence, coercion, and intimidation in the months leading up to the 1977 elections, the PPP still was able to obtain 29.29 percent of the vote.[12] Therefore, the New Order regime escalated their efforts toward the marginalization of Islam as a force for institutional and extra-institutional political opposition following the 1977 election.

The New Order regime began a campaign to socialize *Pancasila* as the foundational ideology of the regime and the nation.[13] The campaign culminated in the August 1982 order that all parties adopt *Pancasila* as their *azas tunggal* (sole foundation) in the run up to the 1982 elections. This meant that the PPP, which formerly had been designated as the Islamist party, had to formally abandon Islam and eliminate direct references to Islam from its charter. After the New Order forbade parties to use Islamic symbols, the PPP was forced to change its designated symbol from the Ka'bah[14] to the star, one of the symbols of *Pancasila*. This might beg the question of why, at this point, Suharto did not eliminate the PPP. It provided a useful pressure valve for political frustrations and a safe channel for Muslims to exercise their political ambitions.[15]

After the political parties adopted *Pancasila* as their sole foundation, the ruling was extended to all organizations in the 1985 *Undang-Undang Keormasan* (Mass Organizations Law). As a result, all organizations that held both *Pancasila* and Islam in their charters had to abandon Islam. The issue was so contentious that some organizations split over the issue. Himpunan Mahasiswa Islam (Islamic Student Association, HMI), the leading Islamic student association split in two, with the HMI-DIPO accepting the *azas tunggal* ruling and the HMO-MPO choosing to secretly keep Islam in its statutes and go underground. For the modernists, this was especially painful, for it set the *Pancasila,* a creation of man, above the Koran and Islam, creations of God. The very concept of Islamist goals had become seditious. Proposing an alternative vision for society, the implementation of sharia, became akin to calling for the overthrow of the New Order system. Many Muslim activists perceived the politics of *azas tunggal* as an attempt to depoliticize, if not to dethrone Islam.[16] Furthermore, these moves were compounded by the New Order's taboo on discussion of any issues seen to fall under SARA—racial, religious, ethnic (Chinese-related issues), or inter-communal problems (a reference to class conflicts).[17] The New Order was extremely concerned about the potential destabilizing impact of communal, ethnic, or religious conflicts and contended that the prioritization of *Pancasila* loyalty over religion was necessary to prevent SARA-based conflicts.[18] The regime took harsh measures against those who refused to accept *Pancasila* as *azas tunggal* or who defied the taboo on SARA. Many Muslim activists who spoke openly against such policies were arrested and given prison terms.

## Muslim Activists' Response to the New Order System

Muslim activists responded to these state actions in three ways. One group permitted themselves to be co-opted into the institutions and organs of state, so that they could work patiently and quietly over decades to encourage the regime to alter its attitudes toward Muslim interests.[19] A second group recognized the constraints on political participation and worked to improve the socioeconomic welfare of Muslims from a base in civil society. A final group went underground.

### Change the System from Within

Throughout the 1970s and the 1980s, some Muslim activists from Muhammadiyah and the HMI joined Golkar or the bureaucracy in Jakarta and the provinces to have access to channels to improve the well-being of their fellow Muslims. For example, Akbar Tanjung, a former chairman of the HMI, joined Golkar and became minister of youth in one Suharto cabinet. He used that opportunity to recruit his fellow HMI members into the bureaucracy. Some Masyumi members also chose to abandon or, at least postpone the party's Islamist agenda and joined Golkar or the bureaucracy. From this position, they recruited like-minded Muslims into the channels of state and provided them with opportunities for upward mobility.[20] However, these technocrats had little substantive influence over the direction of policy, except in a handful of situations when a bill evoked the ire of pious Muslims, such as the 1973 Marriage Law, which would have largely removed marriage and divorce from the purview of religious courts, and the 1978 Kepercayaan Law, which would have permitted religious mysticism to be recognized as a legitimate belief system by the state. Both of these bills caused no small amount of consternation among many Muslims, for they were viewed as undermining the sanctity of Islam. Both of these bills sparked massive protests. It is important to note that in instances where the New Order compromised, the issues—marriage or conceptualization of religion versus belief—were sociocultural issues, rather than political ones. There was no ideological conflict between depoliticization of Islam and these limited social accommodations.

Some modernist Muslim activists, together with some similarly accommodationist members of NU, joined one of the corporatist associations that

Suharto established to control important Muslim constituencies, including preachers through the Majelis Dakwah Indonesia (Indonesia Dawkah Council, MDI); ulama through the Majelis Ulama Indonesia (Indonesian Council of Ulama, MUI); and later, intellectuals through the Ikatan Cendekiawan Muslim Se-Indonesia (Association of Indonesian Muslim Scholars, ICMI).[21] Others joined one of the many Islamic institutions in Suharto's extensive patronage network, which included schools, publishing houses, think tanks, foundations, and state-sponsored *dakwah* organizations.[22] The purpose of these corporatist and government-affiliated organizations was to co-opt Muslims to the state's viewpoint, to show the state's ideology as fully compatible with Islam. However, it is important to note that many who joined these corporatist associations did not necessarily perceive themselves as co-opted but as taking an alternative route to promote Muslim interests. For example, members of ICMI used their position to advocate for greater *proporsionalisme* (proportionality) in hiring and promoting Muslims vis-à-vis Christians in the upper echelons of civil service, bureaucracy, and organs of state.[23]

*Muslim Civil Society*
While the New Order regime repressed and marginalized Islamist mobilization, it endorsed personal piety, spirituality, and cultural displays of faith. Thus, while it was cracking down with one arm, it was building mosques with the other. In East Java, the number of mosques increased from 15,574 in 1972 to 17,750 in 1979 to 20,648 in 1990.[24] In Central Java, between 1980 and 1992, the number of mosques almost doubled from 15,685 to 28,758.[25] This emphasis on cultural Islam led many Muslim activists to attempt to work for Islam in ways that would not alarm the regime. Since both the Suharto family and the military relied on *yayasans* (foundations) to ensure a steady influx of off-budget monies, the regime never would restrict NGO development in the same manner as the political parties.[26] Moreover, Indonesia was home to the two largest Islamic mass organizations in the world, Nahdlatul Ulama with 40 million Muslims and Muhammadiyah with 30 million Muslims. Thus, it was impossible to limit civil society in the manner seen in many authoritarian regimes in the Middle East. Even during the most repressive years of the Suharto period, one could join NU, Muhammadiyah, or one of the many new Muslim NGOs and work for the socioeconomic, educational, or cultural interests of Muslims.

Muslim activists formed NGOs in the 1970s and the 1980s focusing on social, economic, educational, and cultural issues. Often, they were members of the *Pembaruan* (Islamic Renewal Movement) taking root at that time, which was willing to work within the circumscribed and depoliticized climate of Indonesia to advocate for Muslim socioeconomic and spiritual interests.[27]

These intellectuals were epitomized by modernists like the late Nurcholish Madjid, who argued that Islam could be powerful and substantial without necessarily being institutionalized formally and politically. These new organizations included Lembaga Penelitian, Pendidikan dan Penerangan Ekonomi dan Sosial (Institute for Economic and Social Research, Education and Information, LP3ES), which worked on community development issues; Lembaga Studi Pembangunan (Institute for Development Studies, LSP), which focused on urban issues; and Perhimpunan Pengembangan Pesantren dan Masyarakat (Center for Pesantren and Community Development, P3M), which endeavored to improve the quality of education at Islamic schools.

NU chose to abandon institutional and party politics in favor of working within civil society. By the early 1980s, it had lost its base of dominance within the Ministry of Religious Affairs. The PPP lacked the capacity to function as an effective opposition party, for it was wracked by political infighting and faced a mountain of regulations constraining its activity. According to Kyai Abdurrahman Wahid, the former chairman of NU,

> If NU allowed itself to stay in the formal government-sanctioned political structure, it would be increasingly compromised and unable to protect its interests or the interests of the ummat... the formal institutions allowed by the government were set up to support the New Order development program and served to proscribe independent political behavior... Thus, to avoid government manipulation, NU would leave politics.[28]

These issues were compounded by the marginalization of NU within the PPP and within the government itself. In referring to the treatment of NU, Dr. Bahtiar Effendy, a professor of political science at the Universitas Islam Negeri-Syarif Hidayatullah, remarked,

> I never understood why NU was not accommodated by Suharto... NU was willing to do anything to get that opportunity... they were willing to accept *Pancasila* as the sole ideology, even though they were not forced to do it. NU's political role during the New Order regime was taken over by former Masyumi politicians, who were members of Muhammadiyah. NU's role was limited in PPP and that alone was unsatisfactory because PPP was controlled by former Masyumi and Muhammadiyah.[29]

Thus, NU ended its formal role in Indonesian politics and chose to *kembali ke kittah* 1926 (return to its original 1926 charter), which established it as a mass organization that provided Islamic education and social welfare assistance for its roughly 40 million members. Individual members of NU continued as parliamentarians within the PPP, but NU as an organization pulled out. After NU accepted *Pancasila* as sole foundation and withdrew from politics, some argue that its influence in politics increased, for NU's apolitical position as a member of civil society permitted leaders like Wahid to appropriate the *Pancasila* and other New Order concepts to advance its own interests.

Although Muslims could form NGOs, no movement could openly advocate a political role for Islam, sharia, or an Islamic state. Some conservative modernists, like Mohammed Natsir, the former chairman of Masyumi, also followed the civil society path and formed organizations for *dakwah* like Dewan Dakwah Islamiyah Indonesia (Islamic Propagation Council of Indonesia, DDII) in efforts to improve piety and promote correct Islamic practices. The DDII utilized a varied *dakwah* strategy, including working in schools, *pesantren* (Islamic boarding schools), and on campuses throughout the country.[30] The DDII preached that it was incumbent on all Muslims to support sharia, pray five times daily, adopt Islamic forms of dress, segregate by sex, and use the Arabic greeting—*wa'assalam alaikum* (peace be unto you)—in addressing their fellow Muslims.[31] Although the organization retained Masyumi's belief that democracy was superior to the authoritarianism of Sukarno and Suharto, it differed fundamentally from Masyumi. As a result of the repression and marginalization experienced by these modernists, their perspective on Islam became more conservative, narrow, and more closely identified with Wahabiism. Moreover, the tone of publications became increasingly paranoid, centering on perceived threats from Islamic liberalism, Shiism, Christian and Jewish conspiracies to undermine Islam.[32]

Overall, NGOs had to be exceedingly careful when criticizing the regime. Leaders of NU and Muhammadiyah had some leeway due to the size of their organizations; yet, they were cautious. Syafi'i Ma'arif, chairman of Muhammadiyah from 1999 to 2004, explained that when Muhammadiyah members wrote articles critical of governmental leaders or policies, "we used pseudonyms so the police would not arrest us." [33] The DDII was one of Suharto's most caustic critics, but it criticized the regime in an innovative way, by using international issues as a way to indirectly target offensive domestic actors—Christians, secularists, feminists, and Muslim progressives.[34] As a result of their criticism, the DDII was monitored by the state and was condemned to the political wilderness until the mid 1990s, when Suharto attempted to co-opt Islamists in a last effort to shore up more support for his regime. Finally, other Islamists who criticized openly and directly through newsletters and mosque speeches, such as Irfan Suryahardy, now known as Irfan S. Awwas, were sent to prison for extended terms on subversion charges.[35] Most Muslim NGOs avoided direct, public criticism of the regime, rather than risk being labeled anti-*Pancasila*.

*Biding Time in Study Circles*

While some Muslim groups accepted the constrained atmosphere for political Islam and either joined the government or worked for Muslim interests from civil society, others refused to accede. These groups were driven underground, and their activities increasingly centered on mosque networks. Rather than work for their goals through the crippled party system or by forming apolitical NGOs, these activists chose to voice their protest in mosques, *pengajian* (teachings), *halqah* (small religious study circles), and the more secretive *usroh* (family) groups.[36] Those Muslims who sought a political role for Islam would meet in small groups, in mosques, *pesantren* (Islamic boarding schools), and homes for discussions on enhancing personal piety and an inner rejection of the ideology of *Pancasila* as the sole foundation.[37]

Study circles were most popular in and around college campuses, since student political expression was forbidden under the 1978 *Normalizasi Kehidupan Kampus* (Campus Normalization Law, KNN). Since Suharto banned formal student politics, political activity was channeled through campus mosques and small faculty-level or department-level prayer rooms.[38] Young people needed an outlet for their political aspirations, and they found it in the one area where the state could not fully monitor.[39] Study materials often included the political writings of Mawdudi, Muslim Brotherhood activists such as Hasan al Bana and Syed Qutb, and Iranian revolutionaries such as Ali Shariati and Murtaza Mutahhari. For the most part, the gradualist scholarship of al Bana had greater resonance than the revolutionary writings of Qutb. Many student organizations utilized the study circle format, including leftists and Christian groups as well as Muslims from across the politico-religious spectrum. In seeking to depoliticize university campuses, the Suharto regime inadvertently engendered the conditions for a thriving counter-culture of political Islam, much of which rejected *Pancasila* as sole foundation and supported Islamization of the state.

One notable example, the Salman movement, formed discussion groups on public university campuses that sought to formulate political and economic policy for the future, when the political system would be more receptive to Islamization. These study circles are often grouped together under the name of Gerakan Tarbiyah (education movement). Martin van Bruinessen lists four characteristics of the movement:

> They are highly critical of the secular state and believe that only a state based on sharia can be just. They consist of relatively closed groups and avoid contact with outsiders. They assert that Islam is a total way of life and demand that their members conform to Islamic norms in all aspects of life. They exercise strict control of their members and demand high standards of Islamic morality[40]

The most motivated Gerakan Tarbiyah activists organized themselves into study circles of five to ten people, where they would meet several times a week to study the Koran and the teachings of notable scholars.[41] According to Mutammimul Ula, one of the founding members of the PK, a political party that would emerge from this movement following Suharto's resignation,

> Suharto was repressive against Islamic powers. That means the government did not give them access to politics. At that time, the government imposed *Normalizasi Kehidupan Kampus* where students were forced to devote all to academic life and avoid doing politics. We could not let campus life stagnate. Therefore, we chose the peaceful and spiritual way by establishing study circles to enhance student understanding of Islam. In this way, the movement started.[42]

An entire segment of society with alternative visions for the role of political Islam in the state found their voices in the study circles; yet, it was a voice that perceived the state as following an illegitimate path. The state responded to this movement by attempting to infiltrate the study circles and repress them, but these activities only increased the influence of these movements among students, who were angered by the injustices of the Suharto regime, cut off from alternative ideologies, and hungry for simple solutions.[43]

Hizbut Tahrir, a transnational Islamist organization originally founded in Jordan that aims to establish a pan-Islamic caliphate, also arose from study circles at Gadjah Mada University (UGM), Airlangga University, and Bogor Agricultural University (IPB). This organization is quite unique for it existed as a campus movement within a campus movement, the Lembaga Dakwah Kampus (Campus Dakwah Organization, LDK). According to Ismail Yusanto, one of the founding members of Hizbut Tahrir in Indonesia,

> In the Suharto era, we could not expose Hizbut Tarir in name. We had activities in many cities, but we could not do it as Hizbut Tahrir. We had many activities under the LDK name or as *yayasans*. In Bogor, we used the name of *yayasan kemudi* or The Association of Former LDK activists... For the first ten years, we focused on gathering followers on [college] campuses. We then entered other centers of gathering—offices, mosques, *pesantren*, and also senior high schools. How? Through basic training. We have special training on four main topics—Islam, personality, sharia, etc... we were recruiting and gathering... from campuses and other avenues.[44]

However, during the Suharto era, Hizbut Tahrir could not operate openly as Hizbut Tahrir and proclaim its goals of a pan-Islamic caliphate and the implementation of sharia. It could covertly gather followers but could not openly articulate its goals.

It is important to note that while Gerakan Tarbiyah activists and Hizbut Tahrir activists had radical goals, they used systemic methods. One reason for this lies in their ideological training. Gerakan Tarbiyah was strongly influenced by the Muslim Brotherhood, particularly the writings of Hasan al Bana, which call for a nonviolent, gradual approach to achieving an Islamic state. Likewise, Hizbut Tahrir also has a three-step approach to achieving the pan-Islamic caliphate, the first stage of which involves interacting with fellow Muslims and educating them in the organization's beliefs. As a result, they too were willing to work slowly, gathering followers and supporters in a grassroots bottom-up approach to societal transformation.

In the post-Suharto era, radical Islamist groups would emerge from exclusive Salafi *halqah* and secretive *usroh* groups. Some were closely affiliated with the remnants of the Darul Islam movement and such leaders as Abu Bakar Basyir and Abdullah Sungkar, who would later go on to found Jemaah Islamiyah.[45] Basyir and Sungkar and several other former political detainees created a network of *usroh* of devout Muslims in and around Central Java. While some of the members were quietist, others had been previously detained for alleged involvement in radical Islamist activities during the 1970s.[46] Participants sought to deepen their Islamic knowledge, rejected the legitimacy of *Pancasila,* and were committed to the struggle for the implementation of Islamic teachings and Islamic law.[47] To that end, members were divided into *usroh* or families that would assist one another to remain on the path of religious and moral self-improvement, and in so doing, they eschewed all contact with people outside the network.[48] Another radical Islamist group, the Al Sunna Communication Forum (FKAWJ) and its Laskar Jihad militia were born out of the Salafi study circles of the Jama'ah Ihya al-Sunnah (The Community of the Revival of the Sunna) movement led by Jafar Umar Thalib, a Yemeni-educated Indonesian of Arab descent. Still others such as Negara Islamiyah Indonesia (Indonesian Islamic State) were born from study circles as well.

*Co-optation and Overtures to Muslim Interests*

By the late 1980s, it was impossible to ignore the resurgence of faith that was taking place among Indonesian Muslims. In the years after Islamist organizations accepted *Pancasila* as *azas tunggal,* the New Order began to slowly relax its attitude toward Islam. Whereas it had long resisted policies such as the establishment an Islamic bank and the equalization of Islamic courts with civic ones, Suharto shifted his position to "partially accommodate" Muslim interests.[49] These included the passage of a National Education Law in 1989, which put religious education on par with secular education, the equalization of religious courts with civil courts in 1991, the reversal of the state policy banning headscarves on college campuses in 1991, the issuance of a joint-ministerial decree regulating the collection and distribution of *zakat* (alms) in 1991, the establishment of an Islamic bank in 1991, and the ending of the national lottery in 1993.

Suharto also adopted a more religious lifestyle. Some observers have attributed this to an instrumental effort to woo pious Muslim voters at a time when support from the military was flagging.[50] Others believe that he grew genuinely more religious as he grew older and his health began to wane. He began studying the Koran and took his family on the Hajj to Mecca. The sum total of these actions reduced the climate of mutual suspicion and hostility that had characterized state-Islamist group relations over the previous 20 years. Suharto now believed that co-optation was the best strategy for coping with the Islamic resurgence among Indonesian Muslims.

These efforts were epitomized by the creation of Ikatan Cendekiawan Muslim Se-Indonesia (Indonesian Association of Muslim Intellectuals, ICMI) in 1991 as a vehicle to redress the strained relationship between Muslim activists and the regime.[51] ICMI was not an autonomous organization representing the political interests of the Muslim community but instead a corporatist organization dominated by technocrats and bureaucrats loyal to Suharto.[52] Its purpose was to co-opt Muslim support and contain Muslim opposition, while ceding no real power, influence or support to political Islam.[53] Yet, Muslim intellectuals and officials who joined ICMI saw it as a channel to recruit Muslim colleagues into the higher echelons of the state bureaucracy, as ministers, governors, and bureaucrats.[54] ICMI was instrumental in the establishment of new Islamic institutions such as Bank Muamalat, an Islamic bank, the *Republika Daily*, the ICMI newspaper, and Center for Information and Development Studies (CIDES), the ICMI think tank. The establishment of ICMI gave Muslims another institutional channel through which to mobilize to work toward their goals, but these aims could not be politico-Islamist in nature; they had to coincide with those of the regime.

However, this co-optation worked imperfectly. By the mid-1990s, Muslims leaders from NU, Muhammadiyah, and from inside the ICMI were calling for political reforms. A democracy movement was slowly gaining steam within civil society itself, led by Abdurrahman Wahid, chairman of NU, and, later, Amien Rais, chairman of Muhammadiyah. After the leaders of NU and Muhammadiyah criticized Suharto and called for greater political openness and democratic reform, Suharto directed his efforts toward courting Islamist support, permitting the political Islamists he had previously repressed, monitored, and marginalized to "come in from the cold."[55]

Starting in 1993, Suharto intermediaries, Major General Prabowo Subianto, Suharto's son-in-law and Special Forces commander; General Faisal Tanjung, armed forces commander; and Din Syamsuddin, a Golkar member and Muhammadiyah activist, held several secret meetings with two hard-line Islamist organizations: Komite Indonesia untuk Solidaritas Dunia Islam (Indonesian Committee for Solidarity with World Islam, KISDI) and the DDII.[56] These Islamist groups were willing to work to contain the emerging democratic opposition in return for political patronage.[57] Since they had been long labeled as extreme right and barred from any political access, both groups accepted this bargain and others followed. However, this did not imply that Suharto gave them access to the levers of power or policymaking.[58] According to Fadli Zon, a KISDI activist and a member of Golkar in the late New Order period,

> I think [the 1990s] was a learning period for the Islamist groups. These groups had a hope but not a really a thought out plan. They hoped, they wanted policies friendlier to Muslims. Their expectations were simple. Just be friendly to Muslims. Maybe, the next step would have been to influence policy. But at that time, there were no significant ways to influence the government.[59]

In sum, the New Order sought to disempower and depoliticize political Islam in order to eliminate its ability to present an effective opposition to the regime. The lack of institutional channels for participation had enduring ramifications, for marginalization engendered alienation and radicalization. By eliminating channels for politico-Islamists to work through the system toward their goals and claiming the very goals were seditious, it limited the opportunities for these movements to find any satisfaction using systemic methods. Like a band-aid hides a cut, Suharto's policies merely hid political Islam from view. However, it not only did not disappear, but the perspective advocated by many underground Islamist movements became more conservative, rigid, and Middle Eastern-oriented than those that existed prior to the New Order. In effect, the policy of marginalization and depoliticization radicalized many who aspired to an alternative Islamist vision for society.

### State Capacity

The Indonesian state under Suharto had a mixed capacity. On the one hand, it had a strong presence in the ensuring of public goods. On the other hand, it was far better in ensuring that no one challenged the state without consequences than it was in satisfying popular demands for consistent provision of law and order. At times, it was complicit in the violence. Likewise, the New Order accomplished sweeping socioeconomic goals in reducing poverty, advancing education, and ensuring food security. However, at the village level, it was helped by the mighty efforts of Nahdlatul Ulama and Muhammadiyah, which filled in the holes left by the state in the provision of education and health care by providing those services for the poor. Due to the state's successes in these areas, it gained performance legitimacy.

## Law and Order

While Malaysia and Turkey encouraged peaceful mobilization strategies and discouraged violent ones, bringing the forces of their security apparatus to bear on radical Islamist movements, the Indonesian state repressed Islamist groups and sought to discredit political Islam by linking it to extremist activity. In doing so, it did not necessarily distinguish between groups peacefully advocating for political Islam and radicals willing to utilize violence. Both were perceived as threats.

There was also state-sponsored violence. Elements within the military and civilian bureaucracies readily employed paramilitaries, militant youth groups, and even thugs to defend their interests and to take action to discredit those persons and groups (Islamist groups, political parties, labor groups) who they perceived as a threat to those interests. This contributed to lawlessness at the local level. It would be a mistake to characterize the New Order regime as suffused in violence. Instead, it would be more accurate to state that Suharto's regime faced periodic outbreaks of violence, some a result of militant Islamist movements, and others the result of its own strategic manipulations.

Overall, the Indonesian state was reasonably effective at institutionalizing its mechanisms of control throughout the Indonesian territories to prevent large-scale outbreaks of communal *religious* violence.[60] However, the state's behavior also inflamed localized violence. The Suharto regime responded to threats from Islamist mobilization by what was termed "the security approach." When conflicts broke out, Angkatan Bersenjata Republik Indonesia (Armed Forces of the Republic of Indonesia, ABRI) responded harshly. However, despite the consequences of stepping out of line, periodic explosions of violence by radical Islamist groups occurred throughout the New Order regime.

### A General Assessment of Law and Order Capacities

The New Order regime portrayed itself as the guardian of stability, security, and prosperity and defender against lawlessness. It based its legitimacy on performance in these areas and set up the institutional apparatuses to ensure it.

The territorial structure of the military created a military command that paralleled the civilian bureaucracy. This structure enabled the military to respond efficiently to any major outbreaks of conflict. The military was fused with the police, and thus, it was responsible for handling internal and external security matters. Over time, the military evolved into an instrument for maintaining Suharto's grip on power and the most powerful institution in the country.[61] The territorial commanders exercised paramount authority in their respective districts as well as a great deal of political influence.[62]

Through its territorial system, the military was able to observe radical groups as well. General Saurip Kadi explains,

> During the to period, there was military presence, the mayors, governors, ministers, down to the village heads. In every village, there were sergeants charged to monitor the villages. It means that every activity of the people was monitored by the military. There were clear lines of communication between those sergeants and the intelligence officers. They could see what was going on in the villages. Due to this structure, it was very easy to monitor them.[63]

Kadi also notes that the military responded in different ways to members of radical groups, not always immediately resorting to repressive tactics. "Sometimes, they would arrest them and hold them in jail without trial. Sometimes, the intelligence services would go undercover, joining the group, or the Islamic boarding school under suspicion. Sometimes, they would recruit or utilize agents internally within the *pesantren*."[64] The Badan Kordinasi Intelijens Negara (State Intelligence Coordinating Agency, BAKIN) co-opted members of militant organizations as informants. Moreover, the New Order regime was adept at controlling the use of weapons and disrupting those groups that were perceived as potential threats to the state.

Although the military was viewed as competent in the provision of law and order, the police force was not. While the tradition of militias existed in Indonesia since the Japanese occupation, they continued to function during the New Order period, in part, because the police insufficiently enforced law and order. "During the New Order, law enforcement was so ineffective that civil society organizations had to do it on their own. People would not go to the police to report a crime. They didn't feel their security was adequately ensured by the police."[65] Moreover, the legal system was widely seen as corrupt. As a result of this ineptitude on the part of the police, many organizations including Islamist groups empowered their militias to mete out justice and ensure the security of their members.

Some of the strategies employed by the security services also contributed to violence and disorder. The New Order regime also used a host of covert tactics including "manipulation of competing elites, blackmail, threats, extortion, kidnapping, counterfeiting, employment of hoodlums, incitement of violence and murder."[66] Moreover, it also employed paramilitaries, youth groups, and *preman* (thug) militias to instigate violence in order to justify the repression of protests and to take actions to remove and/or discredit potential rivals.[67] Peaceful demonstrations would suddenly turn violent, and the original participants could not explain it. Journalists would report how villagers noted seeing trucks of men, of outsiders, brought to their village or neighborhood, just before a riot would break out. These tactics were used throughout the New Order period. The use of paramilitaries trickled down to the political parties, which organized youth militias to defend their interests. For example, Golkar would use Pemuda Pancasila to intimidate people into voting for Golkar and to harass potential opposition.

*Periodic Outbursts of Violent Mobilization*
Although BAKIN attempted to infiltrate and monitor radical groups, the security apparatus was always better at responding to acts of violence than it was at preventing it.[68] The late 1970s and 1980s were characterized by a string of violent incidents attributed to radical Islamist groups. In each case, the state identified and arrested the perpetrators, but more incidents followed. This led many to believe that the state was behind these incidents, to draw attention to the boogeyman of militant Islam in the same way it had attacked the threat of communism.

The most notable example of state involvement concerns the arrests of 185 people accused of belonging to a movement popularly referred to as Kommando Jihad, which called for an Islamic state in Indonesia and was responsible for a string of bombings of cinemas, night clubs, and churches. There is considerable evidence that the movement was part of an elaborate sting operation by Ali Moertopo, Suharto's special operations manager, to lure former Darul Islam members out of hiding under the guise of stamping out the last remnants of the communist movement in Indonesia.[69] The Kommando Jihad issue had several ramifications. First, it allowed Suharto to claim credit for the arrests of radical Islamists in the run up to the 1977 election. Second, it provided an excuse for the state to crack down on outspoken, nonviolent Muslim activists.[70] Finally, Moertopo's operation renewed old ties and fostered new ones among radical Islamists living in different regions of the country: Java, Sumatra, and South Sulawesi.[71] Moreover, many of the students in the study circles perceived the Darul Islam rebellions of the 1950s as an indigenous effort to struggle for Islamic values while fighting repression. Thus, "these ideas, combined with the anger generated by the arrests made in the name of Kommando Jihad and the relationships forged among prisoners, helped to radicalize a new generation."[72]

In some instances, the state responded quite effectively. In March 1981, a group led by Indonesians who had lived and studied in the Middle East, referred to by authorities as the Imron Group, attacked a police station in Bandung to seize the weapons stored there.[73] After security forces arrested several dozen Imron members for their complicity in the attack, Imron hijacked a Garuda Airlines jet to exchange hostages for his imprisoned followers.[74] Military Intelligence Chief Benny Moerdani, together with a hostage rescue team composed of Kopassus (special forces) members, rescued the hostages and arrested the five hijackers.[75]

There were other occasions where it seems that the state was absent from the provision of law and order, especially with regard to violence against churches. A survey in *Tempo Magazine* indicated that church burnings increased exponentially during the Suharto period compared with the first 15 years following independence. During the New Order era, 398 churches were burned between 1965 and 1997, while 131 churches were burned between 1995 and 1997 alone.[76] Indonesian Democratic Party statistics similarly cite 600 churches burned during the Suharto era.[77] Christian sources put the figure at more than 500.[78] In contrast, only two churches were burned in the first 15 years after independence. Journalists were advised against reporting on the burnings, for doing so would be a violation of SARA. Yet, the magnitude in which these church burnings were taking place indicates an inability on the part of the military to respond effectively to the problem.

### State Overreach: Repression Goes Too Far
During the 1980s and the early 1990s, the state escalated the brutality of its crackdowns against potentially radical Islamist groups. For example, in 1989, clashes broke out between the armed forces and members of a hardline Islamist community in the village of Talagsari, in Lampung, southern Sumatra, affiliated with the Ngruki *usroh* movement.

> Warsidi, the man who had donated the land for the community was summoned to appear before the local military commander. When he refused, nine of his followers were arrested. Fearing an impending attack, the community armed itself... When the sub-district commander went to speak with Warsidi the following day, he was hacked to death. The following day, the compound was overrun by the military. It is estimated that at least 100 people were killed, including women and children.[79]

This event was a clear indication that, despite the efforts of the Suharto regime, radical groups were forming in Indonesia either underground or in some of these Islamic communities. The brute force of the crackdown further radicalized the movement.

Another notable example of overreach was what became known as the "Tanjung Priok massacre." Tanjung Priok was part of a campaign against the study circles, *pengajian,* and outspoken mosque preachers in the mid-1980s. The event was provoked when two military subdistrict command officers entered the *As Sa'adah* prayer house without taking off their shoes and allegedly used gutter water to remove several posters on the wall before arresting several dozen mosque officials and study circle members. After a soldier was attacked, and his motorcycle was burned by local residents, the police detained four men.[80] Muslim activists organized efforts calling for the release of the arrested men. Following a teaching session at *As Sa'adah* where anti-government speeches were broadcast over loudspeakers, several hundred people marched to the local military and police headquarters to demand the four men be released.[81] Armed soldiers blocked the roadway ahead of them, while armored vehicles moved into the rear cutting off their avenue of retreat.[82] The soldiers, armed with automatic weapons, opened fire. Army troops shot as many as 200 protestors, and many more were wounded.[83] Families reported that 171 activists went missing in the days after the massacre took place.[84]

In subsequent weeks, there was a rash of fires and bombings in Jakarta and Central Java, including an office building, a major shopping complex, a building that housed the state-run radio and television stations, several bank branches, and most shocking, Borobodur, an ancient Buddhist temple. The police and the military could do little to prevent these actions from taking place. In fact, their actions may have exacerbated them. The Tanjung Priok incident caused a massive public outcry, which pitted the victims' families against General Benny Murdani, the armed forces commander, and a Catholic, who sanctioned the imprisonment of 45 residents of Tanjung Priok on charges of "inciting" the attack on the police station.[85]

*The State's Use of Preman and Paramilitaries*
Over the decades of the New Order regime, the state frequently employed paramilitaries and vigilantes and hired unemployed young men to do their dirty work in intimidating and discrediting members of the opposition. There is ample evidence that the government frequently employed those paramilitaries in both the Aceh and East Timor secessionist conflicts; in labor conflicts in Sumatra in the early 1990s; in the run up to the 1997 elections, to intimidate and harass members of the opposition PPP; and, most notably, in the raid against PDI headquarters in 1996.[86]

Between 1995 and 1997, there was a marked increase in the number of riots, particularly in towns across Java. In numerous instances, analysts contend that unnamed elites initiated and inflamed the violence, especially a series of riots that targeted Chinese-Indonesians in East and West Java. On October 10, 1996, the city of Situbondo, in East Java exploded into riots after a judge sentenced a Muslim man, Saleh, to five years in prison for blasphemy. At the conclusion of the riots, 20 churches, five Catholic schools, a Christian orphanage, a pool hall, a video arcade, dozens of Chinese stores, and a courthouse were damage or burned; five people died in one of the churches that was set on fire. An investigation by the National Human Rights Commission concluded that the riot had been instigated by unknown provocateurs of unknown origin.[87] An independent investigation by NU concluded similarly. The army chief of staff, Hartono, likewise agreed that "some people have been coordinating a certain mission here to create instability."[88]

Evidence to support the allegations of provocateurs came from journalist interviews with the Situbondo villagers, who indicated that the majority of the rioters were not local people but black-clad men brought in aboard three trucks from outside the town.[89] According to these journalistic accounts,

> Their leaders blew whistles directing their troops to their targets; a truck dispensed gasoline for petrol bombs. By the time the police arrived, the rioters had moved on to neighboring towns, where they carried out a similarly well-planned program of terror against Christian churches and schools.[90]

The speed at which the riot became inflamed, the trucked-in demonstrators (who appeared before the riots began), and the ease with which they then went to other towns indicated that the violence had been engineered by outside forces.[91] Leaders of NU claimed that the riots had been initiated to incite hostility between Christian supporters of Megawati Sukarnoputri and Muslim supporters of Abdurrahman Wahid.[92] Further evidence to support this hypothesis came in October and November of 1996, when information filtered out of East Java prisons that several NU youths, who had been arrested for participating in the unrest, were being tortured, and one man, Ahmad Siddiq, died in prison allegedly from torture at the hands of Christian army officials.[93] To counter those efforts, Wahid apologized to the victims and sent NU's Ansor youth militia to guard area churches in East and Central Java, which served to calm tensions in those provinces.

In December 1996, riots again exploded in Tasikmalaya, in the province of West Java, following an incident where Rizal, a Muslim *santri* and son of a police officer, was accused of stealing money from his fellow *santri* at a *pesantren* and subsequently beaten by two young instructors. When the instructors came to the police station in response to a formal summons from the police, Rizal's father beat them, along with the *kyai* who accompanied them.[94]

> On December 26, 3,000 gather, and students demand that the police apologize. A small group began to riot throwing stones at the police station, churches, and other buildings before setting them on fire. Four people die. In total, seven department stores, six banks, eight car dealerships, three hotels, 12 churches, four factories, the police station, six bank offices, and 89 stores are damaged or burned as a result. [95]

Observers again became suspicious, when it became clear that, as in Situbondo, several of the youths arrested and charged with instigating the riots were members of Nahdlatul Ulama's student organization.[96] Wahid's supporters were informed by their sources in Indonesian intelligence that the riots had been carried out by anti-Wahid agents.[97] In other words, elements in the state security services were using "provocateurs" to discredit Wahid, who was positioning himself as a key leader in the pro-democracy movement and attempting to position NU as the peaceful, tolerant, pluralistic organization to lead the charge for reform from its base in civil society. Similar riots occurred in Purwakarta, West Java (October 31–November 2, 1997); Pekalongan, Central Java (November 24–26, 1997); Jakarta (December 24, 1997); and Rengasdenklok, West Java (February 1, 1998). Since one was forbidden to discuss religious conflict, under SARA, this spate of riots was attributed to the economic grievances of the Muslim majority.

In sum, the state's capacity to keep law and order was varied. On the one hand, it prevented large scale outbreaks of communal conflict from taking place; no lawless areas emerged where state authority could not penetrate. For the most part, it respond effectively to outbreaks of violent Islamist mobilization, which assuredly contributed to the decision on the part of many Islamist movements with radical predilections to stay underground until more fortuitous circumstances presented themselves. On the other hand, it overreached and utilized excessive force when it cracked down on study circles and Islamic communities. This had the effect of further marginalizing and alienating Islamists, which may have contributed to some groups' decision to use violence. The state was highly effective in ensuring that large-scale communal religious conflicts did not break out. However, it was ill equipped to cope with a serious local issue—the ongoing rash of church burnings and riots. Finally, there is compelling evidence that the state utilized paramilitaries to attack and discredit potential opposition figures. This served to further inflame the violence that continued, at a low hum, throughout the New Order and contributed to the breakdown of security that occurred following Suharto's resignation.

## Social Welfare

When states can provide a measure of education and welfare, this increases popular perceptions of their legitimacy, while, reducing opportunities for radical Islamist groups to recruit followers by supplanting the state and thus gaining the legitimacy reserved for the state. The New Order played a central role in the provision of education and welfare, while Islamist groups supplemented its efforts at the local level. The regime secured its legitimacy by its ability to successful ensure stability and continued prosperity. The provision of universal primary education, self-sufficiency in rice, and the drastic reductions in poverty were the hallmarks of the Suharto era. At the local level, the regime enacted a series of policies referred to as INPRES (Presidential Instruction), which provided funds for improved infrastructure and development assistance to local governments. By the mid-1980s, the state had built health care clinics in every subdistrict and paved roads to connect rural areas to urban centers.[98] The government sought to ensure that all children, even those living in the most remote areas, had access to inexpensive primary education and built thousands of new elementary schools to fill the demand for education.[99] However, the government did not do it alone. It shared its efforts with the two Islamic mass organizations: NU and Muhammadiyah played leading roles in social welfare in villages, towns, and urban neighborhoods throughout Indonesia. Due to the combined efforts of the state, NU, and Muhammadiyah, there was little room for radical Islamist groups to make inroads at the state's expense. While they could set themselves apart, they did not play a meaningful supplemental role. Any legitimacy they gained was from the alternative vision of an Islamic society they promoted, not from social services.

If we examine its 32-year tenure, the New Order regime had many notable successes in education and poverty relief. By 1990, 97 percent of all Indonesian children attended primary school, and 95 percent of all Indonesian children were literate.[100] The Suharto regime succeeded in bringing down poverty levels from 60 percent in 1965 to 16 percent in 1996, according to World Bank measures.[101] By 1985, the country had achieved self-sufficiency in rice. They accomplished this goal by a variety of methods, including researching varieties of high yielding rice, investing in upgrading irrigation networks, and temporarily subsidizing fertilizers and pesticides.[102]

While pockets of malnutrition existed, there was no evidence of famine outbreaks. These factors all had an effect on life expectancy, which increased from 40.7 years in 1950–1955 to 62.4 years in 1990–1995.[103]

Beginning in the late 1970s, the New Order escalated hospital and clinic construction, building over 26,000 public health care centers and sub-centers.[104] Yet, despite these efforts, the New Order regime faced difficulties in providing local health care because the funds allotted to *bupatis* (regents) for health care were frequently siphoned off for other purposes; only 25 percent was passed along to the local health care centers.[105] This remained true until the mid-1990s, when the regime introduced a health card, which entitled the poor to free government health services.[106]

The shortcomings in the health care sector at the local level led the populace to rely more on the services provided by NU and Muhammadiyah, which ran networks of health care clinics and hospitals. Unlike Turkey and Malaysia, parties were forbidden to work at the grassroots level in providing such services. However, NU and Muhammadiyah maintained a strong and vital presence at the local level. Both NU and Muhammadiyah clinics in rural areas had the capacity to provide inexpensive or free health care services to the poor.[107] According to Mariah Ulfah, chairwoman of the Fatayat Welfare Foundation, poor members of NU had access to subsidized medicines at NU hospitals and clinics.[108] Treatment that might cost 50,000rp at a private or government hospital would cost 20,000rp at an NU hospital.[109] The provision of these services was one mechanism through which NU and Muhammadiyah retained the loyalty of their members, who sought out NU and Muhammadiyah hospitals and clinics to provide them with medical services at a reduced cost. In doing this, these two organizations supplemented the government in a meaningful way.

### Education

One of the most notable achievements of the New Order regime was the establishment of free universal primary education in the 1980s. While junior secondary school was also compulsory, school fees also applied. However, due to the marked economic growth that began in the 1970s, school fees were not a major source of contention.

The New Order regime made the development of a modern national education system one of its top priorities in order to reinforce the depoliti-cization of Islam, to co-opt existing Islamist groups to its viewpoint, and to increase economic opportunities for Islamic school graduates. After the state set the goal of universal primary education, the number of students attending public school rose significantly. However, the state also sought to extend control over the madrasa (Islamic day school) sector in order to reorient Islamic education toward rationalist and scientific approaches, as a replacement for the static teaching methods of the traditionalist schools.[110] To that end, the state standardized the madrasa curriculum and provided financial benefits to those madrasas that adopted them.[111] New state-run Islamic schools were established with a curriculum divided into 70 percent general core courses and 30 percent religious studies. The purpose behind these changes was to make the diploma a student received from the madrasa equal to one received from a public school and to permit switching between public and Islamic schools throughout one's educational career.[112] Due to these changes, the prestige of a madrasa education increased as more madrasa graduates are were accepted to secular colleges and universities.[113]

The state also sought to play a role in the development and training of future *pesantren* teachers. To that end, they expanded the State Islamic University (IAIN) system, which has produced a highly educated cadre of graduates trained in Islamic theology, law, and pedagogy, yet also exposed to theories of social science, philosophy, and other non-Islamic intellectual influences.[114] After the conclusion of one's studies at IAIN, they have the option of continuing at public universities for advanced studies. As a result of the changes to and improvements in the IAIN system, the caliber and educational sophistication of the Islamic school teachers increased, and from this, the quality of Islamic education improved.

The efforts of the state were supplemented by the Islamic mass organizations NU and Muhammadiyah. NU ran an extensive network of *pesantren* in small towns and rural areas while Muhammadiyah ran private schools and madrasas in urban areas. NU's *pesantren* network, comprising 69.28 percent of all Islamic boarding schools in Indonesia, served to supplement the state's provision of education among the poor and the rural inhabitants of Indonesia.[115] Some of these, like *pesantren Salafiyah Syafiiyah Sukorejo* in Situbondo have approximately 9,000 students and a university campus. While NU schools were divided between those who agreed to the state's curriculum and those who retain independence, all Muhammadiyah schools accepted the state's curricular recommendations. They made the school day longer in order to add time for religion courses. Both Muhammadiyah and NU schools were typically cheaper than government schools.

### Monitoring of Islamic Schools

The *pesantren* in Indonesia have a long tradition of independence. Thus, the Indonesian government could not extend control over the *pesantren* in the manner of Turkey and Malaysia. Yet, the *pesantren* were regulated more heavily than the madrasas of Bangladesh or Yemen by means of co-optation.

If the New Order could not mandate curricular guidelines for *pesantren* and enforce them, it could seek to provide incentives to incorporate *pesantren* into the national education system. While some Islamic schools accepted co-optation, this was often done by a matter of degrees. For example, within NU, some schools agreed to accept the state's recommended curriculum and state aid, after NU had difficulty providing sufficient funding.[116] More frequently, *kyai* accepted state patronage but retained the existing NU standard curriculum.[117] Still other *pesantren* took a middle path of sorts, accepting state funding and modernizing their teaching methods to an extent.

> *Pesantren* education has become more streamlined. There are still *pesantren* where students are tutored in the traditional way, reading out a text individually, in front of a teacher, who makes corrections… but most also have classroom teaching with a fixed curriculum. And most offer general subjects besides the classical Islamic subjects.[118]

Over time, more began to adopt the government's recommended curriculum in order to remain competitive with the madrasas. Numerous *pesantren* opened up their own madrasas as part of their school system to obtain government funding or modified their daily study routines to permit their students to visit public schools outside the *pesantren* during the day.[119] Even among those who chose to stay independent, the existence of the IAINs provided opportunities for the incorporation of *pesantren* into the state system. For example, although *Pesantren Sidiogiri* in Pasuran, East Java rejected the state's curriculum in order to teach a more solid religious curriculum, it established relations with the State Islamic University-Malang to provide its students opportunities for advanced studies.[120]

The government sought to provide a measure of funding for Islamic schools in their bid to influence them to adopt an integrated curriculum. Both NU and Muhammadiyah, for example, received partial funding from the government for their schools, but this tended to be on a project basis and often, had political motives. Abdul Mukti, chairman of Muhammadiyah's youth wing, explained why Muhammadiyah received funding for its schools during the Suharto period:

> Muhammadiyah was a nonpolitical organization that focused on social services. Suharto liked that. Furthermore, many of the bureaucrats in the government were either former members or active members of Muhammadiyah. For this reason, Muhammadiyah could work more closely to the government. Since NU had affiliated with the PPP at that time and the opposition, they did not receive as much money.[121]

Syafi'i Ma'arif, chairman of Muhammadiyah from 2000 to 2004, also noted that due to the number of Muhammadiyah members who were civil servants in the government, the organization was able to lobby their members in pertinent ministries for increased funds for education.[122]

In addition to the Islamic schools run by the two major mass organizations, some radical Muslims, such as Abdullah Sungkar and Abu Bakar Basyir, used that opportunity to open their own Islamic boarding schools, such Ngruki near Solo. In doing so, however, they were not attempting to supplant NU, make inroads at the state's expense, or even gain a significant number of new recruits. Instead, they worked within the old Darul Islam and the hard-line wing of the Masyumi community to keep successive generations faithful to a more literalist and formalist interpretation of Islam. These schools attracted those who categorically rejected *Pancasila* as *azas tunggal* and sought an Islamic state. Not surprisingly, they received no state funding.

In sum, the Indonesian state gained its legitimacy, largely, from its ability to provide for sustained economic development, poverty relief and education. Over the 32 years of the Suharto regime, poverty rates dropped drastically, the country became self-sufficient in rice, literacy rates rose into the high 90s, and primary education became almost universal with 97 percent of all of-age youths enrolled. As a result, radical groups could not use these channels to make substantial inroads or legitimacy and popularity gains, as they did in Bangladesh, Pakistan, or Yemen. However, they did work effectively to keep their own communities faithful to formalist and literalist versions of political Islam. The state was assisted by NU and Muhammadiyah in offering supplemental social services at the local level. The Indonesian government gained legitimacy from its ability to ensure success in providing education and combating poverty on a macro-level. NU and Muhammadiyah supplemented at micro-local level.

## External Forces

If states lack the capacity to provide security, education and social welfare, one is more likely to see intervention by destructive external forces, which will exacerbate violent mobilization already taking place. The Suharto regime's shortcomings in the provision of law and order did not lead to intervention by external forces such as international terrorism or Afghan veterans. However, this was, in part, a matter of historical context and timing. The Soviet-Afghan war ended in formally 1989, but many of the fighters stayed through 1993. In the case of Indonesia, Abu Bakar Basyir and Abdullah Sungkar, the heads of Ngruki *pesantren* and founders of Jemaah Islamiyah, had fled Indonesia for Malaysia in 1985, after being released from prison, where they were held after being arrested in the Moertopo sting operation for being members of Kommando Jihad. In Malaysia, they spearheaded efforts to send Indonesians to Afghanistan, using Malaysia and Singapore as the primary travel conduits. These men and many of their followers, waited to return to Indonesia until Suharto resigned in May 1998. They established Jemaah Islamiyah only in the mid-1990s. When Suharto fell, the JI designated Indonesia as the primary recruiting ground. However, there were no terrorist actions taken until after Osama Bin Laden published his Declaration of War in 1998. Therefore, as a matter of historical timing, Jemaah Islamiyah was not prepared to launch actions and did not accept terrorism as their preferred method when Suharto was in power.

The major external force that impacted the New Order regime was the 1997 Asian Financial Crisis. Although Indonesia sought help from the IMF early, shortly after Thailand floated the baht, it made little difference. Suharto refused to enact those elements of the IMF program that would adversely affect his family and cronies; prices on staple foodstuffs rose some 80 percent and unemployment increased.[123] Suharto's legitimacy began to plummet. Students began to demonstrate on their college campuses, calling for reform. Riots broke out in major cities and towns. Then, on May 12, 1998, snipers killed five students at Trisakti University. Although he vigorously denied it and today is widely perceived as a scapegoat, circumstantial evidence, at that time, pointed to Suharto's son-in-law, head of Kopassus (special forces), Prabowo Subianto. Members of his cabinet and the Muslim community began openly calling for Suharto to resign. With the New Order regime no longer able to keep rice bowls full, ensure prosperity, or keep law and order, Suharto obliged on May 20, 1998. In the aftermath, there was a mushrooming of both peaceful and violent mobilization.

At the beginning of this chapter, the following question was posed: if states seek to positively influence Islamist mobilization, do opportunities for participation matter? The answer is a resounding "yes." The New Order refused to permit those who sought a political role for Islam or the implementation of sharia law to participate in politics through institutionalized channels unless they abandoned those views and accepted the state's vision. Even in the relatively open civil society, their opportunities were constrained. They could not lobby. They could not articulate critical views in writing without fear of repercussions. There was no way for those who sought a political role for Islam to register their grievances openly through political processes and have them addressed. The key problem in the case of Indonesia during the New Order was not one of the failures to provide public goods; it was the decision to marginalize this segment of the population. The banning of Masyumi eliminated an important channel for

Muslims advocating a political role for Islam to work for their goals. The decision to force all parties and movements to adopt Pancasila as their sole foundation made those very goals seditious.

The Suharto regime primarily sought to discourage violent Islamist mobilization through the "security approach." This had mixed results. The territorial system of the military and the efficient intelligence services surely discouraged certain groups from considering the violent path. It was also adept at preventing outbreaks of large-scale communal violence. There were no lawless regions where state authority could not penetrate or did not dominate. Yet, at the same time, it was unable to end the rash of church burnings. Moreover, violence occurred periodically throughout the Suharto era. In most instances, although the state could not prevent the incidents, it identified and arrested those responsible for them. However, the Suharto regime also failed to distinguish on several occasions between the potential threat posed by political Islamists in study circles versus radical Islamists undertaking bombings. Thus, it cracked down too severely in cases like Tanjung Priok, which set the stage for subsequent campaigns of retaliatory bombing. Elements within the New Order also sought to discredit potential opponents by employing paramilitaries, youth militias, and gangs of hooligans. This only served to inflame Christian-Muslim tensions.

The Suharto regime deserves high praise for its work in combating poverty and ensuring a measure of education and social services. This capacity enabled the regime to claim legitimacy on a performance basis, as effective authoritarian states must, if they seek to survive. In addition, NU and Muhammadiyah played important roles in supplementing the state's provision of health care, education, and community services at the local level. As a result, radical Islamist groups were unable make substantial legitimacy gains at the state's expense. Instead, their legitimacy came from their alternative vision for society and state, which they advocated in their *usroh* and *pesantren*.

This chapter endeavored to show the shortcomings of effective authoritarianism, to illustrate why it is not sufficient for states to simply maintain effective capacity, to keep the repressive apparatus strong and provide ample public goods to appease the population. The New Order case showed how states, which proceed along this path are never able to eliminate violence by radical groups. In fact, the state's policies actually contribute to the very radicalization they are try to prevent. When the Asian Financial Crisis hit in late 1997, the New Order could not longer provide public goods and it lost its performance-based legitimacy. In those last days, the elements in the security services began to arm paramilitaries to discredit the pro-democracy movement, hoping that the populace, fearful of mob rule, would demand a restoration of authority. Instead, Indonesians demanded participation and reform.

# CHAPTER 4

# The Incredible Indonesian Journey: Aspiring beyond the Ineffective Participatory State

On May 20, 1998, Suharto resigned from office after 32 years in office, leaving his vice president, BJ Habibie, to govern the country. Facing demonstrations and without a strong following from the military, Habibie initiated a process of political liberalization to accommodate the demand for reform. Islamists, in particular, used this newfound political openness to mobilize to achieve their politico-religious goals through newly available channels. They established political parties, civil society organizations, media publications, and umbrella organizations to coordinate activities among dozens of like-minded groups.

The immediate post–New Order period can be likened to removing the lid on a boiling pot. Indeed, institutionalized Islamist mobilization increased with political liberalization. There was also a similar bubbling over of violent mobilization. The extent of violence including riots, violent demonstrations, communal violence, and acts of intimidation was surprising given the military's territorial function remained intact. Yet the military and the police were divided and factionalized. In numerous cases, it seemed as though the military was overwhelmed, unable, and perhaps sometimes unwilling to step in to restore law and order. In 1999, communal conflicts broke out in West Kalimantan, Maluku, North Maluku, and Central Sulawesi. Although the conflicts were rooted in economic insecurity and often elite competition, those in Maluku and Central Sulawesi became framed in religious terms because churches and mosques were often targeted. The state seemed powerless to stop the violence.

At the same time, the Indonesian government was beset by a complex array of socioeconomic problems. Poverty rates increased from 16 percent in 1996 to 23.4 percent in 1999.[1] Pockets of malnutrition emerged, most notably in the outer island provinces. When Indonesia initiated regional decentralization policies in 2001, the responsibility for providing education devolved to the provinces, which led to an increase in school fees in some areas. The overall perception of the state's ineffectiveness increased with the state's retrenchment. Radical groups sought to take advantage of the state's lapses to gain support, especially in conflict areas, but their ability to do so was limited by the key roles of Nahdlatul Ulama (NU) and Muhammadiyah in supplementing the state. Yet, the state's shortcomings in offering social services did not have the same impact as in Yemen or Bangladesh because of the unique strength of Indonesian Islamic mass organizations.

Between 1998 and 2003, Indonesia faced significant pressure due to the potent combination of political liberalization; economic crisis; and the degradation of its capacities to provide security, education, and social welfare. Indonesia has improved significantly since then. It has transitioned to a democracy, which has since become consolidated. Efforts to maintain law and order and deliver education and social service improvements have begun to bear fruit under the leadership of President Susilo Bambang Yudhoyono and Vice President Jusuf Kalla. The communal conflicts in Maluku and Central Sulawesi have been resolved. Access to education has been expanded.

This chapter shows how opportunities for political participation encourage Islamist groups to utilize peaceful strategies. However, participation alone will not discourage those radical groups who would take the law into their own hands. Only improvements in capacity will do that. This chapter highlights the great variation within the ineffective participatory model and the ability of a state to encourage political engagement while, at the same time, working to improve its capacities. This chapter will highlight Indonesia's accomplishments and ongoing challenges.

## Political Participation

Islamist groups engage the political system in four main ways: by forming political parties and contesting elections, by forming alliances to achieve favorable policies, by working through local governments to pass legislation, and by mobilizing through civil society. Islamist organizations often work in large coalitions to pressure the national and local legislatures on specific issues. However, they also work with political parties, when their goals coincide. In these instances, political parties mobilize within the legislature, while Islamist NGOs lobby, hold demonstrations, send petitions, and participate in hearings. This high level of engagement enables Islamist groups to make incremental gains.

The immediate post–New Order period was marked by a lifting of restrictions on participation and the establishment of new laws to regulate the conduct of parties and elections. The November 10–13 meeting of the Majelis Permusyawaratan Rakyat (People's Consultative Assembly, MPR) led to the rescinding of the controversial 1985 Mass Organizations Law, which stipulated that all NGOs and parties were required to adopt *Pancasila* as their sole foundation. The repeal of the Mass Organizations Law meant that Islam was once again a permissible ideology for parties and NGOs. As a result, this period saw a proliferation of parties and organizations, which explicitly adopted Islam as their foundational ideology. In this open political environment, Islamist groups recognized the opportunities for political participation, reacted strategically, and began to mobilize through the new available channels. Islamist political parties formed and readied themselves for new elections to be held on June 7, 1999. The Dewan Perwakilan Rakyat (People's Representative Assembly, DPR) passed a new election law, which established a mixed system combining elements of both single member district and proportional representation. A new Political Party Law stipulated that parties must have branches in half of the districts in one-third of Indonesia's provinces to qualify for the national ballot and pass a 2 percent electoral threshold to contest future elections.

This period was also marked by the mushrooming of a more politically engaged civil society, including new progressive Islamic organizations such as Jaringan Islam Liberal (Liberal Islam Network, JIL) and the open emergence of hard-line Islamist organizations such as Hizbut Tahrir. Demonstrations became daily events. Indonesia faced increasing instability because the institutions of state were unable to cope with the explosion of political mobilization.

### Indonesian Political Parties

In the first six months after Suharto's resignation, approximately 141 new parties formed. Of these, 48 parties were certified by the Team of 11 to participate in the 1999 elections; 18 of these were Islamist in orientation.[2] Many of these new Islamist parties targeted the old modernist or traditionalist constituencies, but others tapped into new support bases among pious Muslim intellectuals. PPP, the amalgamated Islamic party from the Suharto period, did not disband. Instead, it sought to engage in the new political system. Other parties like Partai Keadilan (Justice Party, PK) emerged from the Gerakan Tarbiyah study circles that thrived during the Suharto era in campus mosques and prayer rooms in the public university campuses. Table 4.1 shows how the traditions of Masyumi and NU were each revived by multiple parties.

**Table 4.1**  Islamic and Islamist parties descended from Masyumi and Nahdlatul Ulama

| Party name | Party affiliation |
|---|---|
| Partai Amanat Nasional (National Mandate Party, PAN) | Masyumi[3] |
| Partai Bulan Bintang (Crescent and Star Party, PBB) | Masyumi |
| Partai Syarikat Islam Indonesia (Islamic Union of Indonesia Party, PSII) | Masyumi |
| Partai Politik Indonesia Masyumi (Indonesian Political Party-Masyumi, PPIIM) | Masyumi |
| Partai Kebangkitan Bangsa (National Awakening Party, PKB) | Nahdlatul Ulama |
| Partai Solidaritas Uni Nasional Indonesia (Indonesian National Solidarity Party, SUNI) | Nahdlatul Ulama |
| Partai Kebangkitan Ummat (Revival of the Ummat Party, PKU) | Nahdlatul Ulama |
| Partai Nahdlatul Ulama (Nahdlatul Ulama Party, PNU) | Nahdlatul Ulama |
| Partai Persatuan (Unity Party) | Nahdlatul Ulama |

Interview, Husnan Bey, editor-in-chief of *Majalah Pakar*, the PPP magazine, May 2006, Jakarta.

Political Islam was mobilizing institutionally through the political party system. These parties can be divided into two categories: parties that kept *Pancasila* as their ideology but were based in Muslim communities and parties that adopted Islam as their sole foundation and sought greater Islamization of society, if not an eventual Islamic state. The two most notable *Pancasila*-Muslim parties were Partai Kebangkitan Bangsa (National Awakening Party, PKB), led by Abdurrahman Wahid, and Partai Amanat Nasional (National Mandate Party, PAN), led by Amien Rais, which were open to both Muslims and non-Muslims. Wahid's PKB is culturally and historically linked to Nahdlatul Ulama with a base of support centered in NU communities in East and Central Java, while PAN's base of support is among urban Muhammadiyah members. While PKB has maintained a *Pancasilaist* stance, PAN has moved closer to the Islamist parties. Other Islamist parties were exclusive and formalist, for they sought to create an Islamic society and state through the legislative process. Partai Persatuan Pembangunan (United Development Party, PPP); Partai Keadilan (Justice Party, PK); and Partai Bulan Bintang (Crescent and Star Party, PBB) are the most significant parties in this category.[4] They were exclusive, for they restricted their membership to Muslims and set the Koran and the Sunna as their sole foundation.[5]

In the aftermath of the Suharto regime, the PPP sought to refashion itself to market itself as the Islamist party best able to represent the interests of all Indonesian Muslims. It sought to shed its image as the institutional Islamic party of the Suharto regime and readopted Islam as its ideology and the Ka'bah as its symbol. Of all the Islamist parties, the PPP has the most diffuse support across Muslim groups in Indonesia, with strongholds in the outer islands and among rural and elderly voters.[6] PBB, in contrast, sought to position itself as the successor party to Masyumi and court members of the old Masyumi community networks.[7] PBB denied that it sought to turn Indonesia into a formal Islamic state but supported the implementation of new regulations to reflect Islamic values, such as incorporating the Jakarta charter into the constitution.[8]

Finally, PK is a cadre party that emerged from the Gerakan Tarbiyah movement. PK is unique among the Islamist parties because it also runs an extensive network of *dakwah* activities, including schools, day care centers, and proselytizing. It holds regular meetings for its members to improve their religious understanding. Mutammimul Ula, a founding member of PK, contends, "We had to convince Indonesian Muslims, as the majority, to seek access to politics and policy through peaceful means."[9] In the run-up to the 1999 elections, Indonesians who sought a political role for Islam could join or vote for the PPP, PBB, and PK, or one of the smaller Islamist parties. Although this party system was a new channel, Islamist groups utilized it. In the 1999 elections, political Islam was well represented.

### Elections

The 1999 elections were widely categorized as free and fair, with only minor incidents of reported abuse in some of the outer islands. In contrast to the 1955 election, where parties espousing an Islamic state took nearly 40 percent of the vote, in 1999, Islamist parties garnered only 17.7 percent of the vote.[10] That vote share rises to 37.4 percent when PAN and PKB are included

**Table 4.2**  Indonesia's 1999 election results: People's Representative Assembly[11]

| Party | Percentage | Number of seats | Ideology |
|---|---|---|---|
| PDI-P | 33.73 | 153 | Pancasila |
| Golkar | 22.46 | 120 | Pancasila |
| PKB | 12.66 | 51 | Pancasila |
| PPP | 10.72 | 58 | Islamist |
| PAN | 7.12 | 34 | Pancasila |
| PBB | 1.94 | 13 | Islamist |
| PK | 1.52 | 7 | Islamist |
| Other 41 Parties | 9.85 | 26 | Varied |
| Total | 100.00 | 462 | |

Of all of the Islamist parties, only the PPP and PBB crossed the electoral threshold. However, the Islamists reacted strategically. They used their vote share to maximize their influence on key issues. For example, the PPP and PBB put forth a resolution calling for the restoration of the Jakarta Charter, which stipulated that all Muslims must follow the sharia.[12] While this initiative was rejected by all the other parties, the move signaled that they would work for their goals through the legislative system.

The year 2004 was largely referred to as the "Year of Voting Frequently," as Indonesians elected representatives for the national DPR; the new Dewan Perwakilan Daerah (Regional Representative Assembly, DPD); the provincial Dewan Perwakilan Rakyat Daerah (Provincial Parliament, DPRD I); and the district Dewan Perwakilan Rakyat Daerah II (District Parliament, DPRD II). The year 2004 also marked the first time in history that Indonesians would vote directly to elect their president. For the Islam-affiliated parties, the 2004 elections were largely a repeat of 1999, with Islamist parties obtaining 18.11 percent of the vote in 2004, versus 17.7 percent of the vote in 1999. When one includes the inclusive PAN and PKB, the total for the Muslim parties are 35.12 in 2004 compared with 37.4 percent in 1999. Table 4.2 compares the results of the 1999 and 2004 elections, where the top five parties from 1999 (Golkar, PDI-P, PAN, PKB, and PPP) all suffered significant losses in 2004, regardless of religious or ideational standing.

Two new parties, Pancasilaist Partai Demokrat (Democrat Party, PD) and Islamist Partai Keadilan Sejahtera (Prosperous Justice Party, PKS, formerly known as PK), gained substantially in this election due to voter dissatisfaction

**Table 4.3** Indonesia's legislative election results compared: 1999 and 2004

| Party | Votes 1999 | Votes 2004 | Net gain/loss | Ideology |
|---|---|---|---|---|
| PDI-P | 33.73 | 18.53 | −15.2 | Pancasila |
| Golkar | 22.46 | 21.58 | −0.88 | Pancasila |
| PD* | — | 7.45 | — | Pancasila |
| PKB | 12.66 | 10.57 | −2.09 | Pancasila |
| PAN | 7.12 | 6.44 | −0.68 | Pancasila |
| PPP | 10.72 | 8.15 | −2.57 | Islamist |
| PBB | 1.94 | 2.62 | +0.68 | Islamist |
| PK-PKS | 1.52 | 7.34 | +5.82 | Islamist |
| Total | 100 | 100 | | |

*Democrat did not exist in 1999.
Source: Compiled from Leo Suryadinata. *Elections and Politics in Indonesia* (Singapore: ISEAS, 2002), 103, and R. William Liddle and Saiful Mujani, "Indonesia in 2004: The Rise of Susilo Bambang Yudhoyono." *Asian Survey* 45, no. 1 (2005): 120.

with the established parties (PDI-P, Golkar, PAN, PKB, and PPP). Scholars also attribute the rise in PKS vote totals to the party's decision to alter their strategy to appeal not only to Gerakan Tarbiyah members but also to Muslims more broadly. Thus, they deemphasized sharia and focused instead on mainstream political concerns. One senior member of the DPR from PKS explained, "We've done our research. The majority of Indonesians don't care about sharia. They care about jobs and poverty and that agenda should be delivered by PKS."[13]

This changing strategy and subsequent increase in support for PKS is a strong indication of the power of participation in the party system. The effect of PKS has been to take an underground movement centered in college campus study circles and channel it into the political arena. PKS, together with the PPP, PBB, PAN, and PKB, represents varied streams of political Islam with differing degrees of appeal. Each of these streams is actively participating through institutionalized political channels, by forming political parties, contesting elections, and once government, advocating for specific legislation and inserting religious provisions into legislation. In doing so, these parties have enabled Islamists to feel enfranchised within the political system. However, this is not their only contribution. Islamist parties have not only sought to make gains from elections but also to push their visions and their political agendas both at the national and local levels. Since no single party obtained a majority in either the 1999 or 2004 elections, Islamist parties have proven an important force in coalition politics nationally and locally.[14]

### Alliance Building

Islamist parties have had the most success and gained the most leverage in working toward their goals when they formed strategic alliances with Golkar, Demokrat, PAN, and PKB at the national and local levels to win elections, to leverage their influence in the legislature, and to pass legislation. Table 4.4 will give a sample of these alliances.

**Table 4.4** Islamist party alliances

| Alliance description | Parties involved | Purpose | Success |
|---|---|---|---|
| Poros Tengah (Central Axis) | PPP, PK, PBB, PAN, PKB, parts of Golkar | To prevent Megawati Sukarnoputri from becoming president in 1999 | Yes |

*(Continued)*

**Table 4.4** Continued

| Alliance description | Parties involved | Purpose | Success |
|---|---|---|---|
| Fraksi Reformasi (Reform Fraction) | PAN and PK | To maximize PK and PAN's influence in the DPR and to provide PK cadre with a legislative training | Yes |
| Governing Alliance | Demokrat, PKS, Golkar, and PBB, PPP, PBR | To maximize influence by joining the governing coalition with the Demokrat Party | Yes |
| Local Level Electoral Alliances | All parties make these alliances | To win elections | Mixed results |
| Alliance to pass the 2003 Education Bill | PPP, PBB, PK, PAN, Golkar and eventually PKB | To ensure the passage of article 13 (1) in the education bill requiring all students to be taught religious studies by a member of their religion | Yes |
| Alliance to pass the 2006 RUU-Anti-Pornografi-Pornoaksi | PKS, PPP, PBB, PAN | To pass of a bill that would limit access to pornographic materials and restrict the ill-defined "pornographic acts" | No. Golkar, PKB, and PDI-P refuse to join the pro-bill alliance |
| Alliance to pass the 2008 RU-Anti-Pornografi | PKS, PPP, PBB, PAN, PKB, Golkar, and Demokrat | To pass of a bill that would limit access to potentially "pornographic materials," including arts, videos, and lyrics | Yes |
| Local Level alliances to pass sharia-inspired legislation | PKS, PPP, PBB, with either local officials from Golkar, PAN, or PKB | To pass legislation to regulate daily religious practice, personal modesty, and religious study in schools | The majority are successful |

Perhaps the two most notable alliances successes were the 1999 *Poros Tengah* (Central Axis) and the issue-based alliance to pass the 2003 National Education Bill. Both of these instances showed Islamist parties that they are best able to achieve their goals when they ally with *Pancasila*-based parties. In 1999, Megawati Sukarnoputri's PDI-P won 33.4 percent of the vote in the legislative elections and believed the MPR would select her to be president. In subsequent weeks, however, Megawati allied herself and the PDI-P closely with religious minorities, which alarmed the Islamist parties, who feared they would again be marginalized if she became president. Thus, the PPP, PK, and PBB formed the *Poros Tengah* coalition with PAN, PKB, and elements of Golkar to put forth an alternative candidate for president. As a result of this alliance-based maneuvering, Abdurrahman Wahid—moderate Muslim cleric, the chairman of PKB, and former chairman of Nahdlatul Ulama—became president. This showed Islamist parties the utility of forming alliances across ideological lines to achieve strategic political and legislative objectives.

Islamist parties also form issue-based alliances with receptive nationalist parties to achieve legislative goals. One example of a successful issue-based alliance is the RUU *Sisdiknas* 20/2003 (National Education Bill) in which Islamist parties and their allies scored a victory in their campaign for the inclusion of the controversial Article 13 (1). The National Education Bill was drafted to set standards for Indonesian education. Article 13(1) stipulated that all students were entitled to religious instruction taught by teachers from their faith. Since public schools already provided religious education, this bill was aimed at private schools, which had greater freedom in offering religious education. If the bill passed with Article 13(1) included, religious private schools would be obligated to provide religious education for those students whose faith differed from the schools' mandate.[15] This article ignited controversy between Muslim groups, who saw the article as preventing apostasy, and Christian groups, who resented that they would face the lion's share of the burden in implementing the rule to accommodate the thousands of Muslims attending Christian schools.[16]

All Islamic and Islamist political parties in parliament, save PKB, strongly supported the inclusion of Article 13 (1), but they did not have sufficient votes to pass the bill without making alliances with nationalist parties.[17] Thus, PK, PPP, and PBB formed an alliance with PAN and Golkar. PKB joined too in the final weeks. Islamist NGOs pressured the DPR to pass the bill with the article intact, holding several major rallies in June of 2003 to show their support to the bill. It is estimated that tens of thousands of Muslims attended the rallies.[18] While Nahdlatul Ulama opposed the bill, Muhammadiyah, Hizbut Tahrir, and Gerakan Tarbiyah endorsed it.[19] An interreligious coalition called the Cipayung forum mounted an opposition to the bill, but it lacked comparable parliamentary support.[20] Due to extensive parliamentary and extra-parliamentary lobbying, the DPR endorsed the bill, and then President Megawati Sukarnoputri signed it into law.[21]

The Islamist parties continue to utilize alliances even if they do not always win. It is important to note that they can only pass sharia-inspired legislation nationally if it is moderate enough to attract the nationalist or inclusive Islamic parties like Golkar, PDI-P, Demokrat, PKB and PAN. For example, in 2006, the same coalition of parties, PKS, PPP, and PBB, joined with PAN and Demokrat to attempt to pass the Anti-Pornografi Pornoaksi (Anti-Pornography Pornoaction Bill, RUU-APP). They failed, for they were unable to convince PKB, Golkar, or PDI-P to support the controversial bill, which would have curtailed women's rights, banned a wide array of sexual practices, and potentially infringed on the cultural expression of non-Muslims in the name of limiting access to pornographic materials and ill-defined pornographic acts.[22] This was an important learning experience, for when the bill was reintroduced in 2008, although it still contained contentious elements, most the pornographic acts clauses had been removed. As a result, Golkar, which had been seeking to burnish its own Islamic credentials in the run-up to the 2009 legislative elections, threw its support behind bill.

Through alliances, Islamist parties not only seek to influence electoral outcomes but also to impact legislative politics in an Islamic direction. Greg Barton explains,

> Islamists have great faith in the power of law to change behavior . . . Even as minority players, Islamist parties will seek out strategic alliances that will afford them the opportunity to achieve incremental amendments to national laws through the legislature. They understand that laws, once passed through the legislature, are not easily repealed and that the cumulative effect of many small amendments can be considerable.[23]

Husnan Bey affirms this sentiment, "We will build it brick by brick. This is education. This is pornography. This is something else. We will build this nation that way. Then, my child or grandchild will have an Islamic society."[24] Islamists understand that incremental legislative change often results in the state implementing many aspects of sharia even if it is not labeled as such.[25] They utilize alliances and the legislative process to work toward their goals.

### Legislation at the Local Level

The end of the New Order sparked a significant increase in political participation at the provincial, regency, and district levels. When Islamist parties found it difficult to enact sharia-inspired legislation at the national level, they turned their efforts toward passing them at the regency or district levels. While these efforts tend to be spearheaded by the PPP and PKS, regulations are often implemented by sympathetic legislators, mayors, and regents from Golkar, PKB, or PAN.[26] At the local level, Islamists have had a succession of victories in implementing certain portions of their political agenda, including improving Koran literacy and enforcing Islamic dress (see Table 4.5).

**Table 4.5** Local government regulations on morality and Sharia

| Region | Name of Regulation | Details of Regulation |
|---|---|---|
| Padang, West Sumatra | Mayor's Instruction No. 451.422/Binsos-III/05 | Muslim residents required to wear full Islamic dress. Non-Muslims encouraged to follow |
| West Pasaman Regency, West Sumatra | Part of regency's "Return to the Mosque" Program | Female students at Islamic schools required to wear full Islamic dress. Male students required to wear long sleeve shirts and pants |
| Solok, West Sumatra | Local regulation from 2000 | Male and female residents required to wear full Islamic dress and read the Koran. |
| Tangerang City, Banten | Tangerang City Regulation No.8/2005 | Part of regulation calls for the arrest of suspected prostitutes working in public places |
| Cianjur Regency, West Java | Agreement between Cianjur Legislative Council & 36 orgs, (Muharram 2001) | Local government employees required to wear full Islamic dress on Fridays and study Islam for an hour each day. Female local government employees must wear headscarves. No activities during the call to prayer |
| Indramayu Regency, West Java | Regent's call launched on Indramayu Regency's 475th anniversary (2001) | Local government employees required to wear Islamic dress on Fridays, fast on Monday and Thursday, and read the Koran for 30 minutes each day. No activities during call to prayer |
| Tasikmalaya Regency, West Java | Regent's Circular Letter No.452/SE/04/Sos/2001 | Local regent recommends all female Muslim students wear Islamic dress and requires all women to wear headscarves |

*(Continued)*

**Table 4.5** Continued

| Region | Name of Regulation | Details of Regulation |
| --- | --- | --- |
| Pamekasan Regency, East Java | Regent's Circular Letter No.50/2002 | All government employees required to wear full Islamic dress on Fridays and study Islam for an hour each day. Female government employees must wear headscarves. No activities during call to prayer |
| Maros Regency, South Sulawesi | Regent's Circular Letter dated Oct. 21, 2002 | All government employees required to wear full Islamic dress on Fridays and study Islam for an hour each day. Female government employees must wear headscarves. No activities during call to prayer |
| Maros Regency, South Sulawesi | Maros Regulation, December 2005 | All students must pass a Koran literacy test to advance to the next grade. Promotions for local government employees if they can read the Koran |
| Gowa Regency, South Sulawesi | Local tradition and community agreement | Female local government employees must wear headscarves. No activities during the call to prayer. Hour of Islamic study required each day |
| Gowa Regency, South Sulawesi | Gowa Local Regulation No. 7/2003 | Primary school students must pass a Koran test before advancing to the next grade. |
| Gorontalo Regency, Gorontalo | Gorontalo Local Regulation No. 10/2003 | Part of regulation prohibits a woman from going out late in the evening without her husband |

*Note:* This chart is a sample of government regulations relating to issues of morality and sharia.
*Source:* Chart taken from Van Zorge and Heffernan and Associates, "Creeping *Sharia*?" *Van Zorge Report* VIII/8 (May 9, 2006): 7.

According to Dr. Saiful Mujani, a professor of political science at UIN Syarif Hidayatullah and a resident of Tangerang, where several of these provisions have been enacted, efforts at shariatization are not being initiated necessarily by the political parties, but instead from a coalition of Islamist organizations, including Hizbut Tahrir, Persatuan Islam (Persis), the *Tarbiyah* movement, elements from Muhammadiyah, and the fundamentalist wing of the Muslim Student's Association (HMI-MPO).[27] These groups, Mujani argues, pressure the DPRD I and DPRD II for shariatization. "They're demanding that the local governments behave like the Angel Gabriel at the local level. The local governments are responding to this by [enacting] the laws. This is happening and is supported by PKS."[28] Yoyoh Yusroh, a member of the DPR from PKS, explains the PKS position on local shariatization, "Perhaps, friends in the regions perceived that the local community was conducive [accepting of the idea for the implementation of sharia-inspired initiatives]. PKS could not work on it alone because we are aware that we are only part of the parliament in the regions."[29]

Mohammed Kaththath, head of Hizbut Tahrir, explains how his organization, in coalition with others, works with either elements of the government bureaucracy or the parties to push for the enacting of sharia-based initiatives at the local level.

> In the regencies, there is usually the local Council of Ulama (MUI) and leaders of local Islamist parties. We help them to promote sharia. We campaign for sharia in the regions by forming sharia care forums. Recommendations for the implementation of sharia usually come up in the forum's meetings. Forum leaders bring the recommendations to local councilors or government officials. We also send delegations from Jakarta to discuss with local governments and council officials on sharia. We hold street protests when necessary. We cooperate in these efforts with PBB, PKS, and PPP.[30]

Some radical Islamist groups have attempted to intimidate the majority into accepting these regulations without protest, breaking up counterdemonstrations and issuing threats.[31] These groups are not simply content with lobbying local and national legislatures, submitting petitions, and drafting legislation. Instead, they mean to mobilize through all available channels, including the violent ones. These actions continue due, in large part, to the reluctance of the local governments to take a firm stand against acts of intimidation because they fear being labeled un-Islamic. This has enabled those groups to push the boundaries of acceptable behavior. However, these concerns have not stopped progressive Islamic civil society from counter-organizing to push for the repeal of these initiatives.

In 2006, opposition to these laws in Tangerang coalesced into an organized coalition led by progressive Islamic NGOs and women's NGOs from Tangerang and Jakarta under the name of Takdir. Participant organizations include Kaki Lima, Kalyanamitra, KePPak Perempuan, Lembaga Bantuan Hukum-Asosiasi Perempuan untuk Indonesia Keadilan-Jakarta (LBH APIK-Jakarta),

Perempuan Bantuan Hukum dan Hak Asasi Manusia Jakarta (PBHI), Federasi Serikat Patani Indonesia (FSPI), Mitra Perempuan, the Wahid Institute, Yayasan Jurnal Perempuan, and Yayasan Pengabdian Hukum Indonesia (YAPHI).[32] Takdir has appealed to the Department of Home Affairs and has filed briefs with the Supreme Court, claiming that the Tangerang regulation is not only a violation of the Indonesian Criminal Code, but also is unconstitutional insofar as it unfairly targets women.[33] However, it remains to be seen to what extent Takdir will be successful in its repeal efforts.

While some of these initiatives limit civil liberties under the guise of sharia, they also make a discussion of sharia part of the public discourse.[34] After three decades of repression and underground organizing, Islamists are finding their voice by engaging in the political system, mobilizing either as civil society organizations or political parties, and, in the process, they are courting debate over the interpretation of Islam and sharia in Indonesia. In the process, they are pushed to engage in debate with nationalist parties, women's groups, progressive civil society groups, and Nahdlatul Ulama and Muhammadiyah—both of which have rejected the implementation of sharia-inspired legislation at the local level. Furthermore, these regulations prove to Islamist groups that they can influence the political agenda through peaceful and systemic means.

In sum, after the fall of Suharto, the Habibie regime permitted new channels for participation and the government repealed those laws limiting politico-Islamist participation. The vast majority of Indonesian Islamist groups have utilized those channels to work for their goals. When Islamist political parties and NGOs could not enact sharia initiatives at the national level, they took the issue to the local level and sought allies with the nationalist parties in order to enact sharia regulations in the provinces, regencies and districts. While the trend toward peaceful Islamist mobilization is increasingly positive, it is clear that some Islamist groups also rely on threats, intimidation and violent demonstrations to pressure the government to adopt sharia initiatives. As democratic institutions have consolidated, these incidents have become much less frequent. However, acts of violence still occur due to state's difficulty in taking a consistently firm stand against radical activities. The state must not only encourage Muslim groups to mobilize peacefully by providing channels for political engagement but also seek to discourage the violent path.

## State Capacity

The resignation of Indonesian president Suharto in May 1998 opened up a political vacuum. Facing an economic crisis and a political crisis, the Indonesian state quickly became overwhelmed. It retrenched in the provision of security, education and social welfare at a critical time. Issues of state capacity have been a significant challenge for Indonesia, particularly in the first six years following the end of the New Order regime. While Muhammadiyah and Nahdlatul Ulama supplemented state efforts, radical Islamist groups like the Laskar Jihad (Holy War Militia) also gained popularity for their work protecting Muslims in conflict areas.

## Law and Order

Issues of law and order are widely recognized as one of the most severe challenges Indonesia has faced. State lapses emboldened radical Islamists to utilize violence and intimidation to target minority religious sects, to crack down on vice, and to temporarily supplant the state in the provision of security in conflict areas. In 2006, interview respondents highlighted issues of law and order and poverty as the two most significant problems for Indonesia. Many drew a direct link between the state's lapses in law and order capacity and increased radicalism. Indonesian scholars, journalists, politicians, and NGO leaders have characterized the state as "weak," "not firm," "inefficient in law and order," "incompetent," "ineffective," and "soft," to name several common criticisms.[35] As in the Turkish case, the responses of the Indonesian state to the breakdown of law and order at times exacerbated violent mobilization. Elements in the security forces took sides in several conflicts and gave funds, arms, and training to radical Islamist or Christian militias. In addition, the Indonesian state faced tremendous challenges, for it was coping with communal conflict breaking out in multiple provinces almost simultaneously.

This section first examines two cases of communal conflict, in Maluku and in Central Sulawesi. It contends that in these cases, the failure of the state to restore security facilitated the arrival of radical Islamist groups, most notably, Laskar Jihad, who supplanted the state in these two provinces. This enabled them not only to gain a significant measure of respectability for protecting Muslim interests when the state could not, but also the opportunity to persuade Muslims in conflict areas of the superiority of sharia.[36] Second, it explains how the state has inadequately ensured the security of religious minorities and how this has enabled radical Islamist groups, often working in coalition with one another, to push the boundaries of acceptable behavior to their advantage. Finally, it analyzes how the state's failures in law enforcement have emboldened radical groups to use violence and intimidation to enforce the vice laws.

## *Maluku*

The Maluku conflict broke out in January of 1999, after a fight between a Muslim minibus driver and a Christian passenger led to street battles between Christian and Muslim gangs. The fighting quickly spread from the city of Ambon to the surrounding districts and neighboring islands. Both sides inflicted heavy casualties on each other in the initial stages of the fighting. It is estimated that between 5,000 and 10,000 people were killed and nearly 700,000 displaced in the Maluku conflict.[37] The immediate causes of this conflict have been attributed to communal frustration due to (a) the effects of Suharto's transmigration policy, which relocated thousands of Muslim Butonese, Bugis, and Makassarese (BBM) to Maluku to relieve overcrowding in Sulawesi; (b) the degeneration of bureaucratic power-sharing arrangements between indigenous Muslims and Christians during the 1990s; (c) competition over resources; and (d) competition over civil service jobs.[38] However, the conflict quickly became framed in religious terms, as churches and mosques became targets of rioters, and riots coincided with religious holidays.

It quickly became clear that security forces, both military and police, were overwhelmed, unable, and, in some cases unwilling to take the necessary measures to restore law and order.[39] Gerry Van Klinken explains that the conflict in the province of Maluku should be first understood as an example of state failure to provide for the security of the Ambonese people.[40] Badrus Sholeh, a researcher on social conflicts at the Center for Peace Studies at the Institute for Social and Economic Research, Education and Information (LP3ES) concurs, "The origin of Laskar Jihad and the *mujihideen* [groups] lies in the weakness of the state and lack of law and order." [41]

The incapacity of security forces can be attributed to several factors. First, in the early months of the conflict, the security forces were undermanned and, as such, lacked the capacity to contain the rapidly spreading violence. In March 1999, shortly after the first outbreak of conflict, the combined number of troops from the army and police amounted to 5,300 in a territory with a population of two million spread over hundreds of islands; by November, the number of troops had increased by only 700 persons.[42] These issues were compounded by a lack of infrastructural capacity. The jail at Ambon's police station could hold only 20 detainees; the fire department had only two fire engines; Ambon suffered from a severe lack of fire hydrants; and the disaster relief coordination service lacked sufficient transportation to assess the magnitude of the crisis—they did not even have a motorcycle.[43]

Second, there were also issues concerning troop management and impartiality. The troops faced problems due to "contamination," as Christian and

Muslim members of the security services sided with members of their respective faiths. Allegations were levied on different organs of the security services. It was widely reported that Brimbob (the police mobile brigade), which was 75 percent Christian sided with Christian Ambonese, while Kostrad, which was majority Muslim, sided with Muslim Ambonese.[44] Given the troop arrangements, perhaps these instances of contamination were not surprising.

> Although all military units were mixed and regularly rotated from one area to another, soldiers naturally became acquainted with the residents in the villages they defended and were often given food, drink and cigarettes by the villagers. It was not unusual that when clashes took place that soldiers sided with the villagers they had been meeting on a daily basis, with the result that Muslim soldiers sometimes defended Muslim villages against Christian attacks and Christian soldiers defended their friends against Muslim attacks.[45]

It would be a mistake, however, to assume that all soldiers sided with their religious kin. There were many reports of troops acting impartially in arresting Muslim and Christian militia members, but there were also numerous instances where troops stood by as clashes took place or failed to intervene when armed men approached a targeted area.[46]

A third factor compounding the incapacity of the military and the police to cope with the violence was, ironically, the much needed police reforms taking place at that time. In October 1998, the military and the police were separated into two distinct security apparatuses, with the domestic security function being assigned to the police and the external defense function to the military. As a result, both forces faced an acclimating period with regard to their new roles and frequently clashed over resources and law enforcement issues.[47] This impeded coordination between military and police officials, which, in turn, hampered their ability to end to the fighting. Worse, clashes between military and police units were all too common in this initial period.

Finally, there is evidence that some elements in the military wanted the conflict to continue. Repeatedly, scholars and journalists cite the fact that Laskar Jihad was permitted to depart for Maluku over the orders of the president, that they received weapons on arrival and that these were standard military weapons as evidence of military involvement.[48] One TNI general explained that, "The problem was the military elite close to the old regime. To protect the old regime, they wanted to make the state weak. To do this, they made horizontal conflict. If they did not do this, they feared they would all be in jail now."[49] There are many stories of well-armed, well-built men clad in black, who attacked Muslims living in Christian areas, burning their homes and mosques.[50]

Laskar Jihad came to Maluku to protect Muslims, after perceptions spread that Muslims were being brutalized, and the state was unable to come to their rescue. As the violence continued, numerous groups began to demonstrate, including members of Islamist political parties and various Islamist organizations. The massacre of approximately 500 Muslims in Tobelo by radical Christian militias led to calls for jihad to defend Muslims. The Forum Komunikasi Ahlus Sunna wa'al Jama'ah (Sunna Communication Forum, FKAWJ) and its Laskar Jihad militia coordinated many of these efforts. They held demonstrations at Senayan in front of the DPR and the presidential palace calling for a jihad in Maluku and trained 3,000 fighters at their camp in Bogor. In mid-2000, Laskar Jihad left the port of Surabaya for Maluku, despite the fact that President Abdurrahman Wahid issued a direct order to the military chief in East Java to stop the militiamen from boarding the boats.[51] Since they claimed to be on a humanitarian mission, the armed forces allowed them to enter.[52] The arrival of several thousand Laskar Jihad marked a substantive shift in the conflict, as the fighters reinforced the Muslim side.[53] Laskar Jihad inflicted heavy casualties on the Christian communities and displaced thousands of Christians, causing the national government to impose a civil emergency in the province.[54] Although President Wahid declared a state of emergency in June 2000, it had little imphact as more Laskar Jihad forces entered the region.

Dr. Azyumardi Azra contends, "Laskar Jihad asserted that since [President Abdurrahman Wahid] failed to keep law and order, they would defend Muslim interests. They had a goal outside of that too. They wanted to show that Islamic law was better than secular law."[55] Therefore, they imposed strict sharia in the areas that they controlled. Since the state could not ensure the security of Muslims, Laskar Jihad would do it for them, thus advancing their goal of shariatization in the process. There is evidence that elements of the military backed Laskar Jihad. From 1999 onward, regular meetings occurred between Ja'far Umar Thalib, head of Laskar Jihad, and retired military elites, who indicated they would back Thalib's efforts to defend Muslims against Christian attacks.[56] Laskar Jihad fighters received military training before their departure, weapons upon their arrival, and, once in Maluku, backing from military personnel.[57]

In addition to Laskar Jihad, other radical Islamist groups also came to Maluku, including Laskar Jundullah; KOMPAK, a radical offshoot of the DDII; and Jemaah Islamiyah. While each group claimed it sought to protect Muslims, all contributed to the violence and disorder that characterized Maluku at that time. Laskar Jihad became known for taking over Christian villages, razing villages, and conducting forced conversions.

Jemaah Islamiyah and KOMPAK often killed Christians and mounted attacks on priests, seemingly more dedicated to eliminating their enemy than converting them.[58] After the arrival of Laskar Jihad and other radical Islamist militias, the violence again increased, with Christians bearing the brunt of the casualties. The dominant role played by Laskar Jihad and the escalation of the violence forced a more calculated government action. In 2001, the state renewed its own efforts to reestablish security and its own legitimacy in the province by sending a Joint Battalion, a centralized mobile reserve drawn from elite forces of the three services, which responded aggressively to the threat posed by Laskar Jihad and other militias and was successful in reducing the level of violence.[59] In November 2001, however, the Joint Battalion was withdrawn after it gained a pro-Christian reputation for its frequent attacks on Laskar Jihad. In June 2002, the state again attempted to reestablish law and order, this time through a mixed security/mediation solution. They established a "Security Restoration Operations Command," in order to improve coordination between police and military officials in the province and brought the factions to the negotiating table. This two-point strategy contributed to an improved perception of the state and security forces and led to the signing of the Malino peace pact in February 2002. However, this was an uneasy peace and sporadic incidents of violence would continue for the next few months.[60] The police could not stop Laskar Jihad from carrying out acts of violence on Christian targets until the October 2002 Bali Bombing prompted them to disband. Since the withdrawal of Laskar Jihad, the Maluku security apparatus has become increasingly effective and violent mobilization on both sides has decreased significantly.[61]

## Poso

The communal conflict in Poso, which ran from 1998 to 2002, is a similar story to the conflict in Ambon. Like Ambon, the conflict in Poso began as a recurring series of clashes between rival youth gangs in December 1998, which escalated into attacks on villages and neighborhoods by armed militias and paramilitaries.[62] While there are varied estimates, the most reliable say that approximately 1,000 people were killed; many more injured; and over 100,000 displaced during the fighting.[63] After the signing of the Malino Agreement, sectarian conflict diminished substantially. Here too, we see the shortcomings of the state in its inability to prevent the escalation of the conflict. Due to these failings, radical Islamist groups exploited the state's weakness for their own ends.

The Poso was sparked by a combination of local factors, including (a) economic competition over land and cash crops between indigenous

Pamona and Bugis and Javanese transmigrants, (b) competition between government officials over bureaucratic positions, and (c) the disintegration of bureaucratic power-sharing arrangements between indigenous Muslims and Protestant Christians. With the implementation of regional decentralization, competition for bureaucratic positions now suddenly involved higher stakes, and electoral campaigns became struggles between Christian versus Muslim factions.[64] The Poso conflict was not overtly religious in nature, but became framed in religious terms, as certain district- and provincial-level Protestant and Muslim politicians incited, and at times, organized riots and other incidents of violence in order to intimidate their opponents.[65] It is important to note that, in many of these instances, the offending politicians were arrested, tried, convicted, and sentenced to prison terms of several years.[66]

According to Badrus Sholeh, "It should have been very easy for security forces to stop the violence. Poso is a very small place. [Central Sulawesi] is a small region. Compared with Maluku, Poso should have been easier."[67] One regional representative speculated that the security service response to Poso was slow in coming because, unlike Maluku or the Jakarta bombings, Poso attracted little international attention.[68] Military and police competency was inconsistent. According to Human Rights Watch, when security forces were deployed in a timely manner and behaved professionally, outbreaks of communal violence were halted quickly.[69] However, there were often delays in sending additional troops, and attacks on villages by Christian and Muslim militias were allowed to rage for days.[70]

It became evident the state lacked the capacity to resolve the conflict following the Kilometer 9 incident,[71] where Christian militias attacked the Walisongo Pesantren in Sintuwulemba village, where Muslims had taken refuge.[72] In the ensuing months, JI and Mujahideen KOMPAK sent teams charged with recruiting and training fighters and, in the case of KOMPAK, distributing aid assistance. Laskar Jihad sent a contingent of between 100 and 150 fighters in July 2001. While all shared the common goals of protecting Muslims, many in JI believed they could use Poso as a secure base for their activities. To that end, JI's activities also included intensive *dakwah* to shore up support for Islamic law. Until the arrival of JI and Mujahideen KOMPAK, Muslim fighters in Poso relied on traditional weapons such as spears, knives and fish bombs.[73] However, after they received instruction in tactics, explosives, and firearms from JI and KOMPAK trainers, they had a clear military advantage.

At the end of 2001, the state began to increase its efforts to provide security in Poso, recapturing their mandate from the jihadi groups through a joint security-mediation process. Susilo Bambang Yudhoyono, then coordinating minister for political and security affairs, and Jusuf Kalla, then coordinating minister for people's welfare, negotiated a cessation of hostilities and disarmament of the warring sides at Malino. The Malino declaration agreed that both sides would cease all forms of conflict, obey efforts to enforce the law, ask the security forces to maintain law and order, reject involvement by foreign parties, return all belongings to their respective owners, return displaced peoples to their homes, carry out religious laws according to mutual respect, charge the government to carry out the rehabilitation of the economy, and forgive for the sake of peaceful coexistence.[74] To ensure security, the national government sent two battalions of army and police forces, comprising mostly Christians, to nearby Tentana, while Muslim troops took over the guard posts erected by Laskar Jihad and other militia forces.[75] Despite the continued presence of radical Islamist forces, Malino helped to reduce the violence.

However, in contrast to Maluku, the Malino accords did not lead to the end of the violence. From 2002 to 2007, Poso faced a second threat that locals refer to as "the terror." Although police strength was increased to 2000 persons, compared with 400 at the outbreak of the crisis, it was difficult to discern the root causes and main actors.[76] Theories included elite manipulation, lingering remnants of radical Islamist movements and illegal logging syndicates interested in the ebony trade. In comparison with the communal conflict where Christian and Muslim gangs were pitted against each other, the terror was characterized by attacks from small armed groups and was largely one sided, with Christians as the primary victims.

Incidents included the killing of 13 Christian villagers in Poso and Morowali by masked gunmen in October 2003; the bombing of a minivan in November 2004, that killed 6 people; a bomb in May 2005 of a market in the nearby town of Tentana that killed 23; the beheadings of three school girls in October 2005; the bombing of a Palu market on December 31, 2005, that left 8 dead; and two homemade bombs that killed a man and a woman in September 2006.[77]

The beheadings of the children mobilized the government to act, and they sent a police counterterrorism team to investigate.[78] It became evident that Jemaah Islamiyah's Poso *wakalah* (subbranch), together with members of mujihideen KOMPAK, was responsible for the attacks.

Over the course of a year's investigation, the police compiled a list of 29 suspects believed to be responsible for the majority of the attacks in Poso since 2003.[79] For several months, the police attempted to convince the listed militants to turn themselves in with no success. On several occasions, militants clashed with the police, burning two policemen's homes and a sentry post.[80] Finally, on January 11 and 22, 2007, the police launched two operations to arrest those responsible for the terror attacks, in both instances under live fire from the militants. The operations led to the arrest of 8 militants and the deaths of 14 militants and one policeman.[81]

In examining police behavior, we do see improved capacities. The police conducted the investigation systematically and attempted to negotiate for the militants' surrender for several months, before using force. Its actions have had several important ramifications. According to the International Crisis Group,

> Since January 2007, the radical Islamists responsible for the terror crimes have been identified, arrested, tried and convicted without backlash. The Jemaah Islamiyah administrative unit has been at least temporarily destroyed. The government initiated vocational training programs aimed at ensuring young men have access to career opportunities so they will not be tempted to join militant groups.[82]

As a result of the government programs and the police effectiveness, no serious acts of violence have taken place in almost two years. Poso was the last of the "lawless regions." Since January 2007, there are no lawless regions of Indonesia where state authority does not dominate.

### Attacks on Minorities

At the same time as Indonesia's security services have grown increasingly more effective in maintaining law and order at a macro-level, the government and the police have faced another problem—a rash of vigilante violence. This is well recognized by the public. "In one poll, respondents listed police passivity as a major factor in outbreaks of public disturbances."[83] Since 2005, the main source of violent Islamist mobilization has been coalitions of radical vigilantes that have taken the law into their own hands, attacking churches operating without proper permits and Islamic sects deemed "heretical," such as Lia Aminudin's Kingdom of God, al Qiyadah al Islamiyah, and Ahmadiyah. In November 2007 alone, radical Islamist vigilante groups attacked five different religious minority groups, which authorities had labeled as "deviationist," and the police did little to stop them.[84] These incidents exposed lingering problems in the maintenance of law enforcement. In these instances, radical Islamist groups assumed they could act with impunity, and, in some instances, they have been empowered in their efforts by the Indonesian Ulama Council (MUI), a quasi-government fatwa-issuing body.

One example is the forcible closure of churches in West Java. In March 2006, the ministries of home affairs and religious affairs issued a joint regulation to foster religious harmony by improving the regulation of the building of houses of worship. It required those seeking to establish a new church, temple, or mosque to obtain identity cards from 90 proposed users, the written support of at least 60 other community members, and the approval of a newly established provincial- and district-level body, the Forum for Religious Harmony.[85] Although this joint regulation was meant to be an improvement over a restrictive 1969 law, minority religions still faced difficulties in gaining approval for new houses of worship.[86] This reality led some Christians living in Muslim majority regions to bypass the regulations and establish private informal churches in their homes.

The presence of these unauthorized churches angered hard-line groups, who decided that if the government would not enforce the laws on community approval, they would do so.[87] According to the Communion of Churches and the Indonesian Bishop's Conference, between 2004 and 2008, 108 houses of worship were forcibly closed, ransacked, threatened, or burned, most notably in West Java.[88] In West Java, the hard-line Anti-Apostasy Front forcibly closed dozens of unauthorized churches. On several occasions, the police either refused to intervene or actually provided the hard-liners with an escort.[89] While the house churches were operating without proper permits, the West Java police's toleration of Islamist vigilante organizations taking the law into their own hands enabled those groups to push the boundaries of acceptable behavior. It showed these groups that they could undertake these actions without repercussions.

Another example is the issue of Jemaat Ahmadiyah Indonesia (Indonesian Ahmadiyah Community, JAI), an Islamic sect that is considered heretical by many Muslims, for it contends that another prophet, Mirza Ghulam Ahmad, followed Prophet Muhammad. The underlying controversy has been whether or not to ban Ahmadiyah as a heretical Muslim sect or to permit the movement to continue to exist in Indonesia, since the Indonesian Constitution guarantees freedom of religion. However, within this debate, the most serious overarching issue is whether Islamist vigilante coalitions will be allowed to take the law into their own hands to redress what they see as the inadequacies of government policy. In their zeal to pressure the government to ban Jemaat Ahmadiyah Indonesia, radical Islamist groups have attacked Ahmadiyah compounds and forcibly closed Ahmadiyah mosques. The issue is further complicated by the fact that MUI supports a ban on Ahmadiyah, and MUI members have been present at anti-Ahmadiyah demonstrations and attacks on Ahmadiyah property. Thus, it has been a struggle for both the government and the police to take firm action against these coalitions.

The most recent round of attacks on Jemaat Ahmadiyah Indonesia began in 2005 in Parung, West Java, where JAI members were holding their annual meeting. Members of the Forum Ulama Ummat Islam (FUUI); the Front Pembela Islam (Islamic Defenders Front, FPI); and the Lembaga Penelitian dan Pengkajian Islam (Institute for the Research and Study of Islam, LPPI) broke into the compound, armed with stones and batons; damaged buildings; and set fire to the women's dormitory.[90] Eight people were wounded before the Bogor police arrived, but the police made no arrests.[91] In the ensuing days, all Ahmadiyah members living in the compound were sent to their respective hometowns, and the local administration banned the sect from conducting any activities in its regency.[92] No arrests were ever made. That same month, MUI issued a fatwa declaring that Ahmadiyah was a deviationist stream of Islam, and its members were apostates.

In subsequent months, attacks on Ahmadiyah compounds occurred in Cianjur, West Java; Lingsar, on the island of Lombok; Praya village, on the island of Lombok; and South Konawe, South Sulawesi. Local police began to act more effectively after civil society leaders pressured the government to take action. In Cianjur and Mataram, suspected attackers were arrested. However, in Cianjur, the regency administration banned Ahmadiyah and its teachings.[93] Despite the arrests, radical Islamists felt emboldened by the decision of the local governments, felt empowered by the stance of MUI, and saw mob violence as a viable tactic to use against Ahmadiyah.

In 2008, the Yudhoyono government issued a joint-ministerial decree, which sought to chart a middle ground on the Ahmadiyah issue. It prohibited the sect from proselytizing, but stopped short of banning JAI. Vice President Jusuf Kalla took a firm stance that Ahmadis should continue to have the right to worship in their homes and mosques so long as they did not try to convert others.[94] The decree evoked the ire of many radical Islamist groups. According to Khoirul Roes Soetardjo, chairman of FPI-Solo Branch and secretary general of Laskar Umat Islam (Islamic Paramilitary Militia), two of the radical organizations involved in the anti-Ahmadiyah activities, "We demand a presidential decree to disband Ahmadiyah as soon as possible. If the people of Ahmadiyah don't want to return to the right path, the government must open political asylum to other countries. If the Ahmadiyah want to live in Indonesia, they can do so, but they cannot claim to be Muslims."[95]

Although government officials warned the public not the engage in criminal actions against JAI, the decree itself left the door open for radical Islamist groups to take the law into their own hands. In public statements, a spokesman from the Ministry of Religious Affairs said, "We'll let the public act as the watchdog. They can file reports to law enforcers whenever they see JAI followers violate the decree. Whether or not they are guilty of violations will be decided by the courts."[96] In response, Islamist vigilante militias took the law into their own hands and, in direct violation of the decree, set about forcibly closing Ahmadiyah mosques. Reports of police reactions were mixed. In some instances, the police were accused of standing by and permitting the violence to continue, while in others, they reacted swiftly by sending personnel to guard Ahmadiyah mosques and enclaves.[97] In June 2008, radical Islamist vigilantes forcibly closed Ahmadiyah mosques and office headquarters in Cianjur, Makassar, and Tangerang. A mob in Palembang attempted to march on an Ahmadiyah mosque, but police personnel stopped them with water cannons.[98]

Also in June, the Islamic Defenders Front and Laskar Pembela Islam (Islamic Defense Militia, LPI) attacked a peaceful demonstration held by the pro-Ahmadiyah coalition, Aliansi Kebangsaan Kebebasan Beragama dan Berkeyakinan (National Alliance for the Freedom of Religion and Belief, AKKBB), injuring 12 members, including old men, women, and children. According to Mohamad Guntur Romli, a member of AKKBB, who was beaten in the attack, "It was a peaceful rally. Some of us planned to have family gatherings afterwards. I planned to entertain my nieces with a ride around Monas in a (horse-drawn) buggy after the rally. Therefore, we were not prepared when the FPI attacked us."[99] This incident prompted a public backlash against the radical militias. Following the attack, President Susilo Bambang Yudhoyono gave a news conference where he made a clear statement that Indonesia was a lawful state, not an anarchic one, and that violence would not be tolerated. Subsequently, the coordinating minister for political, legal, and security affairs examined the prospects of banning the FPI, and the police made major national-level arrests.[100] On June 5, the police arrested 59 men at FPI headquarters and declared 10 of them suspects in the attack, including FPI chairman, Habib Rizieq Shihab.[101] Subsequently, the police arrested Munarman, boss of the LPI. In October 2008, Habib Rizieq Shihab and Munarman were each sentenced to a year and a half in prison.

Thus, although the government and the security services have become much more effective in ensuring macro-level law and order, radical Islamist groups are still able to take advantage of state-level lapses to take the law into their own hands. In refusing to arrest the perpetrators of anti-Ahmadiyah violence in Parung, the Bogor police inadvertently empowered the radical militia coalitions. Likewise, in failing to immediately establish a proper implementation mechanism for the joint-ministerial decree and offering the public a role in enforcement, the government allowed radical

Islamist groups to step in and do it for them. The law and order issue remains a significant one for the Indonesian government. A survey in *Kompas,* the Indonesian paper of record, indicated that 86 percent of respondents felt concern over the militarism of Islamist organizations.[102] Azyumardi Azra contends, "Rule of law and consistency of law enforcement is key in dealing with radical groups. When groups use violence to achieve their own ends the government should bring those groups to justice."[103]

### The Complicated Picture of the Islamic Defenders Front

Radical Islamist groups also have their grievances with the government in its failure to enforce the law, which has led some like the Islamic Defenders Front to take the law into their own hands. Aside from the Ahmadiyah issue, the FPI is best known for attacking bars, cafes that sell alcohol, and gambling dens. It contends that it is countering social ills, carrying out the Koran's dictates of *amar ma'aruf nahi munkar* (enjoining the good and discouraging the bad) and working for the implementation of sharia. Azra argues, "Groups like the FPI appeal to the police to enforce the laws prohibiting gambling and regulating drinking, but they do nothing. Now, the FPI feels like they have to do it themselves. If the government could reduce these social ills, groups like this would lose their raison d'etre."[104] This view is confirmed by Khoirul Roes Soetardjo, chairman of the FPI for the Solo area, who lamented the unwillingness of the police to take on vice: "It is not that the police can not do their job. They can eradicate the wickedness, but they just don't want to do it." According to Soetardjo, the FPI repeatedly asks the police to undertake anti-vice actions before it involves itself.

> It's not like that we jump down to the street and commit violence. That is the wrong perception. The first thing we do is that we convey to bureaucracy or police in letters that there is wickedness in a certain spot, and we ask them to clamp down and close down the spot. If they do not respond to our first letter, then we write [three more] letters to remind them. If they still do not respond to the fourth letter, we go straight to the wickedness spot and take matters into our own hands.[105]

Since its inception, the FPI has been linked with elements within the military and the police, most notably General Wiranto, the former armed forces commander, and Nugroho Djayusman, the former Jakarta police commander. The organization maintains close ties with the police. While Soetardjo may be upset regarding the inadequacies of the police, police personnel rarely intervene to prevent the FPI from attacking bars or gambling houses. In fact, the close ties have allowed the FPI to conduct its raids with a large measure of impunity. Given this degree of influence, it is encouraging that the public, the police, and the Yudhoyono government have reacted so strongly to the attack on the AKKBB demonstrators.

In sum, after the fall of Suharto, the Indonesian state retrenched in its ability keep law and order in the face of communal conflict, vigilante violence, attacks on religious minorities, violent demonstrations, and repeated raids on cafes, bars, and gambling houses. These failures of capacity were due to a combination of factors, including the separation of the police from the military; insufficient manpower in the face of multiple conflicts; and intervention by elements of the military, who sought to foment conflict to avoid further pressures for reform. When it became clear that the state could not reestablish security in Maluku or Central Sulawesi, radical Islamist groups traveled to the conflict areas in the name of protecting Muslims. However, their arrival served to increase the overall climate of violence and instability in the conflict areas. When the state committed to ensure security with the enforcement of the Malino agreements and subsequent increase in troop presence, religious violence decreased significantly, and since 2003, it has remained low. This is a significant accomplishment—the Indonesian state has progressed a great deal from the instability that characterized the transitional period.

However, on law and order issues, challenges still remain. Most recently, Islamist vigilante coalitions have used state lapses to create an atmosphere of intolerance toward religious minorities in certain provinces. When the police refused to arrest the perpetrators responsible for the attack on the Bogor Ahmadiyah compound and the local government banned the group, this emboldened them to repeat the same actions elsewhere. Moreover, radical groups have taken the law into their own hands with regard to enforcing regulations on vice, in the face of state neglect. The sum of these instances clearly indicates that when the state fails to ensure law and order, radical Islamist groups will either do it for them or take advantage of those lapses to pursue their interests. As a result, violent Islamist mobilization will increase. However, when the state takes a firm position with regard to the boundaries of acceptable behavior, radical groups will cede to the state's authority.

### Social Welfare

In the first six years following the end of the New Order regime, the state retrenched substantially in the spheres of education, health care and poverty relief, which caused it to lose a measure of performance legitimacy as the provider of the people's well-being. Although the state attempted to improve this perception by initiating education and social development projects, many of these were not widely successful due to high levels of corruption and mismanagement. However, these incapacities did not lead to radical groups making substantial inroads by supplanting the state in the provision of education and welfare. As in the Turkish case, this is largely due to the efforts of mainstream Islamic civil society, most notably NU and Muhammadiyah, which have a combined membership of approximately 70 million Muslims. However, radical groups used these state lapses to improve their credibility in conflict areas.

During the first year of the Asian Financial Crisis, poverty rates increased significantly. Urban poverty rose from 11.1 million people in February 1996 to 19.1 million in February 1999, while rural poverty increased from 26.6 million persons affected to 36.7 million persons affected.[106] The percentage of chronic poor also increased from 3.2 percent in 1996 to 9.4 percent in 1999.[107] Prices on essential staples such as cooking oil, rice, and noodles rose, including a 300 percent increase in the price of rice alone, which adversely impacted the population and led to an increase in malnutrition.[108] The Asian Financial Crisis also affected the health care distribution networks. State-run hospitals faced shortages of medicines and health care supplies as well as an overall degradation in the quality of existing machinery.[109] Moreover, most of the public lacked health insurance, making health care costs prohibitive.

In response, the state initiated the *Jaring Pengaman Sosial* (Social Safety Net, JPS) programs, which targeted the key issues of employment, food security, education, and maternal and child health in order to reduce the impact of the crisis on the poorest Indonesians.[110] Although poor families did benefit to a certain degree, the JPS programs were poorly implemented; mismanaged; and suffered from leakage, corruption, and under-coverage.[111] State programs targeting reductions in urban poverty, subsidies on rice, and the development of rural infrastructure faced similar challenges.[112] These capacity failures engendered a lack of confidence in the state's ability to provide for the social welfare of the population.

Recently, the state has implemented several new programs targeting the poor, including direct cash transfers and state health insurance. To address the issue of health care access, the Yudhoyono government implemented the Askseskin national health insurance program, which offers health care assistance to the 76.4 million Indonesians living below the poverty line.[113] However, like the JPS, this program has faced problems with mismanagement as non-poor are purchasing admission to the program from corrupt neighborhood officials, which is stretching the program's capacities, and hospitals report not being paid.[114] Another more successful example has been in the sphere of poverty relief. According to Kevin O'Rourke, "The state has tried to provide a cash subsidy for the poorest. This is tangibly felt. With each phase of the program, the delivery mechanism has improved. The money goes from the finance ministry directly to the post offices, which reduces the opportunities for leakage. This makes it more directly administered, and this is appreciated."[115] As a result of these new programs, perceptions of state capacity are improving, although it remains weaker in these areas than Malaysia or Turkey.

*The Role of Islamic Mass Organizations and Islamist Groups*
A wide variety of Islamic and Islamist groups have supplemented the state's provision of social services, especially in the first six years following the end of the New Order regime. The most omnipresent among these have been NU and Muhammadiyah. As the Asian Financial Crisis and subsequent state retrenchment affected the health care distribution networks, resulting in shortages of medicines and supplies, members of NU and Muhammadiyah relied more heavily on these organizations for health care assistance. According to Dr. Din Syamsuddin, chairman of Muhammadiyah, "Muhammadiyah has 250 health centers and 116 hospitals and clinics. Some of these clinics give free services in poor areas."[116] NU also has an extensive network of inexpensive hospitals and clinics to supplement the state's efforts, including family health clinics, HIV clinics, and clinics for broken families.[117] Since one in three Indonesians belongs to either Nahdlatul Ulama or Muhammadiyah, this enabled them to play a vital role in supplementing the state in health services efforts. Both organizations have also provided supplemental poverty relief as well. According to Syafi'i Ma'arif, the chairman of Muhammadiyah from 1999 to 2004, during the Asian Financial Crisis, Muhammadiyah collected food and clothes from different sources and distributed them in the areas where they were badly needed.[118] Local leaders of NU also offered assistance to their affected members during the economic crisis.

Radical Islamist groups have largely been limited in their ability to make inroads at the state's expense in the social welfare sector, due to the roles played by NU and Muhammadiyah. During the communal conflicts in Maluku and Poso, however, Laskar Jihad was able to use the state's retrenchment to improve its own standing in the local Muslim communities. Before sending a militia, it first sent doctors.[119] Laskar Jihad used the provision of social services and education to integrate into local communities and establish roots in its areas of operations.[120] In both Maluku and Poso, this made Laskar Jihad a valuable ally in Muslim communities, for it was supplanting the state in three key ways: by providing security, education, and social welfare. This move also served to increase its popularity among Muslims in Jakarta.

## Education

At the time of the Asian Financial Crisis, the Indonesian government also faced significant problems with regard to education. According to then minister of education Juwono Sudarsono, approximately 5 million children dropped out of school between the onset of the crisis in 1997 and 1999.[121] The policies of regional decentralization under presidents Wahid and Sukarnoputri gave regional governments the authority to determine the budgetary allocation for education in their areas. It was not uncommon for local officials to choose to spend the majority of their revenues on budgetary items that were likely to have a quicker and more stimulating effect on the economy than education, unless local voters pushed for better schools.[122]

In 2002, a clause was inserted into the Constitution requiring the national and regional governments to spend 20 percent of their annual budgets on education beyond the payment of teacher salaries.[123] The national budgetary allocation for education increased steadily, finally reaching the 20 percent marker in 2008. However, to date, the corresponding requirement for regional governments has not been enforced. The state performance in education has varied by education level and by region. In 2006–2007, 94.7 percent of Indonesian children attended primary school; this number decreased to 66 percent for junior secondary school and 52.6 percent for senior secondary school.[124] The 2003 National Education Bill requires all Indonesian children from ages 7 through 15 to participate in basic education, with grades one through nine being compulsory. However, the drop between the primary and junior secondary levels shows that this requirement has also not been enforced. There is also variation in attendance for primary and secondary school across regions, with 96 percent turnout in Central Kalimantan and Aceh compared with 78 percent in Papua.[125] Between 2003 and 2006, although 25 out of 33 Indonesian provinces increased their rates of student attendance in junior secondary school, 6 provinces still had junior secondary rates below 60 percent.[126]

The state has begun to remedy these educational disparities through a series of programs. First, it established a program of nine years of free basic education for all school-aged children in 2005.[127] Initially, this program ran into problems of implementation and mismanagement, for numerous public schools still required students to pay "entrance fee," and building maintenance fees, often amounting to between 200,000 and millions of rupiah.[128] As of 2008, of the 33 provincial governments, however, only 6—South Sulawesi, Central Sulawesi, West Java, Jakarta, Banten, and North Sumatra—have successfully implemented free education.

To discourage schools from charging fees, the state has also implemented the *Bantuan Operasi Sekolah* (BOS) program, which gives participating public and private schools 235,000 rupiah per primary school student and 324,500 rupiah per junior secondary student per year to offset any revenue lost.[129] A 2006 program covers the costs of textbooks for poor families. Laboratory, library, and sanitation facilities have also been improved. These programs have increased perceptions of state effectiveness, and the Yudhoyono government has reaped legitimacy gains as a result. According to the Indonesian Survey Institute, the BOS program received a 94 percent positive rating in a December 2008 survey, while overall perception of state performance in education averaged a 74 percent approval rating between 2005 and 2008.[130]

*Islamic Education*
Throughout Indonesian history, Islamic boarding schools (*pesantren*) have played a key role in supplementing the state's education efforts. With the changes in the educational system and the removal of Suharto era education subsidies, *pesantren* education became cheaper than public education. However, education quality at Islamic boarding schools varies. Some *pesantren* like *Sunan Pandanaran* in Yogyakarta, *Pondok Modern Gontor* in Ponorogo, and *Salafiyah Syafiiyah Sukorejo* in Situbondo are renowned for the high quality and integrated education they provide. However, *pesantren* also face funding shortages and are often criticized for providing substandard education often due to insufficient resources. According to statistics provided by the Education Management Information System (EMIS), there are 14,067 registered *pesantren* currently operating in Indonesia. Of these, 69.28 percent of them are affiliated with NU.[131] The remaining 30.72 percent are run by Muhammadiyah; organizations affiliated with the Prosperous Justice Party; more puritanical organizations like DDII, al Irsyad, or Persis; or they are unaffiliated.

Unlike Malaysia or Turkey, the Indonesian state lacks the capacity and the resources to monitor the 14,067 registered *pesantren*. While the state stipulates the curriculum for all madrasas, the *pesantren* have been free to accept the state's curriculum, open up madrasas that teach the state's curriculum while maintaining their own traditional studies, or keep the traditional curriculum. Former minister of religious affairs Said Agil Husin Al-Munawar stated that the government can only reach out to perhaps 5 percent of the total *pesantren*.[132] Moreover, a significant proportion of *pesantren* remain unregistered. The Ministry of Religious Affairs is currently in the process of conducting a census on all *pesantren* to better monitor and address the needs of the *pesantren* and their students.[133]

The state is, however, growing more adept at monitoring madrasas and *pesantren* that have madrasas on their premises. According to Mutasim

Billah of *Pesantren Sunan Pandanaran,* which has its own madrasa, they receive monthly visits from the Department of Religion to ensure they are following the curriculum.[134] The state also visits independent *pesantren,* which do not accept the state curriculum, to offer them certification in the form of packets A, B, and C that students can use to study for the appropriate national certification exams for primary, lower secondary, and upper secondary school, respectively.[135] The national certification program is a key reason why the state is undertaking the census. It seeks to address criticisms that Islamic school students are graduating without the necessary skills to obtain employment or pursue higher education.

In Indonesia, the number of radical Islamic boarding schools is small because of the combined roles of the state and mainstream organizations like NU and Muhammadiyah, which dominate the Islamic education marketplace. However, the problem of radicalism in the *pesantren* still remains, thus necessitating the state's continued monitoring of these *pesantren.* After the first Bali bombing, the police identified and stepped up surveillance efforts of *pesantren* it identified as radical, focusing on both the "Ngruki network" of *pesantren* where several of the Bali bombers studied and a handful of NU *pesantren.* The police initiated undercover operations, posing as students or *bakso* (meatball soup) vendors. However, the state has been unable to prevent the spread of radical *pesantren.* After the tsunami in Aceh, two *pesantren* opened in Aceh that were affiliated with Jemaah Islamiyah.

While some have advocated curricular reforms as a solution to radicalism in the *pesantren,* it is not simply a matter of convincing these schools to adopt the state's curricular recommendations. Several schools within the radical Ngruki network, including Al Mujihideen and Ngruki utilize the state's recommendations to ensure they remain accredited and that their students may to pursue higher education.[136] Both Ngruki and Al Mujihideen receive regular inspections from the Department of Religion. Ngruki leaders are suspicious of the government's monitoring efforts. According to Ali Usman, head of the Ngruki Alumni network,

> The government has always monitored Ngruki. It sent teachers from the Department of Religion to teach students and to monitor us. The government officials sometimes drop in. Or they send spies. How do we know they are spies? They come to the *pesantren.* The beard is there, the prayer mark [on the forehead] is there. And then they smoke. Since it is forbidden to smoke in Islam, we know they are not real Muslims.[137]

This indicates the problem of radical *pesantren* will not be solved by the state forcing a change of the formal curriculum or by monitoring alone.

Badrus Sholeh contends that the answer for the state lies in engaging the radical *pesantren,* improving funding of all *pesantren,* and monitoring the graduates of the radical *pesantren.* "Ngruki received funding from Al Haramain and from the Middle East. The government needs to increase funding for the *pesantren.* It is better if they receive government monies than from the Middle East."[138] To that end, it is important that the state provide the schools with technology and reading materials that might enable them to arrive at a more open point of view independently. Finally, it is important that the state also monitor graduates of radical *pesantren* to see if they are joining radical Islamist organizations. Perhaps a combination of these tactics will prove more effective.

In sum, in the first six years following the fall of Suharto, the state struggled to provide education and social services. While the state has had good intentions with regard to social safety net and health care programs, these projects are often poorly implemented and mismanaged. Under the administration of Susilo Bambang Yudhoyono efforts to provide education, health care, and poverty relief have improved, albeit to varying degrees.NU and Muhammadiyah have assisted the state during these crucial years in providing public goods to the poor, which limited the ability of radical Islamist groups to make popularity gains at the state's expense during the initial transition period. The state has also attempted to better monitor and assist *pesantren* in recent years. However, this is an uphill battle, as the state lacks the capacity to monitor 14,067 *pesantren.* While it has attempted to monitor radical *pesantren,* they are aware of these activities. The state may need to switch tactics and engage these *pesantren* to diffuse the threat posed by them.

## External Forces

External forces have exacerbated the violence in Indonesia to a greater extent than Malaysia or Turkey. The two factors that will be discussed in this section overlap: the Jemaah Islamiyah terrorist network and Afghan veterans. The Afghan veteran phenomenon is of key importance to understanding the role played by external forces. Many of those mujihideen, who went to fight in Afghanistan, developed extremist viewpoints and founded radical Islamist organizations in their home countries. In multiple cases, these organizations have been willing to use violence to achieve their goals of an Islamic state.

Indonesia is no exception. Almost every radical Islamist group that has been active in the *reformasi* period has Afghan veterans as founding members. Ja'far Umar Thalib, commander of Laskar Jihad, fought in Afghanistan in a Saudi government-affiliated battalion. Leading operatives from Jemaah

Islamiyah also received training and fought in Afghanistan, including Hambali, former head of Mantiqi 1, and Imam Samudra, who was recently executed for his role in masterminding the 2002 Bali Bombing.[139] Laskar Jundullah chief-of-staff Muchtar Daeng Lao is also an Afghan veteran. All three organizations played key roles in exacerbating the communal violence during the Maluku and Poso conflicts. In 2002, Laskar Jundullah, with assistance from Jemaah Islamiyah, bombed a MacDonalds in Makassar and a car dealership owned by then coordinating minister for the people's welfare Jusuf Kalla, thus contributing to the overall climate of lawlessness in Indonesia at that time.

Jemaah Islamiyah was founded by two Indonesian clerics, Abdullah Sungkar and Abu Bakar Basyir, in Malaysia, and since then, the organization has spread across Southeast Asia and Australia. The Jemaah Islamiyah terrorist network is the single greatest exogenous actor responsible for the exacerbation of Islamist violence in Indonesia. It donated over $18,000 to the Maluku jihad; its members participated in conflicts in Maluku and Poso; and they have been responsible for a string of bombings throughout Indonesia.[140] JI is most famous for carrying out the October 2002 bombing of the Paddy Bar and the Sari Club in Kuta Beach, Bali; the 2003 bombing of the JW Marriot Hotel in Jakarta; and the October 2005 bombings of the Kuta Central Square and two restaurants in Jimbaran Bay, Bali.

According to Nasir Abas, the former head of Jemaah Islamiyah's Mantiqi 3, JI did not start out conducting terror activities against civilian targets, but this changed following Osama bin Laden's 1998 statement, which said that it was permissible to do so.[141] Although Abas himself disagreed with the statement, others in the group, most notably Hambali, head of Mantiqi 1, began planning operations. "Hambali said he wanted to bring the Ambon conflict to a national conflict. He wanted to provoke Christian-Muslim conflict all over Indonesia. After his ideas were rejected in a meeting, he decided to do it by himself. He used his own Malaysian and Singaporean guys from Mantiqi 1 and some disloyal members of Mantiqi 2 [which comprised Indonesia]."[142] Hambali's first target was Medan, which had significant percentages of Muslims and Christians and a long-standing reputation for religious tolerance. In 2000, he and his followers carried out a series of church bombings in the city. However, the bombs prompted the city residents to close ranks and forswear violence; no one linked it to terrorism.[143] Later that same year, on Christmas Eve, they carried out a series of bombings of 38 churches. While these incidents clearly exacerbated the level of violence, they did not succeed in inflaming Christian-Muslim tensions. In fact, in the long term, these events served as a unifier among Muslims and Christians, for in subsequent years, Muslim organizations from Nahdlatul

Ulama and Muhammadiyah to the FPI assist the police in guarding the nation's churches so that Christians can celebrate Christmas safely. Thus, in this case, Islamic civil society reinforced the efforts of the state.

The overall increase in state effectiveness in law and order can be seen with regard to Jemaah Islamiyah and its affiliates as well. Since the first Bali bombing in October 2002, the police have significantly improved their investigatory and monitoring capacities. Arrests have crippled Jemaah Islamiyah's ability to conduct major operations and caused the organization to become fragmented. Jemaah Islamiyah has not succeeded in carrying out any large-scale bombings since 2005. Following the arrests of the members of the Poso *wakalah* in January 2007, most small scale attacks by Jemaah Islamiyah have also ceased. The overall effectiveness of Densus 88 can be seen from an internal change in JI strategy. Jemaah Islamiyah has shifted its attentions now to winning the ideological war, setting up boarding schools, establishing new militias, and developing a publishing industry to win hearts and minds. According to the International Crisis Group, Jemaah Islamiyah is now in a "building and consolidation phase, which, for the most part means that it is unlikely to be interested in large, expensive operations that could further weaken its support base."[144]

In conclusion, with the liberalization of the Indonesian political system, Islamist groups reacted in a strategic manner by taking advantage of the opportunities offered by the new political system. Some movements formed political parties and contested elections, while others worked from civil society by pressuring national and local legislatures to pass sharia-based legislation or to reject it, to combat corruption, to ban pornographic materials, or to reform the education system. This chapter illustrates how institutionalized political participation encourages peaceful Islamist mobilization.

However, political participation alone was not sufficient. Indonesia struggled to maintain law and order especially between 1998 and 2003. The state's inability to restore security after the outbreak of communal conflicts in 1999 led to radical Islamist groups supplanting the state in the provision of law and order to ensure Muslim safety and show the supremacy of Islam and sharia law. This intervention served as a wake-up call to the central government, which established workable agreements to end the conflicts through a combination of increased troop presence and inter-party mediation. The Indonesian government should be praised for its great strides in maintaining law and order on a macro-scale. Now, the main issues are micro-issues—how to curb the activities of radical vigilante coalitions that have used the permissive nature of law and order to target specific minorities. Perhaps most telling, when the police have arrested leaders and members of the militias, there have been no reprisals. They have ceded to

Indonesian law. According to Dr. Bahtiar Effendy, this indicates, "if the state acts like a state, then there is respect. Then you know what you cannot do. Indonesia is not an Islamic state. Either you abide by Indonesian law or go elsewhere."[145]

Indonesia's record in providing education and welfare is mixed. While the state retrenched following the fall of Suharto, it has never ceded spheres but instead has put forth numerous theoretically promising yet poorly implemented initiatives. While this caused the state to be perceived as ineffective, radical Islamist groups could rarely take advantage of the state's lapses to increase their own popular support, due to the dominant supplemental efforts of NU and Muhammadiyah. In Maluku and Poso, however, Laskar Jihad was able to supplant the state by offering security, education, and medical care. In recent years, under the administration of President Susilo Bambang Yudhoyono, the state's provision of education, health care, and poverty relief have begun to improve, thus resulting in increased perceptions of effectiveness.

As a result of the security lapses, Indonesia had to cope with intervention by external forces, most notably Afghan veterans and Jemaah Islamiyah. JI exacerbated violent mobilization nationally by conducting a string of bombings throughout Indonesia to foment national inter-religious conflict. This effort backfired. In solving both Bali bombings, the police have shown high competence, which has, in turn, led Indonesians to express increased confidence in their capacities to protect them. According to a survey conducted by the Indonesian Survey Institute in 2006, 69 percent of Indonesians feel the police are doing a "good" job.[146]

In conclusion, the Indonesian experience highlights the challenges of the ineffective participatory state. In the post–New Order era, the Indonesian state provided multiple channels for institutionalized participation, and the vast majority of Indonesian Islamist groups have chosen to work through them. However, a minority did not. Although Indonesia effectively encouraged peaceful Islamist mobilization, it has not sufficiently discouraged the use of violent strategies. Today, radical Islamist groups still take advantage of lapses in law and order to push the boundaries of acceptable behavior. However, a vast improvement has been made since 2002, when violence in the name of Islam was at its peak. Over the past decade, Indonesia has transitioned from an effective authoritarian system into an ineffective participatory one. As the state continues to improve its firmness in law and order and competence in social service delivery, it may soon transition again into an effective participatory system.

# CHAPTER 5

# The Effective Participatory State of Malaysia

Among all the cases in this book, Malaysia has the lowest incidence of violent Islamist mobilization. Authoritarian regimes that argue that political liberalization would unleash violent Islamist mobilization and revolution need only to look at Malaysia, an effective participatory state that provides opportunities for institutionalized political participation while refusing to tolerate those groups that use or threaten violence. Malaysians have a great deal of faith in their institutions as channels for political activity. Malaysia has a long history of coalition governance through the institutions of parties and the legislature. This historical legacy has had a profound impact on how Islamist groups mobilize. In contrast to Turkey and Indonesia, Malaysia is governed by a dominant coalition, the Barisan Nasional (National Front, BN), since 1974. Prior to that, another multiethnic coalition, the Alliance, governed the country from independence in 1957 to the 1969 race riots. Thus, interethnic coalition governance has been institutionalized within the political system. This is a fact that is also accepted by the Partai Islam se Malaysia (Malaysian Islamic Party, PAS), the main Islamist opposition party, which also forms coalitions in its contests for political gain.

It is important to note that Malaysia is not as liberal or democratic as post-New Order Indonesia or Turkey. It is often characterized as a "semi-democracy" for combining democratic institutions and procedures with curbs on the freedom of speech, the press, and assembly. Elections are free but not fair, because districts are often gerrymandered to favor the BN. Islamist organizations have been banned if they have been deemed to subscribe to "deviationist" ideas. However, there is a strong tradition of what Dr. Shamsul Amri Baharuddin terms "oppositionism." Both political parties and Islamist groups can mobilize as loyal opposition. Islamists in particular have made significant progress incrementally over the past 25 years. Furthermore, opposition parties make gains in the national legislature and win control of state legislatures and state governments. Islamist groups use these channels to work toward their goals.

More so than Indonesia or Turkey, the Malaysian state is highly effective in ensuring security, poverty relief, and education for all Malaysians. There are no lawless areas where state authority does not dominate. The state security services capably monitor the activities of Islamist groups due, in large part, to the intelligence training they received from the British during the Emergency, when the nation battled a communist guerrilla insurgency. Furthermore, the Malaysian government is highly adept at offering social services. The state dominates in both education and social welfare, with Islamist organizations playing a supporting role. Thus, it is clear to Malaysians that the state provides for their needs. As a result, Islamist groups are unable to make substantial legitimacy gains at the state's expense. Although Malaysia faces threats from Jemaah Islamiyah (JI) and Afghan veteran groups, JI has yet to carry out a bombing in Malaysia. In 2001 and 2002, the police arrested members of Jemaah Islamiyah and the Afghan veteran group Kumpulan Mujihideen Malaysia (Malaysia Mujihideen Group, KMM).

By providing opportunities for participation through institutionalized channels, Malaysia has encouraged Islamist groups to mobilize using peaceful strategies. Islamist groups have reacted strategically and used these channels to win victories on key issues. However, the state has no tolerance for those groups that employ violence. This chapter contends that the state's capacity to ensure security and provide a measure of education and welfare has prevented radical Islamist groups from making inroads to threaten state legitimacy. It has made the cost of employing violence too high.

## Participation

Since the birth of the *dakwah* (Islamic propagation) movement in the early 1970s, Islamist groups have come to embrace political participation as the best and most effective means to achieve their goals.[1] *Dakwah* organizations participate in the Malaysian political system in several ways: joining either the United Malays National Organization (UMNO), the dominant Malay nationalist Islam-friendly party in the governing coalition, or the bureaucracy to push for greater Islamization; joining opposition parties such as PAS and contesting elections; forming electoral pacts and alliances among opposition parties to leverage their influence; and lobbying for political goals from a base in civil society. Despite the fact that Malaysia is a single-party dominant political system, *dakwah* movements have secured victories and pushed for the enactment of Islamization policies and Islamic institution building, by either being co-opted into the government or joining the opposition. While the opposition parties cannot lead governing coalitions, they have an important impact on the political system and Islamist mobilization strategies. According Dr. Chandra Muzaffar,

> The institutionalized channels for participation are a very important part of why Malaysia has such a tradition of peaceful Islamist mobilization. The very fact that PAS is around curbs the potential for violence. PAS is a safety valve for religious groups. The religiously inclined can also join the government through institutions such as the Islamic and Moral Education Department (JAPIN); Department for the Advancement of Islam (JAKIM); Islamic Dakwah Foundation of Malaysia (YADIM) and the Malaysian Institute for Islamic Understanding (IKIM). [2]

Dr. Shamsul A.B. concurs, noting that "Malaysia has structures for participation. You can get things done by working through the parties and NGOs." [3] This sense that one can work through the political system to achieve one's goals has only increased under the leadership of Prime Minister Abdullah Badawi. Datuk Shahrir Samad, a backbencher within the UMNO party, explained that "political system has grown more participatory under Badawi. He believes in our institutions."[4]

## Co-optation

One of the main ways that Malaysian Islamist leaders and groups have worked to achieve their goals is by affiliating themselves with UMNO and the bureaucracy. The Islamic resurgence became a potent force in Malaysia as early as 1971 due to the soul searching that followed the 1969 race riots. As in Indonesia, organizations formed in and around college campuses. By 1975, *dakwah* movements had found their sociopolitical niche and began to criticize the government, calling for less corruption, greater transparency, and more substantial efforts at Islamization.[5] Angkatan Belia Islam Malaysia (Malaysian Islamic Youth Movement, ABIM) was the most influential of the *dakwah* organizations and sought to integrate the concept of *dakwah* with the multiethnic, multireligious reality of the Malaysian context. Other groups had formed abroad, had developed Islamist viewpoints more closely identified with the Middle East, and were active in underground study circles. The government felt pressured to respond to these groups. Rather than actively repress them, the state sought to partially accommodate them and, after Mahathir Mohammed became prime minister in 1981, to co-opt them. To that end, the government identified the *dakwah* movements' moderate elements and brought them into the mainstream to ensure their compatibility with the government's developmental goals.[6] This co-optation was a form of representation and participation. It provided amenable groups with political access necessary to accomplish long-held goals.

The major co-optation coup occurred in 1982, when Anwar Ibrahim, the former president of ABIM, agreed to join the government. Anwar brought many ABIM colleagues with him into the government bureaucracy and ruling coalition, although some members left ABIM and joined PAS.[7] In previous years, the government had taken several symbolic measures to show support for Islamization. However, these policies escalated beyond symbolism following Anwar's entry into the government. Table 5.1 shows the effect of Anwar and ABIM's co-optation on government Islamization efforts, most notably the rapid establishment of new Islamic institutions.[8]

**Table 5.1**  Malaysian government Islamization policies[9]

| Year policy enacted | Explanation of policy |
| --- | --- |
| 1974 | Government establishes Pusat Islam (Islamic Center) to coordinate all national Islamic activities |
| 1975 | Ministry of Education increases the budget for training of Islamic school teachers |
| 1977 | Government directs all of its women employees to dress modestly |
| 1978 | Government declares plan to revise the national legal system to bring it more in line with sharia |
| 1979 | Government launches National Dakwah Month |
| 1979 | Government announces plan to establish the Southeast Asian Islamic Research Center |
| 1980 | Government declares policy to remodel Malaysia's economic system as an Islamic one |
| 1981 | Islamic radio and TV programs increase on government-run channels |
| 1981–1982 | Islamic Resources Group and Special Enforcement Group are established |
| 1981–1982 | Government introduces compulsory course for Muslim university students on Islamic civilizations |
| 1982 | Building of the first Islamic Teachers College costing MR $22 million |
| 1982 | Permanent site is found for the International Islamic Training Camp |
| 1982 | Turf clubs are relocated far from Kuala Lumpur |
| 1982 | Government elevates status of *kadi* (Muslim judges) at par with Western-trained judges |
| 1982 | Government recruits 850 religious teachers |
| 1982 | Anwar Ibrahim joins UMNO and the government |
| 1983 | Government sponsors Islamic Medical Center |
| 1983 | Government refuses to approve new applications for casinos. Bans Muslims from existing ones |
| 1983 | Government employees must attend courses on Islamic law, irrespective of their faith |
| 1983 | International Islamic University is established |
| 1983 | Islamic bank is established |
| 1983 | *Syarikat Takaful,* an Islamic insurance company is established |
| 1984 | Islamic Development Foundation is established |

*(Continued)*

**Table 5.1** Continued

| Year policy enacted | Explanation of policy |
|---|---|
| 1984 | Islamic pawnshop is established |
| 1984 | Ministry of Education allows Muslim students to dress according to the Islamic dress code |
| 1984 | "Pusat Islam" becomes the nerve center of the Islamic bureaucracy |
| 1984 | Official declaration of "Islamization of Government Machinery" |
| 1984 | Government seeks to standardize Islamic Family Law with the passing of the Family Law Act |
| 1985 | Anwar Ibrahim founds the Institute of Policy Development to carry out human development training for student leaders, youth activists, junior managers, and public servants |
| 1987 | International Institute of Islamic Thought and Civilization (ISTAC) is founded as a postgraduate institution |
| 1988 | Declaration is made that "only Islam will get airtime over Radio and TV Malaysia" |
| 1988 | Status of Islamic judges and courts to be at par with their counterparts in the civil judiciary |
| 1988 | Program is initiated to build "Islamic villages" in cities throughout Malaysia |
| 1991 | Family Law Act comes to slowly be enforced |
| 1991 | Government increases regulations on the sale of alcohol and relations between the sexes |
| 1991 | Films and publications are increasingly censored |
| 1992 | Government imposes taxes on cigarettes and alcohol in pursuance of an Islamic value system |
| 1992 | Institute for Islamic Understanding (IKIM) is established |
| 1993 | Administration of Islamic Law Act establishes three main juridical authorities: sharia, religious assembly, and muftis |
| 1995 | Securities Commission establishes the Department for Islamic Capital Markets |
| 1996 | Sharia Advisory Council established for the Department of Islamic Capital Markets |
| 1997 | Government makes Islamic Civilization course compulsory for students of all religions |
| 1997 | Sharia Court Evidence Act is passed into law |
| 1997 | Sharia Criminal Offenses Act is passed into law |
| 1997 | Sharia Criminal Procedures Act is passed into law |
| 2000 | Government increases monitoring at Friday sermons and mosques |
| 2000 | Government proposes to standardize religious school curriculum |
| 2000 | Government drafts the Islamic Aqidah (Faith) Protection Bill to prevent conversions from Islam |
| 2001 | Finance minister launches plan to make Malaysia a hub for Islamic capital market activities |
| 2004 | Prime Minister Abdullah Badawi conceptualizes Islam Hadari as Islam that is consistent with pluralism and democracy |
| 2005 | Islamic Family Law is amended to make it easier for Muslim men to take a second wife and divorce |
| 2008 | National Fatwa Council issues ruling banning Muslims from dressing like tomboys and practicing yoga |

Anwar Ibrahim quickly advanced through the ranks of the bureaucracy following his recruitment and co-optation into UMNO. The government did not use him for his token or symbolic value. Instead, it gave him access to positions of power, influence, and patronage.

> Following his joining of UMNO in April 1982, Anwar contested and won a parliamentary seat and was subsequently named the Deputy Minister of the Islamic Religious Affairs Section within the Prime Minister's Department. Later that same year, he was elected as president of UMNO Youth, making him one of UMNO's five Vice-Presidents.[10]

The next year, he became a full minister, and in subsequent years, he held positions as minister of culture, youth, and sports; minister of agriculture; minister of education; and minister of finance before becoming deputy prime minister in 1993.

Most of ABIM's academics and professionals went to work for the government, particularly in the Ministry of Education, the Ministry of Culture, Youth, and Sports, the Prime Minister's Department, and Jabatan Kemajuan Islam Malaysia (Department for the Advancement of Islam, JAKIM).[11] Many became leaders of the new Islamic institutions. After the state established the International Islamic University of Malaysia (IIUM) in 1983, many ABIM academics joined it, and Anwar Ibrahim served as its second president from 1988 to 1999.[12]

As a result of the co-optation, the once-oppositional ABIM became an officially accepted pressure group in university communities.[13] It also gained a greater share of government patronage and a role in major government projects. ABIM also became involved in the government's institution-building programs and was able to expand its network of schools, training centers, and colleges.[14] According to Yusri Mohamad, the current president of ABIM, "It was easy to achieve our goals when Anwar was in power. More channels were open to us. Islamic credentials were an important factor in any project and ABIM was the reference point."[15] This successful effort at co-optation influenced the perceptions of other Islamic organizations as well. According to Dr. Noraini Othman and Dr. Clive Kessler, "Other groups like Jemaah Islah Malaysia (JIM) are no longer antigovernment. They would like to be part of the game. They would like to be included."[16]

ABIM's influential relationship with the government would end in 1998, when Anwar would be dismissed after a row with Mahathir, arrested on corruption and sodomy charges, and beaten in prison. A reform movement mobilized in opposition to the government's treatment of Anwar

Ibrahim. Anwar was released from prison with a full government apology in 2003. Today, ABIM claims to be a politically neutral organization, neither pro-government nor pro-opposition. However, its members remain influential leaders of Islamic institutions and ex-members currently lead PAS.

## Oppositionism

Islamists frequently work to achieve their goals through institutionalized "oppositionism."[17] According to Dr. Shamsul A.B., "There have always been opposition parties and they play an important role. Opposition parties and organizations can articulate opposition to UMNO, to government policies or to the status quo. In this way, the system is participatory."[18] If Islamist groups or Islamists do not support the status quo, they can register their dissent by joining PAS, by mobilizing through civil society, or by forming coalitions of many civil society organizations to maximize their influence. Among civil society groups, the coalition strategy is employed frequently to lobby both for and against proposed legislation and to advocate the repeal of existing legislation like the repressive Internal Security Act (ISA).

PAS is the largest, oldest, and most influential Islamist opposition party. It was formed in 1951 by ulama from UMNO and, at that time, prioritized both Islam and Malay nationalist causes. This changed in 1982 when PAS' ulama faction shifted its focus to a universalist vision of Islam. According to the PAS 1993 Constitution, its objectives include "striving to build a society and a government where Islamic values and Allah's laws are implemented; and protecting the 'honor,' the independence and the sovereignty of Islam."[19] Its base of support lies in the Malay heartland—Kelantan, Terengganu, Perlis, and Kedah—especially among Muslims who have not benefitted from the New Economic Program.

Nationally, PAS has a significant impact on the political agenda. According to one PAS leader, PAS may not be winning elections, but it is advocating an Islamic agenda and an Islamic message.[20] PAS leaders in Kuala Lumpur and Kelantan contend that the Malaysian government adopted Islamization policies in response to the challenge posed by PAS.[21] Thus, they see themselves as having an impact on politics. Dr. Chandra Muzaffar explains further, "PAS affects change, even if they cannot come to power. PAS has influence. They pressure the government and mobilize the government to act on Islamic issues. The government has to take notice because they represent an important constituency."[22] Dr. Noraini Othman and Dr. Clive Kessler highlight the strength of PAS' influence by noting that "PAS has set the terms of political competition between UMNO and itself, while UMNO plays catch-up. UMNO is becoming a 'me-too' party. PAS sets the discourse and UMNO responds."[23]

The PAS has undertaken Islamization beyond the government policies in the states which it controls. In Kelantan and Terengganu, it passed *hudud* (punishments) and *qisas* (retaliation) laws. However, they cannot be implemented without an amendment to the federal Constitution. In Kelantan, it has passed laws to counteract apostasy by requiring those who wish to convert from Islam to obtain permission from the sharia courts. Kota Bahru, the capital of Kelantan, has been transformed into an "Islamic city" run by sharia law, which includes regulations on prayer, modest dress, separation of sexes, and entertainment.

In recent years, PAS has sought to repackage its message to attract the votes of Malay Muslims who may not support the imposition of strict sharia. PAS has not abandoned its Islamic statist goals; it sees itself as having to introduce Malaysians to sharia and educate them on how sharia would benefit them. To that end, PAS speaks of poverty alleviation, environmental sustainability, and social justice in an Islamic way.[24] Whereas UMNO highlights the promoting of Malay rights and affirmative action policies to promote Malay economic welfare, PAS has sought to repackage itself as the party for all Muslims, regardless of ethnicity.[25] According to Dr. Chandra Muzaffar, "PAS has never rejected democracy. They win at the state level and make gains. If they engage in politics, they make gains."[26]

Another form of oppositionism comes from civil society. Both progressive and ultraconservative Islamist organizations articulate dissent or support for policies through lobbying, submitting petitions and memos to the government, making public statements, holding rallies, holding discussions, and utilizing media outlets. One can find numerous alternatives to the government-sponsored view of Islam within civil society. In keeping with the tradition of Malaysian coalition politics, Islamist groups, including JIM, ABIM, and the progressive Muslim women's organization, Sisters in Islam, frequently utilize coalitional strategies in civil society as well. This strategy serves to maximize the influence of the member organizations while minimizing the likelihood that the government may attempt to proscribe them en masse. According to Zaid Kamaruddin, president of JIM, JIM uses coalition strategies a great deal. For example, JIM is a member of the Allied Coordinating Committee for Muslim NGOs, a coalition of 14 Islamic NGOs, including ABIM, Perkim, and the Malaysian Islamic Chinese Association (MACMA).[27] JIM has also partnered with PAS and 74 civil society organizations to lobby for the repeal of the ISA. This anti-ISA coalition has employed a variety of peaceful strategies, including sending memos to parliament and the human rights commission, lobbying parliament and the UN Human Rights Commission, holding rallies, and submitting petitions to the legislature.[28]

Sisters in Islam also works through coalitions to maximize its influence on particular legislative issues. Most often, it mobilizes as part of a "joint action group" to promote gender equality and law reform.[29] According to Zainah Anwar, executive director of Sisters in Islam,

> Certain groups take the lead on different issues so we share the work. Sisters in Islam takes the lead on Islamic issues; Women's Aid Organization on domestic violence; All Women's Action Society on rape and sexual violence; Women's Center for Change on sexual harassment and constitutional law; Women's Development Collective on gender equality training; and the women's section of the Malaysian Trade Union Congress on working women's issues.[30]

It is clear then that Islamic and Islamist organizations utilize coalition strategies as they work for political and religious change. The manner in which they engage the state through institutionalized political channels can be clearly seen in the debates over the Family Law Act. This act was passed in 1984, implemented in 1991, and amended in 2001, in part, to make it easier for Muslims to divorce and for Muslim men to take a second wife. Since then, Sisters in Islam led efforts by the Joint-Action Group coalition to express opposition to these amendments and lobby for their repeal.[31] It targeted the legislature, female legislators, and the Ministry for Women and Family Development.[32] Although the ministry adopted Sisters in Islam's arguments and lobbied within the government, the religious authorities (JAKIM) refused to alter the objectionable amendments.[33] When this strategy failed, it took the issue to the media to pressure the government to revisit the law. According to Zainah Anwar, "The government is wiling to give hearings and space. Whether they will take action is another story. However, the doors are open. Our system is a flawed system but the space is there. You have to fight for the space and have good arguments."[34]

### Elections

Scholars have different views on the role of elections as a means of participation and democratic legitimation in the Malaysian context. The winner take all arrangement of the electoral districts and extensive gerrymandering disadvantages opposition parties. Dr. Shamsul A.B.

explains that "elections in Malaysia are about social control. Democracy is not about elections. It is about how many ways you can participate. In Malaysia, elections do not equal democracy. All opposition parties were, at one point, part of the Barisan Nasional."[35] Harold Crouch has a more guardedly optimistic view of Malaysian elections, noting that they make the system more responsive even if they cannot effect substantive change.[36] Osman Bakar concurs, "If UMNO wants to win the votes of Malay Muslims, it must show interest in Malay Muslim issues and affairs."[37]

Although parties take part in a rigged electoral game, opposition parties have continued to participate in those elections because they can win control of states, make inroads into state legislatures, and increase their seats nationally. If one examines Tables 5.2 and 5.3, one will see the evolution of BN and PAS electoral gains and losses over time.

As one can see from the tables, the BN has always won a majority in every election. However, PAS and other opposition parties have secured gains that have varied over time. PAS has been able to win seats nationally and at the state level, maintaining almost continuous control over Kelantan since 1959. In the 1978, 1982, and 1986 elections, for example, PAS won more than 50 percent of the seats in Kelantan; between 40 and 50 percent of the seats in Terengganu, Perlis, and Kedah; and between 20 and 33 percent in other peninsular Malay states, despite the extensive gerrymandering of districts that UMNO employed to ensure it maintained its national majority.[40]

This was most acutely seen in the 1999 elections. PAS became the single largest opposition party in Malaysia, for over half of the Malay population voted for PAS, many to register a protest vote against UMNO for the humiliating treatment of Anwar Ibrahim. [41] PAS also attracted Malay

**Table 5.2** Parliamentary election results: Percentage vote share per party[38]

| Political Parties | 1974 | 1978 | 1982 | 1986 | 1990 | 1995 | 1999 | 2004 | 2008 |
|---|---|---|---|---|---|---|---|---|---|
| Barisan Nasional (BN) | 60.7% | 57.2% | 60.5% | 57.3% | 53.4% | 65.1% | 56.5% | 63.9% | 51% |
| Malaysian Islamic Party (PAS) | — | 15.5% | 14.5% | 15.5% | 6.7% | 7.3% | 15.0% | 15.2% | 21.6% |
| Semangat '46* | — | — | — | — | 15.1% | 10.2% | — | — | — |
| Partai Keadilan Rakyat (PKR) | — | — | — | — | — | — | 11.5% | 8.9% | 13.1% |
| Democrat Action Party (DAP) | 18.3% | 19.9% | 19.6% | 21.1% | 17.6% | 12.1% | 13.6% | 9.9% | 14% |
| Others | 21% | 6.9% | 5.4% | 6.1% | 7.2% | 5.3% | 3.4% | 2.1% | — |

*a breakaway faction of UMNO, participated in two elections as an independent party before dissolving in 1996.

**Table 5.3** Parliamentary election results: Number of seats per party [39]

| Political parties | 1974 | 1978 | 1982 | 1986 | 1990 | 1995 | 1999 | 2004 | 2008 |
|---|---|---|---|---|---|---|---|---|---|
| Barisan Nasional (BN) | 135 | 131 | 132 | 148 | 127 | 162 | 148 | 198 | 140 |
| Malaysian Islamic Party | — | 5 | 5 | 1 | 7 | 7 | 27 | 7 | 23 |
| Semangat '46 | — | — | — | — | 8 | 6 | — | — | — |
| Partai Keadilan Rakyat (PKR) | — | — | — | — | — | — | 5 | 1 | 31 |
| Democrat Action Party (DAP) | 9 | 16 | 9 | 24 | 20 | 9 | 10 | 12 | 28 |
| Others | 10 | 2 | 8 | 4 | 18 | 8 | 3 | 1 | 0 |

Muslim voters because it changed its election strategy, joining a multiethnic coalition and deemphasizing its Islamic agenda to focus on broader concerns of social justice, clean government, honest elections, and the rights of the citizen.[42]

The electoral results reflected popular discontent. Although the BN was victorious, UMNO won 76 seats compared with 89 in 1995.[43] PAS won all 8 parliamentary seats in Terengganu, won 13 out of 14 seats at stake in Kelantan, and emerged as the ruling party in both states.[44] PAS also made substantial inroads in Mahathir's home state of Kedah, winning 8 out of 15 parliamentary seats.[45] Nationally, PAS increased its representation in parliament from 7 seats in 1995 to 27 seats in 1999. The BN and UMNO emerged victorious only because they performed well in semi-urban mixed constituencies and in eastern Malaysia.[46]

In the 2004 elections, the BN made up significant ground thanks to four interrelated factors: Mahathir resigned in 2003; the system was gerrymandered further to produce more mixed-urban districts that favored the ruling majority; Mahathir used the events of September 11, 2001, and statements made by certain PAS members to argue that PAS sought the Talibanization of Malaysia; and, finally, PAS alienated voters in Terengganu by focusing too much on *hudud*. With the new prime minister Abdullah Badawi, who was perceived as more open and democratic, at the helm, UMNO reaped an electoral windfall.

In 2008, PAS came back chastened with a universalist message. The new party platform did not mention implementing *hudud* or other aspects of the Islamic criminal code. It addressed varied issues, including electoral reform, clean government, maternity and paternity leave, and environmental reform. The party more than tripled its seats in parliament and retained control of Kelantan. What was surprising about the increase in PAS support was that it was not confined to Muslims. For the first time, PAS attracted a measure of non-Muslim support. Non-Muslim supporters of PAS have been forming "PAS Supporters Clubs" since 2005, attracted to the party because of its commitment to nonracialism. Now, PAS is confronting the reality of 10,000 plus members in PAS Supporters Clubs across the country and is pondering the development of a non-Muslim wing.

### Electoral Pacts

PAS and other opposition parties have also been able to make significant gains when they have entered into strategic electoral pacts. Since 1974, PAS has entered into four such pacts and reaped substantial gains each time. These are as follows: from 1974 to 1978, PAS was in a unity coalition with the BN; from 1990 to 1998, PAS was in a coalition with a new party, Semangat '46, a breakaway faction of UMNO; in the 1999 elections, PAS entered into a multireligious, multiethnic opposition coalition, the Barisan Alternatif (Alternative Front, BA), with the Democratic Action Party (DAP), a Chinese opposition party, and Keadilan, the party founded by Dr. Wan Azizah Wan Ismail, wife of Anwar Ibrahim; and finally, in 2008, PAS joined a coalition with Partai Keadilan Rakyat, and following the elections, with DAP. Each time PAS enters into a coalition, it gains 12–14 seats, supporters, and employs a broader political message that focuses on clean government and social justice—issues that appeal to both Muslims and non-Muslims. These alliances rarely impact policy, but they are often used to increase the influence of the opposition vis-à-vis the governing coalition.[47]

From 1974 to 1978, PAS joined the BN in an effort to promote national unity following the 1969 race riots. During their years in office, PAS representatives in the legislature and the government were permitted to question any initiative or bill on the grounds that it might contravene Islamic teachings.[48] Moreover, PAS used the opportunity in the government to champion the implementation of Islamic law; the establishment of an Islamic university; an increased government commitment to dakwah; and the overhaul of the political, economic, and educational systems to reflect Islamic values.[49] Many of these policies were adopted in some form following PAS' departure from the government.

PAS made significant electoral gains as part of the BA in 1999. This was the first time that PAS and the Chinese-dominated DAP formed a direct electoral alliance with one another. The BA contested 152 parliamentary seats out of 193 and 367 state seats out of 394; it represented the strongest challenge that Mahathir ever faced during his tenure as prime minister.[50] The BA also came to represent many types of dissidents, including disgruntled UMNO supporters; Islamists from PAS, ABIM, and JIM; DAP's Malaysianists; Keadilan's social democrats; concerned Christians; women's groups; and students.[51] Many came to see the BA as a possible alternative to UMNO and the BN, although the BA did not succeed in displacing the BN.

In 2008, PAS, Partai Keadilan Rakyat, and following the elections, DAP formed the most successful coalition to date. The Pakatan Rakyat coalition quadrupled its seats in the legislature, compared with the 2004 results, and won the leadership of five states—Selangor, Kelantan, Perak, Penang, and Kedah. This coalition attracted a great deal of non-Malay support. Whereas in 1999, it was the Malays who had shifted their support to PAS, this time, non-Malays swung to the opposition. The Malaysian Chinese Association and the Malaysian Indian Congress suffered significant defeats, while UMNO only succeeded in gaining about 35 percent of the vote. For the first time, the BN was denied its two-thirds majority.

### Limits on Participation

Islamists in Malaysia cannot participate as freely in politics as compared with their counterparts in Indonesia and Turkey. To correctly portray Malaysia, it is necessary to note the constraints on participation. Thus far, Islamist parties and civil society groups have been willing to work toward their goals through established institutional channels under laws that limit freedoms of speech, assembly, and the press. These laws are enforced, to varying degrees, depending on the prevailing political climate. However, their very existence serves as a constraint to mobilization, as groups must take great care in what they say, where they say it, and in what company, or they may risk imprisonment. The list below summarizes several of the most egregious laws.

1. The Sedition Act of 1948 prohibited speech that could be deemed inflammatory or could promote disharmony or conflict among the races.[52]
2. The amended Printing Presses and Publications Act of 1971 empowers the Ministry of Home Affairs to revoke the licenses of any publications that "alarm public opinion" or are deemed likely to be prejudicial to public order, morality, or security."[53] This promotes self-censorship among the various newspapers and press outlets.

3. The Police Act of 1967 limits freedom of assembly by requiring a permit for gatherings of more than 3 or more people.[54] While local police may withhold permits or revoke them, permits are given quite freely. The Police Act serves as a tool for monitoring.

4. ISA empowers the minister of home affairs to detain someone without trial if he, "is satisfied that the detention of any power is necessary with a view to preventing him from acting in any manner prejudicial to the security of Malaysia or any part thereof or to the maintenance of essential services therein or to the economic life thereof" (Internal Security Act, Section 8-I).[55]

Following a rise in communal protests and demonstrations in 1974, the government amended the Universities and University Colleges Act, which prohibited students from joining political parties, trade unions, or political organizations without the permission of their vice chancellor.[56] Moreover, they were forbidden from stating support for any political party or political group. As in Indonesia under Suharto, the attempted depoliticization of campus life had the effect of channeling political activities and desires through campus mosques and study circles. However, the Razak, Mahathir, and Badawi administrations did not treat political Islam with the level of suspicion that Suharto did. Thus, one did not see the same levels of alienation in Malaysian study circles that one found in Indonesian ones during the Suharto period.

In sum, Malaysia encourages peaceful Islamist mobilization by permitting Islamist groups to participate in politics through a variety of institutionalized channels. They can be recruited into the governing coalition and work to achieve their goals from inside. Alternatively, they can join PAS to advocate for the implementation of an Islamic state and sharia. Although the BN dominates the electoral system, it is possible for opposition parties, most notably PAS, to make significant gains, especially in the face of rising discontent against UMNO or when they enter into alliances with other parties. Islamist organizations can also work in coalition with other like-minded NGOs to lobby for or against specific policies. The government has adopted and implemented numerous policies favored by PAS and Islamist movements, including Islamic institution building, empowerment of sharia courts, and Islamic education reform. This encourages Islamist groups to engage through these channels because they can accomplish goals. However, there are also curbs on assembly, speech, and the press that impede civil society's mobilizing capabilities. Islamist groups must agree to operate under these constraints or opt out of politics altogether.

## State Capacity

More so than Indonesia or Turkey, Malaysia is highly effective in the provision of security, education, and poverty relief and has gained a substantial measure of legitimacy from that success. The state ensures stability and security, which prevents groups from pushing the boundaries of permissible behavior. *Dakwah* groups compliment the state in the provision of services. Furthermore, most of their members have benefited substantially from government development and education policies, and this encourages such complimentary roles to continue. The next section will detail Malaysia's capacities in these areas.

### Law and Order

Malaysia is highly effective in ensuring law and order. In Malaysia, there are no lawless areas where state authority does not dominate, and the general climate of law and order, even in opposition party-governed areas, is strong. Most Malays I interviewed for this book referred to only a handful of incidents of Islamist violence between 1975 and 2006. The Malaysian state has taken several measures to show hard-line Islamist groups that radical activities or revolutionary pronouncements will not be tolerated. When groups threaten violence or employ it, the state acts quickly to ensure order. In contrast with Suharto's Indonesia, the Malaysian police force usually takes care to minimize casualties in its crackdowns, preferring to rely on the law rather than firepower. This section will discuss these methods and then analyze two instances where the state responded to violent Islamist mobilization: the Memali incident in 1985 and the Al Ma'unah incident in 2000.

### Malaysian Security Services, Tactics, and Strategies

Under the leadership of prime ministers Mahathir Mohammad and Abdullah Badawi, brute force repression has been the weapon of last resort. If parties or groups threatened violence, employed violence, began stockpiling weapons, or were believed to have crossed the line between loyal and systemic dissent and antigovernment, anti-system deviationism, the government was prepared to crack down and employ force.[57] Oftentimes, it was not necessary for the government to resort to violent repression. Instead, it would observe, monitor, proscribe, and use the force of the law. Unlike Indonesia or Turkey, Malaysia has a long history of civilian supremacy over the military. Thus, the police has been the arm of the law most responsible for enforcing these measures on a daily basis and is viewed as effective in doing so. However, if demonstrations become violent, the government can call upon the Federal Reserve Unit or the Light Strike Force.[58] Likewise, if severe riots break out, the police can employ the Special Field Force.[59]

According to Dr. Noraini Othman and Dr. Clive Kessler, Malaysia is quite capable in its provision of law and order as a result of its intelligence agencies, most notably the Special Branch, which has an effective surveillance apparatus.[60] This Special Branch of the police is quite successful in monitoring organizational activity to guard against what the state terms *dakwah songsang* (deviant dakwah). The British developed the Special Branch during the colonial period to respond to the threats of communism and radical nationalism. Malaysian Special Branch forces received training in monitoring and interrogation tactics from British intelligence authorities and ranks among the most effective intelligence services in the region.[61] It may infiltrate organizations and parties, monitor speeches given by academics, and observe the activities of activists. Special Branch officers are speculated to serve as chairmen of political parties, both in the BN and in the opposition; in most government ministries; in universities; in civil society organizations; and in private offices.[62] They may pose as telecom officers, students, office boys, and chauffeurs to monitor key figures and groups.[63] Thus, this may deter many radical groups from plotting violent activities; one never knows who is watching or listening.

*The Use of Proscription*

Rather than use violent repression, the Malaysian government will more frequently choose to ban organizations that espouse *dakwah songsang*. This term is used to identify groups that are cult-like, promote anti-system visions of Islam, threaten communal harmony, or adhere to non-Sunni sects.[64] Proscription of Islamist groups began to escalate in the 1980s, for the state claimed that numerous extremist groups had taken root in Malaysia, ranging from doctrinally deviationist organizations to those advocating the overthrow of the government.[65] A government survey noted the presence of roughly 40 *dakwah songsang* movements in Malaysia with an estimated membership of 30,000.[66] Shia organizations were proscribed, in part, for their potential links to Iran and the Iranian revolution, while Ahmadiyah and several Sufi brotherhoods were also labeled as deviant and banned.[67]

The most famous of all Malaysian proscribed movements was the Darul Arqam, which was controversially banned in 1994, and many of its members were arrested under the ISA. Darul Arqam was a prosperous cult-like Islamist organization that preached self-reliance and established communes, businesses, and schools throughout Malaysia. Although Darul

Arqam committed no violence, it was banned allegedly for training a private army and for its increasing cultism. According to government sources, Ashaari claimed he had visions of the Prophet Muhammad and was himself a prophet.[68] Arqam was also viewed as a threat to the political system because it had successfully infiltrated the parties and governing bureaucracy.

> Arqam boldly claimed that 60 percent of the Malaysian population and 80 percent of government servants supported the movement . . . The movement might have further infiltrated UMNO had the UMNO-led government not acted earlier to curtail its influence. If Arqam's claim was even close to the truth, the government might not have been able to stop its activities if the movement became more radical in the future . . . the government estimated that 7000 civil servants were involved in the movement.[69]

Furthermore, the government maintained that group was training militias in preparation for a coup.[70] Evidence of the threat posed by Arqam was sufficient that PAS also supported the ban.

The issue of proscription is a sensitive one. Banning a group can send it underground. For example, a faction of Darul Arqam reemerged in 2000 as the militant cult Al Ma'unah. For the majority of Islamist organizations, the threat of banning, when it is used in tandem with other elements of the Malaysian security apparatus, such as the Special Branch and the Internal Security Act, may serve to discourage the use of violence. In other cases, it may create greater problems in the long run.

*The Internal Security Act*
The ISA is among the most significant weapons in the state security arsenal and a major component of the state repressive apparatus. ISA detainees may be kept in solitary confinement for 60 days and held without trial for up to two years at the discretion of the minister of home affairs. The ISA was enacted during the British colonial period as a response to the communist emergency. However, its purpose shifted in the post independence period from containing communism to maintaining communal harmony.[71] In practice, however, the ISA has been used to intimidate critics, most egregiously by Tun Razak. For example, Anwar Ibrahim, as president of ABIM, was imprisoned for 22 months in 1974. In 1980, local PAS leaders from Kedah were imprisoned under the ISA following their participation in peasant demonstrations.[72] These actions were designed to send clear messages to both groups that criticism beyond a certain point would not be tolerated.

After Dr. Mahathir Mohammad became prime minister and Musa Hitam became minister for home affairs, the use of the ISA dropped significantly from 900 in 1979 to a low of 50 in 1986, 141 in 1991, and 53 in 1993.[73] A majority of those imprisoned during the Mahathir period were labeled as communists, but the ISA was also used against those Islamist groups deemed to be a threat to state security, most notably Darul Arqam in 1994 and PAS-affiliated hard-liners in Memali, who were allegedly stockpiling weapons in 1985. In an attempt to silence influential government critics, Anwar Ibrahim would be imprisoned again under the ISA in 1998. However, this action had the opposite effect as it sparked the *reformasi* (reform) demonstrations nationwide, the founding of the Keadilan party, and the establishment of the BA.[74]

Since September 11, 2001, the Malaysian government has primarily employed the ISA to arrest members of Jemaah Islamiyah and its affiliated local organization, the KMM. In June 2005, of the 115 people imprisoned under ISA, 77 were suspected members of Jemaah Islamiyah or KMM, while in August 2006, 59 out of a total 97 people detained were from the two organizations.[75] The 2008 numbers paint a more mixed picture. In December 2008, of the 46 people detained under ISA, only 16 came from Jemaah Islamiyah; another 13 came from a new radical Islamist organization, Darul Islam Sabah, of which little is known; and 7 were members of various dissident groups.[76] Perhaps ISA employed judiciously and with extreme discretion is an effective tool against those groups that clearly are plotting or have plotted violence. However, it must be used with caution so as to not suppress legitimate dissent or radicalize those with militant views who, to that point, have eschewed violent acts.

## Memali

Violent Islamist mobilization in Malaysia is extremely rare, and in the majority of cases, the state is adept at responding to it in a manner that brings the force of law to bear on radicals while minimizing bloodshed. In the Memali incident, the state departed from this strategy. A radical member of PAS, Ibrahim Mahmud (a.k.a Ibrahim Libya), had gathered followers and began calling for jihad against the government. He called for PAS members to oppose the government in "in every possible way and if necessary, life and property must be sacrificed."[77] Police attempted to arrest Mahmud, but they were prevented by 100 of his followers armed with sharpened bamboo sticks.[78] When the police attempted to arrest Mahmud again, it used excessive force, and 15 civilians, including Mahmud, as well as four policemen were killed.[79]

At Memali, a village in the peninsular state of Kedah, the police showed that it was willing to use force against radical Islamists and that threats to national stability and security would not be tolerated.[80] However, the government lost credibility from that action. Although the government showed it had the capacity to crack down with force, the actual use of that force was interpreted by Malays as a sign of weakness.[81] Mahmud and his followers were viewed as martyrs by many Kedah villagers. One Kelantan-based scholar accused the government of confusing aggressive rhetoric with anti-government intentions.[82] "Indeed he was too aggressive in his speeches and wanted to set up a group of hard-liners within PAS. However, the government cracked down too much."[83] This action cost UMNO the Malay heartland. The government learned a lesson, however, because in subsequent conflicts with radical Islamist groups the state did not crack down in this manner again.[84]

*Al Ma'unah*

The increased effectiveness and change of strategy by the state can best be seen in the case of Al Ma'unah. In 2000, members of Al Ma'unah, a radical Islamist cult, posed as army officers and stole more than 100 rifles and large amounts of ammunition from two army bases.[85] In the following days, the police realized what had transpired and moved against the group, which took two policemen, one army ranger, and one orchard owner hostage; one member of the group was killed when he refused to retreat.[86] After the group surrendered on July 6, the bodies of the two policemen were found tortured and killed.[87] Investigations showed that Al Ma'unah was a break-away faction of Darul Arqam.[88]

The state was effective in dealing with the threat of Al Ma'unah. First, it identified the organization quickly, so as to minimize its ability to conduct any operations with the weapons it had gathered. Second, rather than use excessive force to show that violence would not be tolerated, it used the force of law against the Al Ma'unah members. The members were arrested under the ISA and received court trials. The 3 ringleaders received the death penalty, while 16 members received sentences of life in prison for treason, and 6 others were sentenced to ten years in prison on charges of making preparations for war against the state.[89] Contrary to the state's actions at Memali, this outcome was well received. It also sent a clear message to radical Islamists that they had to abide by the laws of the state.

In sum, the state in Malaysia is highly effective in maintaining law and order. The Malaysian state has a variety of tools at its disposal, which it utilizes willingly but often judiciously. The proscription of groups espousing *dakwah songsang*, the ISA, and the Special Branch are all mechanisms through which the government seeks to maintain security and stability through the force of law. The state has shown that it will not tolerate violent Islamist mobilization or groups that publicly support the government's overthrow. Conversely, the population has shown it will not accept the government's use of excessive force. As a result, the state will crack down most often by employing the force of law rather than physical coercion and repression that could result in massacres. The state and the security apparatus in Malaysia are very strong. The key, however, is that the state must remember the line between anti-systemic extremism and loyal dissent and not seek to quash opposition in the name of security.

## Social Welfare

Malaysia has been an exceptionally effective provider of education and poverty relief, most notably to Malay Muslims. It is important to stipulate at the outset that, by definition, all Malays are Muslims. Numerous Malays depend on the state to provide them with social services and educational opportunities, and many feel a debt of gratitude to the state for enabling their rise to the ranks of the middle class.[90] Malaysia has been highly successful in reducing poverty over the past three decades from 74 percent in 1970 to 6 percent in 1994.[91] According to Dr. Patricia Martinez, "The state ensured a level of wealth and well-being and increased education opportunities. It raised the standard of living for Malays."[92] Islamist groups play a supplemental role, assisting those left behind by the New Economic Policy (NEP).[93] They often obtain small grants from the government on a project basis to run schools, day care centers, and programs for the disabled. The government monitors their activities.

The government's commitment to providing for the welfare of the Malay Muslim population began at independence. However, this mission became a central focus of Malaysian economic policy in the aftermath of the 1969 race riots. Prime Minister Razak believed that poverty was a key underlying cause of the race riots. As a result, his government developed the NEP in 1971 as a program that would eliminate poverty among Malays, especially the rural poor; improve Malay social and economic standing through quotas for Malays in education, employment, and government contracts; enable Malays to have easier access to bank loans and business licenses; and increase Malay ownership of corporate equity.[94]

In rural areas, the NEP enabled farmers to adopt modern techniques for double paddy cropping, irrigation, and draining and the development of a Malay entrepreneurial class that sold food products and handicrafts.[95] The government also created job opportunities for Malay university graduates across majors and across sectors. Many graduates were employed as managers in government agencies, banks, insurance companies, financial institutions, real estate companies, consulting firms, or education and welfare programs that were sponsored by the government.[96] Many of these organizations and institutions were either set up or partially funded by the government through new privatization initiatives.[97]

The NEP enabled the government to have a positive impact on the lives of a majority of Malays. Other programs have contributed to the sense that the government has invested in improving the material and spiritual welfare of Malays. For instance, through the Tambung Haji program, Muslims can save to go on the Hajj to Mecca, and the government provides matching funds. The state also ensures that Malays have easy access to mosques, sharia courts, religious schools, telephone service, business licenses, doctors and clinics, schools, and religious institutions.[98] The dominant role of the government ensures that it has a significant measure of performance legitimacy. As a result, radical Islamist groups cannot make significant inroads and substantial legitimacy gains at the state's expense. Moreover, their members also benefit from the NEP and government programs.

In Kelantan, which is governed by PAS, the state and federal governments share the provision of education and welfare, with Islamist groups playing a supplemental role. According to a senior PAS official in Kelantan, "PAS helps the poor, orphans, and widows. The federal government provides health care through its network of rural clinics."[99] Both PAS and the federal government share the provision of education. PAS also provides free job training programs for women in the fields of tailoring, cooking, and baking and after school programs and job training for youth.[100] PAS may contract out portions of its education and welfare programs to either ABIM or JIM. However, even in a province run by the opposition, it is clear that the federal and state governments are the primary providers for the people's welfare. Thus, radical Islamist groups cannot make substantial inroads in opposition-held provinces either.

*Supplemental Efforts by Islamist Groups*
Islamist groups like ABIM, JIM, Perkim, and Darul Arqam, until it was banned, have provided supplemental social welfare for Malay Muslims. They tend to target those people left behind and those issues not covered by the NEP. Perkim, for example, runs a rehabilitation center specializing in physical therapy for stroke patients and a day care center for special needs children.[101] It also offers education and medical services in rural areas.[102] Perkim receives annual funding from JAKIM to conduct its activities and other grants on a project-by-project basis from the Ministry of Welfare.[103]

JIM runs a program for women pregnant out-of-wedlock to assist them in preparing for motherhood or adoptions; it receives a government grant to assist in its administration.[104] The ABIM runs community development programs in rural areas and examination technique seminars and scholarships for high school students who plan to sit for government examinations.[105] It also runs courses on Islam during Ramadan and receives funding for this program from the Youth Ministry.[106] While most of ABIM's funding comes from member donations and the businesses and schools it runs, it obtains government grants for specific programs on a project-by-project basis.[107]

Since Darul Arqam preached self-reliance, it did not seek government funding for any of its projects. Instead, it ran an extensive network of businesses. Arqam ensured the welfare of its members through the implementation of the concept of *massy* (need-based salary distribution) at its communes.[108] According to this idea, all members received a salary in accordance with their family's needs; a doctor who is single would, therefore, receive less income than an electrician with five children.[109]

### Education

The National Education Policy invested heavily in primary, secondary, and tertiary education for Malays by initiating university quotas for Malays and increasing the number of scholarships available for Malays to study abroad. The number of Malay students studying abroad rose by 65 percent between 1970 and 1975, and by 1979, 66.4 percent of all university students were Malay.[110] By 1989, Malays accounted for 83.2 percent of all students enrolled in science and technology degree programs and 62.8 percent of all arts enrollments.[111]

Education in Malaysia is inexpensive. Students pay yearly entrance and exam fees, but this does not amount to a serious amount of money. The state also provides several programs to aid the poor to defray the costs of sending their children to school, including free breakfast and lunch, uniforms, textbooks, and hostels for students to live if their family's residence is far from a secondary school. School fees can be waived for very poor families. In addition, the state is in the process of improving public transportation in rural areas to increase attendance in secondary schools. Although 92.75 percent of all students attend primary school, this number drops to 82 percent in junior secondary school and 72.45 percent in later secondary school.[112] Malaysia is currently working to make primary and secondary education compulsory.

The government also developed state religious schools as alternatives to private madrasas and to ensure that a moderate, pro-development Islam is taught. There are five types of primary and secondary religious schools in Malaysia: *Sekolah Agama Persekutan* (Federal Religious Schools, SAP); *Sekolah Agama Negeri* (State Religious Schools, SAN); schools run by a state's Council of Islamic Religion; *Sekolah Agama Rakyat* (Community Religious Schools, SAR); and *Sekolah Agama Swasta* (Private Religious Schools, SAS).[113] The state has a centralized standard curriculum for all federal SAPs, state SANs, and community SARs, although the SARs do not consistently employ it.[114] Federal religious schools are federally funded, state religious schools are funded by the individual state governments, and community religious schools are partially funded by the federal government according to per capita per child grants.[115] Private religious schools are eligible for government grants if they agree to register and adhere to national curricular recommendations. The government attempts to monitor private religious schools and community religious schools in order to prevent these educational institutions from instructing students in an antigovernment Islam.[116]

The state has also been responsive to the Muslim desire for improvements in Islamic education. By 1977, under pressure from PAS members in the governing coalition and *dakwah* organizations, the state increased religious studies in the government curriculum and offered Arabic as an elective.[117] Malaysia also sought to develop an integrated curriculum in the 1980s to instill universal religious values in young people and to teach Muslim youths how to correctly practice Islam and how to pray.[118] At the university level, all students are required to take one course in Islamic civilizations, while Muslims are obliged to take Islamic instruction class.

PAS runs a network of madrasas, with a student enrollment of approximately 700,000.[119] In Kelantan alone, PAS runs 90 SARS and 68 *sekolah bantuan,* which combine the government curriculum with that of Al Azhar University. According to an official in the Ministry of Education for Kelantan, these schools receive approximately half of their funding from the federal government, part of which is used to pay teacher salaries.[120] The cost per family is inexpensive, ranging between 80 and 100 ringgit per year (between $22 and $27 USD)which can be reduced if parents have two or more children enrolled in school at the same time.[121] These schools also reinforce the perception of the state as a capable and legitimate actor. According to Abdul Halim Bin Mohammad Naam, assistant director of the Curriculum Division of the Department of Islamic and Moral Education (JAPIM), PAS schools follow the law.[122]

*Supplemental Provision of Education*
Since the 1970s, when the *dakwah* movement took root in Malaysia, Islamist groups centered their activities in the education sector, for education was

seen as a key way to initiate the Islamization of society from the individual upward. ABIM, JIM, and Darul Arqam have all run primary and secondary schools and education programs. ABIM and JIM schools are registered with the Ministry of Education and state-level ministries of religion. They follow the government curriculum in order to obtain government grants and provide their students with the opportunity to attend Malaysian universities. However, they also extend the school day to make more time for Islamic studies. ABIM's private schools are run according to the idea of an integrated curriculum, which Islamizes the philosophy of education and civic concepts.[123] Through this method, one can fulfill the state's curricular requirements while teaching students how Islam relates to each subject. Both ABIM and JIM private schools include classes in Islamic understanding, the Koran, and Arabic.[124] In addition to primary and secondary schools, ABIM runs a network of 409 Islamic preschools to introduce children to basic Islamic concepts at an early age.[125] ABIM also conducts diploma courses in Islamic banking, Islamic politics, and Arabic; programs to assist dropouts; and tutoring for students who failed the national exams but want to retake them.[126]

Darul Arqam schools did not adopt the national recommended curriculum and were not formally registered with the Ministry of Education.[127] Instead, the curriculum centered on Islam. This alarmed government officials because Darul Arqam ran 257 schools in Malaysia with a total enrollment of 9,541 as of 1994.[128] This was another example of the Arqam movement refusing to adhere to government regulations and norms in a manner similar to ABIM and JIM. Since Darul Arqam refused to register its schools, it was difficult keep a watchful eye on them. Furthermore, the state could not have that same positive influence on the well-being of Arqam members.

*Monitoring and SAR Crisis*
The state has sought to effectively monitor activities at private schools and SARs. To gain accreditation, private schools must register with the state's religious department and obtain a license.[129] The state gives an added incentive for registration by allocating grants to private schools.[130] If schools do not adopt the government curriculum, their students cannot sit for the national exams and cannot attend Malaysian universities.[131] As in Indonesian *pesantren* (Islamic boarding schools), this impedes their ability to obtain employment. While many private schools registered, aside from those run by Darul Arqam, a majority of SARs did not. The JAPIM attempted throughout the 1990s to persuade the SARs to adopt the government curriculum to better monitor them, but few SARs acquiesced.[132]

In 2002, the government took a controversial hard-line against the SARs to push them to register and to identify those unduly politicized or radicalized.

It temporarily ended aid to the SARs. This hurt the *rakyat* schools, for they relied heavily on funding from the federal government.[133] Fearing the SARs were indoctrinating their children in radical Islamism, many parents pulled their children out. By February 2003, the beginning of the national school year, 14, 916 out of 24,000 students had withdrawn from the 268 SARs nationwide.[134] At the same time, the state pressured SAR teachers to apply for positions in the national education system with promises of better salaries and training opportunities.[135]

There is consensus that SARs produce youths more likely to support PAS.[136] However, some contend that a minority, perhaps 1–2 percent, of those schools teach radical Islamism.[137] SARs had allegedly become breeding grounds for terrorism as evidenced by the fact that the leadership of the KMM and other terror cells were SAR graduates.[138] Thus far, however, the state has identified and closed only one SAR, Luqmanul Hakim, in the state of Johor for teaching radical Islam. This school warranted the government's attention, for it was started by Abu Bakar Basyir and Abdullah Sungkar, two Indonesian exiles and the founders of Jemaah Islamiyah. Since the onset of the SAR crisis, the JAPIM has sought to become more effective in monitoring the *rakyat* schools; all are now compelled to register, to abide by the government curriculum, and to agree to monitoring by the state.[139]

In sum, the Malaysian state has dominated the provision of education and social services with Islamist groups clearly playing a supplemental role. Through the New Economic Policy and the National Education Policy, the state increased opportunities for Malay Muslims to rise to the ranks of the middle class. Poverty dropped significantly. The Malaysian government benefits from the perception that it takes care of the Malay Muslims. This has inhibited the ability of Islamist groups, radical or peaceful, to make significant inroads at the state's expense. *Dakwah* organizations provide a valuable service, however, in providing education and some social welfare services to those left behind by the NEP. Even in the state of Kelantan, which is governed by PAS, the state government and the federal government share the responsibilities for providing education and social services, thus reinforcing the idea of the state as a caretaker. It creates a sentiment, stated in numerous interviews with Muslim government officials, academics, party officials, and civil society leaders, "Why rock the boat?"

## External Forces

The impact of external forces in Malaysia is minimal compared with external forces in Indonesia or Turkey. Malaysia faces threats from the KMM led by Afghan veterans and from Jemaah Islamiyah. Several top leaders of

Jemaah Islamiyah are indeed Malaysian, including the late Ashaari and Noordin Top, two of the masterminds behind the 2005 Bali bombing. However, while Jemaah Islamiyah has Malaysian members, the organization has never successfully carried out a major bombing or operation on Malaysian soil.

Originally, Mantiqi 1, the branch of Jemaah Islamiyah encompassing Malaysia and Singapore, was the best organized and most capable compared to the other three mantiqis. When Jemaah Islamiyah was founded, Malaysia and Singapore were designated as the "fund-raising region." Following the events of September 11, 2001, the Malaysian government tightened security at U.S.-linked companies and high-profile targets like the Kuala Lumpur International Airport and the Petronas Twin Towers. Moreover, the arrests of Jemaah Islamiyah members in Singapore and Malaysia in 2001 and 2002 and the capture of Hambali, head of Mantiqi 1, so crippled Jemaah Islamiyah's ability to operate in Malaysia that it moved its base of operations to Indonesia.

The KMM is an organization with a core membership of Afghan veterans, including its founder Zainon Ismail and Nik Adli Nik Aziz, the leader of the organization from 1999 until his arrest in 2001.[140] It is loosely affiliated with Jemaah Islamiyah and subscribes to the pan-Islamic jihad ideas of Osama Bin Laden.[141] Malaysian authorities have held the KMM responsible for the assassination of former state assemblyman Dr. Joe Fernandez, the 2001 attack on a Johor police station, the bombing of a church and a Hindu temple, and a botched robbery. Those who have recanted their extremist views have been set free and are monitored. Those who refuse remain in prison.[142]

Nasir Abas, former head of Mantiqi 3 of Jemaah Islamiyah, explains KMM-JI relations through a conversation he had with Hambali, former head of JI's Mantiqi 1.

> Hambali told me stories about Nik Adli. He had relations with Nik Adli. He said there was a group of Malaysians from PAS families, but they did not agree with PAS. Nik Adli, according to Hambali, did not agree with PAS. Those under Nik Adli did not agree with the struggle of PAS in parliament. Hambali could not persuade them to join JI. They formed their own group. But Hambali was able to establish relations between the Nik Adli group and the JI. Between Mantiqi 1 and the KMM.[143]

One PAS official acknowledged the existence of the KMM but denied that the organization represented a legitimate part of PAS: "There are always overzealous fringes that are fed up with the leadership not wanting to take more hard-line stances on government injustices. PAS is demonized through KMM."[144]

In sum, through its effective law and order apparatus, the Malaysian government prevented Jemaah Islamiyah from carrying out operations in Malaysia and, with the aid of Singaporean and U.S. intelligence services, damaged the JI's infrastructure network, causing it to shift its base of operations to Indonesia in 2002. The government was also effective in crippling the KMM by arresting its leaders and members. While the Ministry for Home Affairs had them arrested under the ISA, members were released once they recanted and swore to abandon violent strategies. As of 2005, three members remained in prison.[145]

## Conclusion

Of all the case studies in this book, violent Islamist mobilization is rarest in Malaysia. This is due to a concerted strategy on the part of the state. Although the Malaysian political system is not as democratic and open as that of either post–New Order Indonesia or Turkey, it does provide channels for political participation, and Islamist groups have won numerous small victories by utilizing those channels. They joined UMNO and worked for their goals through the legislature and the bureaucracy. This proved a successful strategy for ABIM from 1982 to 1998 and for PAS from 1974 to 1978. Due to their efforts, over 60 policies to promote Islamization and Islamic institution building were passed nationally between 1974 and 2006.

Islamists also take advantage of the long tradition of oppositionism in Malaysia and work through PAS or as members of Islamic civil society groups. PAS represents a very important channel for peaceful mobilization in Malaysia. It may not gain a majority in parliament, but it wins elections at the state level either in coalitions or independently and governs states. In states where PAS has won, it has implemented Islamization policies, including enforcing modest dress, improving Islamic education, curbing vices, and restricting certain forms of entertainment. PAS also increases its influence and its vote share when it enters into coalitions. The BA and Pakatan Rakyat coalitions of 1999 and 2008, respectively, have enabled PAS to achieve its greatest electoral gains since its inception.

Malaysia's capacities are stronger than those of Indonesia or Turkey. The Malaysian security apparatus has ensured that no lawless areas emerge. Thus, no radical Islamist groups have supplanted the state and made legitimacy gains for their group or their ideology at the expense of the state. It has also enforced law and order more generally to ensure that radical

Islamist groups do not push the limits of acceptable behavior. If groups will not work for their goals through the "acceptable" institutionalized channels, the state will take measures to ban organizations, to monitor them through the Special Branch, or when necessary, to have them arrested and imprisoned under the ISA. Having learned a lesson from the political backlash after Memali, the state now seems to prioritize the minimization of casualties in cases where it cracks down.

The Malaysian state dominates the provision of education and welfare and reaps substantial legitimacy as a result of the successes of the New Economic Policy and the National Education Policy, which decreased poverty and enabled numerous Malays to rise to the ranks of the middle class. Islamist groups play an important role in supplementing the state, targeting those who did not benefit from the NEP. In education, the federal and state governments not only play an important role in public education but also in the provision of religious education. The vast majority of Islamist groups also abide by the state's mandated curricular requirements to enable their students to obtain a tertiary education in Malaysian universities. The state is quite adept at monitoring Islamic schools and has grown more capable since 2001. Although the crackdown on the SARs was excessive, it has enabled the state to ensure that those schools register to facilitate improved monitoring. Given that federal and state governments fund Islamic schools and provide grants to private schools that register, this may prove a benefit in the long term.

Finally, through the effective provision of law and order, Malaysia has also been successful in limiting the influence of external forces. The security services identified and arrested members of the KMM before they could significantly destabilize the country. Furthermore, through cooperation with Singaporean and U.S. intelligence services, Malaysian security forces captured Jemaah Islamiyah members before they could carry out any major operations in Malaysia and crippled the organization's operating capacity in the country.

Can one speak of a Malaysian model that should be widely applied? Perhaps not. Malaysia is a small, ethnically divided country with a long-standing tradition of uninterrupted coalition politics and a unique historical memory. Perhaps, however, the Malaysian case may provide general lessons—about the benefits of the effective participatory model, the importance of channels for political participation, and the necessity of a state's effective capacity—for other states seeking to encourage peaceful mobilization and discourage violence in the name of Islam.

# CHAPTER 6

# Political Access and Public Goods in the Muslim World

The cases of Turkey, Malaysia, and Indonesia have shown that states that both permit institutionalized participation and maintain effective capacity to provide public goods are better able to encourage Islamist groups to adopt peaceful strategies and eschew violent ones. In Malaysia, where both participation and capacity have been present, intervention by external forces did not occur. The experiences of Indonesia and Turkey shows how shortfalls in capacity empowered radical movements to take the law into their own hands, despite the presence of institutionalized channels for participation. This chapter seeks to apply this theory to several cases from the Arab and the larger Muslim world: Kuwait, Bahrain, Bangladesh, and Yemen.

These states can derive lessons from the experiences of Indonesia, Malaysia, and Turkey. Many of these cases are of countries in transition. Bangladesh, which is more democratic than the other cases in this chapter, experienced a coup in 2007 amid skyrocketing corruption and intercene violence. Bahrain is becoming less effective in the provision of poverty relief amid rising unemployment. Finally, Yemen seems to be drifting toward failed state status without reprieve. Although institutionalized channels for participation exist, they are not sufficient to compensate for shortcomings in both law and order and social services.

## Kuwait

Political liberalization in Kuwait is less institutionalized than in Yemen or Bangladesh and yet Kuwait's channels are the most established of all the Gulf monarchies. Whereas Oman, the United Arab Emirates, Saudi Arabia, and until 1999, Bahrain have chosen strategies of political exclusion over institutional inclusion, Kuwait has a functioning National

Assembly. Since its reestablishment at the end of the Gulf War in 1991, the Kuwaiti National Assembly has served as a safety valve for social pressure: when political groups seek to change government policy, they now have a forum in which to express their opinions and through which to pursue their goals.[1] However, this parliament is not as institutionalized as that of Yemen or Bangladesh. It has been suspended twice—once from 1976 to 1980 and again from 1985 to 1991. Moreover, political parties are forbidden, and all candidates must run as members of social movements or as independent individuals. Thus, an important institution is absent in the Kuwaiti system.

Since the National Assembly's reinstatement in 1991, some political progress has been made. The 1992, 1996, 1999, 2003, 2006, and 2008 parliaments have not hesitated to take positions on public issues that may run counter to the government's.[2] Kuwaiti parliamentarians question ministers, appeal to public opinion, air scandals, and generally annoy the government a great deal, but their ability to bring about change is limited.[3] They cannot pass legislation that is opposed by the monarchy.

Various movements represent the different Islamist streams within Kuwaiti society. The Salafi-dominated Islamic Peoples Bloc aims to implement sharia law, the Islamic Constitution Movement (ICM) seeks a gradual Islamization of society, and other movements represent the Shia minority.[4] There is also a liberal faction in the parliament as well. Islamist movements have formed coalitions with secular movements to push legislation such as ones for segregated education facilities. By these alliances, they have a degree of influence over the politico-religious agenda and gain a measure of accomplishment.

This book is not arguing that Kuwait is a blooming "desert democracy." All parliamentary legislation is subject to veto by the Al Sabah ruling family. Kuwait has held so many elections over the past two decades due to the Al Sabah tendency to dissolve parliament when it becomes too obstructionist.[5] However, due to the electoral reforms enacted in 2006 as well as the decision to grant women the right to vote and stand as candidates for election, incremental changes are being made and major grievances addressed. The elections are becoming freer, as evidenced by the gains that the Islamic Constitution Movement and its opposition coalition partners made in the 2006 election, following the regime's dissolution of parliament. Now, the opposition holds a majority in parliament.[6] Moreover, the legitimation of parliament as an institution to channel popular discontent has reduced the likelihood of violent mobilization by Sunni and Shia radical groups. Since Kuwaitis can organize through institutionalized mechanisms to register their grievances, there is less reason to embrace violence.[7] As a result, the popularity of Sunni and Shia radical groups has declined.[8]

Kuwait's security services enable it to maintain sufficient reach of authority throughout the country.[9] There are no lawless regions, where the military or the police cannot penetrate or do not dominate. In the past, when the state cracked down on militancy, it was careful not to follow the Bahraini model and employ brute force repression. Kuwait's security services effectively monitor the many Islamist groups that operate throughout the country. With the rising threat of spillover effects from the insurgency in neighboring Iraq, Kuwaiti security services have been especially vigilant. In early 2005, the Kuwaiti government cracked down on 100 illegal Islamic charities whose fund-raising kiosks had been tolerated on the streets for years.[10] While many of these groups may raise money for worthy Islamic causes, numerous ones also fund the Iraqi insurgency. Local security forces have unearthed various networks recruiting Kuwaitis to fight in Iraq and several local terrorist cells, including a cell of "stateless Arabs," and three affiliated with al Qaeda.[11] Kuwaiti authorities also acted promptly after receiving intelligence that militants were planning attacks on U.S. military convoys to Iraq.[12] However, the full extent of these networks is not yet known. It is certain, though, that the effectiveness of the Kuwaiti security services in ensuring sufficient reach of authority has prevented radical Islamist groups from utilizing strategies of violence.

Of all the countries studied in this chapter and perhaps this book, Kuwait is the most effective provider of social services. It has developed an extensive network of education services, health care, housing, and public assistance due to its great wealth from oil revenues. The ruling Al Sabah family uses the provision of these services to ingratiate itself among the population. Since political participation is limited in Kuwait, provision of education and welfare has been a means of ensuring that the state is considered both legitimate and effective.

Access to education and health care are guaranteed to all Kuwaitis by the Constitution. This includes primary, secondary, and tertiary education as well as clinical-, hospital-, and specialist-based health care.[13] The state pays for schoolbooks, meals, and supplies in the public schools, while students who choose to go religious schools are also subsidized, with the state not only paying for their tuition but also giving them a stipend.[14] The state will pay only half tuition for students enrolling in private Arabic schools, leaving a financial burden that may make many potential Islamic school students choose to attend public religious institutions.[15]

It is important to note that the Kuwaiti government does not discriminate on the basis of sect in social service provision. Thus, Shias have access to the same level of cradle-to-grave benefits as do Sunnis.[16] This gives the Al Sabah regime legitimacy among Shias for its effectiveness. By not marginalizing Shias in the distribution of benefits, the state is able to avoid the sectarian conflicts that have characterized neighboring Bahrain. It also impedes the ability of radical Shia groups to make inroads among Shia by replacing the state in those spheres.

Thus, the state gains legitimacy by providing housing, health care, education, and public assistance to Kuwaiti citizens. Numerous Islamist movements play a supplementary role, most notably the Kuwaiti chapter of the Muslim Brotherhood, which operates in Kuwait as the Social Reform Society.[17] It conducts a vast array of social welfare and charitable activities, including providing assistance during natural disasters, drug treatment, and other forms of social assistance for the poor.[18]

With the exception of the invasion of Iraq, intervention by external forces has been rare in Kuwait for two decades. The Kuwaiti government has kept a keen eye on the events of fellow Arab states and actively sought to prevent infiltration or destabilization. While Kuwait's astuteness has prevented it from succumbing to the violence that has plagued Bahrain, its penchant for jitters has caused it to disband parliament on several occasions for fear of spillover effects from conflicts in the neighborhood. For example, Kuwait disbanded parliament in 1976, in large part, due to fears that the instability plaguing Lebanon could spread to Kuwait.[19] Regional sectarian violence led Kuwait to suspend parliament again in 1986, concerned about Iranian intervention.

Scores of Kuwaitis fought in Afghanistan, yet, unlike in Yemen or Bangladesh, violent Islamist mobilization has been extremely rare. This may be changing. Afghan veterans affiliated with al Qaeda and other militant groups are recruiting Kuwaitis to fight in Iraq.[20] This would be dangerous for Kuwaiti society, if one looks at Pakistan for precedence, where Muslim society in border provinces was radicalized by the Afghan jihad. There are also indications that the violence in Iraq may be spilling over into Kuwait. In 2002 security forces discovered al Qaeda networks inside Kuwait and in January 2005 engaged in several gun battles.[21]

In sum, relative to its neighbors, the Al Sabah regime in Kuwait has provided opportunities for political participation through the institution of parliament. In response, Islamist groups from across the politico-religious spectrum have reacted strategically and are using that channel to foster incremental change. Kuwaiti Salafi movements participate in electoral politics, as does the Kuwaiti branch of the Muslim Brotherhood, Shia movements, and liberal movements, without the fear of crackdown or significant electoral manipulation. Among all security services in the Middle East, the Kuwaiti apparatus is perhaps the most effective in the maintenance of law and order. It also capably provides health care, education, and poverty relief.

Thus, it has a presence in the lives of the masses. The decision to practice the politics of inclusion and nondiscrimination in the provision of public goods has enabled Kuwait to avoid the violence and frustration that has characterized Bahrain. Despite fears, spillover effects from the most recent Iraq war have been minimal. In Kuwait, the state provides opportunities for political participation while maintaining effective capacity. As a result, peaceful mobilization dominates and violence is rare.

## Bahrain

Bahrain experienced sectarian political violence throughout the 1990s and has begun to liberalize as a response. After parliament was disbanded in 1975, the ruling Sunni al Khalifa family monopolized the political sphere, systematically excluding the 70 percent Shia majority.[22] Thus, political exclusion translated into social and sectarian alienation. Unlike Kuwait, there was no parliament to register frustration and dissent. Furthermore, Shias were systematically excluded from intermediate and high-level bureaucratic jobs and were underrepresented in the cabinet.[23] As one Shia merchant told the *Washington Post* in 1995, "We are totally kept out of all the major government ministries . . . If you switch on the TV, there is not a single program that refers to us, our history, our folklore, our geography. We are nothing."[24] Bahrainis saw their country as a "tribal dictatorship," with no opportunity for institutional inclusion. In the 1990s, Bahraini Shias as well as like-minded Sunnis, leftists, and liberals, sought redress through the one channel available to them: petitioning the king. They sent repeated petitions to the king calling for the restoration of the National Assembly and the 1975 Constitution, and improved efforts for economic equality.[25] When this did not elicit results, Bahrainis took to the streets in mass demonstrations, calling for political and economic reforms, in order to show the seriousness with which they took these requests.

The government feared the threat posed by the Shia opposition movement, especially that certain elements might overthrow the monarchy and establish an Iranian-style theocracy in its place. Instead of enabling some degree of institutional inclusion, as the Al Sabah monarchy in neighboring Kuwait had done, the al Khalifa chose to marginalize the Shia movements. Like Indonesia during the New Order era, the regime did not delineate between systemic and anti-systemic movements—both were viewed with suspicion and repressed. Yet, there was significant variation among Shia organizations both in goals and methods. Certain Shia-power movements, such as the Islamic Front for the Liberation of Bahrain, demanded the implementation of sharia and the replacement of the monarchy, if it refused to comply with their wishes.[26] This organization is perhaps best known for bombing a hotel in Manama in 1996. Others like the Bahraini Freedom Movement focused on universal issues such as the restoration of the 1975 Constitution and a more equitable distribution of wealth.[27] Despite the threat of repression, the petitioning and demonstrations continued to occur throughout the 1980s and the 1990s. By the late 1990s, some groups had begun to utilize strategies of violence, including bombings and arson attacks.

With the emergence of a program for political liberalization and evidence of the government's commitment to a policy of greater inclusion, violence decreased significantly. When Shaikh Hamad bin Isa al Khalifa came to power in 1999, he took several measures to foster Shia inclusion, including permitting municipal councils to be elected and increasing the number of seats in the *Majelis al Shura* (Consultative Assembly) to 40, with 21 Shias and 19 Sunnis.[28] At the end of 2000, Hamad appointed 46 members to a Supreme National Committee to draft a charter to formulate a general framework of the future course of the state and the role of its institutions.[29] This charter highlighted the importance of transparency, accountability, equality between the sexes and among ethno-religious groups, equal opportunity for all, and an independent judiciary.[30] Furthermore, it established channels for participation through a two-chamber parliamentary system.[31] With this commitment to political liberalization and institutionalized participation, violent mobilization decreased substantially as Shia movements started to work through the political system.

However, the reforms were not as sweeping as many had hoped. First, from the outset, Hamad limited the powers of the elected parliament by giving the appointed *shura* council equal power. Second, the electoral districts were gerrymandered to favor the sparsely populated Sunni areas, thereby marginalizing the Shia areas.[32] This move led the al Wafiq movement, which is predominately Shia, to boycott the 2002 elections.[33] The 2006 elections increased tensions between the regime and the Shias, in part, due to the leaking of the "Bandar Report," a government attempt to limit Shia electoral gains by supporting Sunni Islamist movements and giving foreign Sunnis citizenship.[34] Although the 2006 election increased the number of Shia representatives in parliament, it did not quiet sectarian tensions. First, out of 11 runoff elections where a Shia candidate contested against a Sunni, the Sunni candidate won 9 of them. Second, in the two years since the election, the primary Shia victor, the al Wafiq movement, produced little in the way of tangible results to improve the livelihood of fellow Shias, which led many Shias to reconsider more militant movements like al Haq.[35] If we compare Bahrain in 2008 to 1998, it is evident that some efforts have been made to promote Shia enfranchisement. However, the measures are insufficient. The prevailing feeling among Shias is that they are still treated unequally, not only in the political arena but also in their treatment by the security services and in the provision of social services. In examining law and order, there are several parallels between Suharto's New Order Indonesia and Bahrain. First, in several areas, Bahrain's security services were quite competent. No lawless regions emerged on the tiny island where state authority could not penetrate; yet, the state did not have a monopoly on the legitimate use of force. Its intelligence network has the capacity to monitor those groups it perceives as potential threats to the state.[36] Yet, much like New Order Indonesia, these heavy-handed security services have been unable to eliminate violence by small, radical underground movements.

In the early years of the Bahraini uprising, police monitored the demonstrations, using tear gas to disperse the participants. This changed in December 1994, when the security services launched a series of raids to arrest key dissidents, which only emboldened Shia activists to hold larger and more frequent mass protests.[37] Between 1994 and 1997, several small underground movements bombed government installations, seven luxury hotels, the Bahrain International Exhibition Center, locally owned commercial buildings, newspaper offices, and the national bank.[38] Shia youths committed numerous arson attacks on women's clothing stores, department stores, and music stores.[39] Molotov cocktails were tossed into a South Asian restaurant, and several supermarkets owned by South Asians were firebombed.[40] The street protests and violence led to the deaths of more than 36 people, a significant number considering that only 600,000 people live in Bahrain.[41] The security services prevented several bombings, diffusing a car bomb set for the Ministry of Justice and Finance and an explosive device discovered in the Traffic Department.[42] However, the behavior of Bahrain's security services mirrored that of Suharto's Indonesia insofar as they often relied on brute force, rather than the force of law, and did not sufficiently delineate between peaceful demonstrators and groups plotting arson and bombings. In September 1996, the prime minister announced plans to divide Bahrain into four provinces, each to be headed by a military governor; yet, even after the state implemented this plan, it was unable to end the acts of violence.[43] While bombings indeed petered out by the end of 1997, the arson attacks continued.

Together with the political reforms, the state enacted several modifications to the security services. Most notably, Bahrain dismantled the state security laws and the state security courts, two of the most hated components of the state's repressive apparatus.[44] At the time, this enhanced perceptions of government acceptability. Violence decreased significantly;

bombings, arson, and riots became rare. However, there is evidence that tensions are running high. In 2004, Shia youths clashed with members of the security services. Riot police still react in a heavy-handed manner to demonstrations as evidenced by their behavior at a June 2005 demonstration, where they beat approximately 50 protestors.[45] It is acts like these, combined with the continued political marginalization of Shias that continues to fuel popular frustrations. If the state continues to disenfranchise Shias, instead of following the example of neighboring Kuwait, some may drift back to the radical movements, losing faith in the ability of peaceful mobilization strategies to produce the desired outcomes.

Like Kuwait, the state in Bahrain provides for education and welfare. In the 1970s, it established an extensive welfare state with free education, health care, and other services for all Bahrainis.[46] If one had an advanced degree, he could obtain a government job. When oil prices fell in the 1980s and the 1990s, this put pressure on the state to rapidly expand its education, heath, and social services to compensate for falling incomes.[47] The regime was forced to make cuts. This led to a declining sense of the state's effectiveness, for children who were raised on full education and social service benefits now had to contend with less. However, even with these cuts, the state never retrenched to the level of Bangladesh or Yemen.

While the state in Bahrain provides health care and educational services, it has not provided comparable levels of public assistance for the poor or the unemployed. Too often, the poor and unemployed are Shias. The unemployment issue was particularly a cause for concern. In the 1990s, unemployment among Shias aged 18–50 exceeded 30 percent, twice the rate among non-Shias.[48] Shias blamed their deteriorating economic conditions on the government's decision to favor Sunni areas over Shia ones.[49] In recent years, however, the government established new job training programs, but there has been a lack of overall investment in a government-sponsored safety net for the unemployed.[50] *Dakwah* groups called *matams* supplemented the state's provision of social welfare services to Shias. The *matams* traditionally have retained a large measure of independence. Each *matam* had its own trust fund through which it collected money and distributed it to the needy in the Shia communities.[51] Given the state's continued suspicion of the Shia, it closely monitored the *matams* for anti-government activities, bringing the income and expenditures of the *matams* under the control of a newly established body, the Higher Council for Islamic Affairs.[52]

Intervention by external forces has been moderate in Bahrain, with revolutionary Iran taking advantage of the feelings of marginalization and frustration among Bahraini Shias. During the 1980s and the 1990s, Iran's

Revolutionary Guards attempted to foment rebellion among Shias. They created a Bahraini branch of Hizbollah, providing military training to its leaders and financial support.[53] At the time of the arrest of 44 Bahrainis accused of being members of Bahraini Hizbollah, it had not committed acts of violence; it had only spread anti-al Khalifa propaganda. Yet, Iranian ties to Bahraini Hizbollah and other anti-government Shia groups exacerbated government fears of overthrow, which led the al Khalifa regime to increase repression and exclusion of Shia.[54] More recently, five men were arrested in 2003, accused of running an al Qaeda cell in Bahrain; in 2004, six more arrests were made.[55] However, al Qaeda has not succeeded in conducting any attacks in Bahrain.

In sum, by limiting channels for participation, al Khalifa restricted the ability of the Shia majority to air its grievances, advocate reform, and work for greater equality. Once the regime opened the system and provided a measure of institutional inclusion, however, it sought to manipulate the system to again limit the influence of the Shia majority. While Shia movements have reacted strategically to the 1999 opening and have sought to use those channels, continued state-sponsored Shia marginalization may backfire, delegitimizing those very channels. The Bahraini state provides public goods but not as effectively or equally as its neighbor Kuwait. While it offers education and health care, it insufficiently provides for the needs of poor and unemployed, most of whom are Shia. This contributes to perceptions of inequality. Moreover, as in the example of New Order Indonesia, although no lawless regions exist in Bahrain, the security apparatus was unable to prevent or end the violence of the late 1990s. The violence only ended once the state attempted to redress concerns of marginalization and unequal citizenship.

## Bangladesh

Bangladesh is an increasingly complicated case. Until 2007, we could say that Bangladesh was the most politically open country among those studied in this chapter. It alone had made a democratic transition. Institutionalized channels for political mobilization exist—it has a multiparty system with two dominant parties, the center-left Awami League (AL) and the center-right Bangladesh National Party (BNP). A host of smaller Islamist parties often play kingmaker roles, most notably, the Jamaat-i-Islami. Bangladesh has had three relatively free elections in 1991, 1996, and 2001, with the BNP and the AL alternating power.[56] There is a vibrant, active civil society at par with Indonesia and Turkey. There is no monarchy or long-standing dictator to constrain the ability of parliament to legislate on a host of issues.

However, in January 2007, a military-supervised caretaker government took power and a state of emergency was imposed.[57] This "soft coup" was conducted in response to rising radical violence and skyrocketing corruption. Begum Khaleda Zia, leader of the BNP, and Sheikh Hasina al Wajed, head of the AL, were arrested and sent to prison, as were scores of other political elites. In 2008, Begum Khaleda Zia and Sheikh Hasina al Wajed were released from prison, and new elections were scheduled for December 29 of that year. Numerous politicians were released from prison in the run-up to the elections, with a resulting electoral victory for the Awami League.[58]

As in Indonesia, Malaysia, and Turkey, Islamist parties have engaged in the political system through the institutional channels. In 2001, more than 15 Islamist parties ran candidates for parliament.[59] Although Islamist parties have typically received only 6 percent of the vote, two have become key figures in party alliances. In 2001, the center-right BNP formed an alliance with Jamaat-i-Islami and Islami Oikya Jote (IOJ). Two Jamaat representatives became cabinet ministers. The alliance and inclusion in the state bureaucracy have enabled these two parties to work through institutional channels to achieve their goals. While the two parties have similar aspirations, the time horizon, structure, and base of membership differ significantly. While Jamaat-i-Islami is a cadre party, which aims to gradually transform Bangladesh into an Islamic state through the parliamentary system, the rural-based IOJ seeks a more rapid transition to an Islamic state.[60]

Unlike the major Islamist parties in Indonesia, Malaysia, or Turkey, factions within Jamaat-i-Islami and IOJ do not believe in democracy so long as the basis for democratic legitimacy lies in the sovereignty of the people.[61] IOJ chairman Fazlul Haq Amini is on record as having said at public meetings in 1999 that "we are for Osama [bin Laden], we are for the Taliban, and we will be in government in 2000 through an Islamic revolution."[62] Both the IOJ and the Jamaat-i-Islami have links to various radical Islamist organizations.[63] This is evidenced by the fact that the seven members of Jama'atul Mujihideen Bangladesh who were arrested in complicity with the 2005 bomb blasts, were members of either Jamaat-i-Islami or its student wing, Islami Chhatra Shabir.[64] IOJ has spearheaded anti-Ahmadiyah campaigns nationwide. Thus, there is no certainty these parties will continue to pursue systemic strategies. In fact, evidence points to a willingness among factions within both parties to use both peaceful strategies as well as violence, intimidation, and threats in pursuit of their goals.

Another problem for Bangladesh is that while institutions exist to channel Islamist participation, the procedures within those institutions have been abused by the major parties. Parliament, in particular, has never functioned properly, for neither the BNP nor the AL will serve as loyal opposition to the other.[65] Since the election of the BNP in 2001, the AL has frequently boycotted parliamentary sessions or walked out of parliamentary debates.[66] The bitter partisanship affects the state bureaucracy channels as well as the mobilization of civil society.[67] Both parties have used large-scale demonstrations and strikes to mobilize supporters against the existing leadership. Until recently, political violence has been a frequent occurrence, one reason for the 2007 "soft coup." The level of gridlock obstructs policy from being enacted, thus making the channels for participation largely ineffective. Furthermore, the politicization of the bureaucratic channels also may impede those Islamists who wish to work with organs of the state on educational, religious, or social welfare issues and yet do not belong to the party currently in power.

The state in Bangladesh has an insufficient reach of authority throughout the country, although to a differing degree than Yemen. This lack of authority has manifested itself in a climate of general lawlessness and decline of the state's reach of authority throughout the country, most notably in the Northwest and the Southeast. The police force is widely considered to be corrupt, ineffective, and tied to gangster networks.[68] While it has had some success in investigating large-scale bombings, this has not extended to prevention. Violence has targeted the Hindu minority, the Ahmadiyah movement, judges, journalists, secular NGOs, and rural women. Governments neither under the AL nor the BNP have been able to restore security. In 1993, Taslima Nasreen, an award winning author, was forced into exile in India after a fatwa was issued against her calling for her arrest and execution. Since 1999, radical Islamists have increasingly targeted secular movements, opposition politicians, scholars, journalists, members of the judiciary, and members of the Ahmadiyah Muslim sect with violence.[69] Writers and journalists deemed "un-Islamic" have been murdered.[70] Attacks on Bengali nationalist and cultural festivals have become commonplace and anti-Hindu violence has also increased.[71] The worst episode in recent years occurred in 2001 following the BNP election victory, when villages were ransacked, Hindu temples destroyed, and over 100 women raped.[72]

In August 2004, radical Islamist groups were implicated in an aborted assassination attempt on Sheikh Hasina al Wajed and the murder of Ivy Rehman, an opposition politician.[73] Despite escalating violence, the BNP-led government denied that radical Islamism existed in Bangladesh and refused to act against the movements.[74] Prime Minister Khaleda Zia claimed on September 6, 2003, "There are no fundamentalists or zealots in this country."[75] However, the following month, the Special Branch of the police authored a report calling for the proscription of several radical Islamist organizations and expressing concern that militant Islamist movements were making such inroads that they may one day challenge the country's sovereignty.[76] However, the report did not prompt the government to reassess its stance.

The state's insufficient reach of authority was most noticeable in the rural western and northwestern regions of Bangladesh, where the radical Jagrata Muslim Janata Bangladesh (JMJB) began to target members of the left-wing Purbo Banglar Communist Party (East Bengal Communist Party) in April 2004.[77] Various newspapers described increasing abductions, torture, the imposition of Taliban-like rule in the villages, and the killing of at least ten people.[78] The erosion of the state's reach of authority is a problem that threatens to undermine efforts at democracy building in Bangladesh. When Muslim militants can attack secular NGOs with impunity, this impedes the development of a functional civil society as well as the distribution of education and welfare services in the rural areas where these attacks are most frequent. The Bangladeshi case illuminates why institutionalization of channels for participation is necessary but not sufficient. While Bangladesh possesses these channels, imperfect as they are, the political parties in parliament have been unable to ensure the state's reach of authority. Due to the inability of the police to stop the violence, the BNP government called upon the military to restore law and order, but with the end of "Operation Clean Heart" in 2003, violence by radical Islamist groups increased once again.[79] The BNP-led government began to take measures to ban the JMJB and the JMB only in February 2005, accusing them of masterminding bomb attacks and killings throughout the country to sow disorder.[80]

However, this did not halt the violence; if anything, these movements chose to up the ante. In August 2005, the JMJB and the JMB set off a coordinated series of 450 bomb attacks at sites throughout the country in less than one hour.[81] In November 2005, a series of bombings targeting judges resulted in the deaths of two lower court judges and two court employees, while ten people were killed in suicide bombings of local bar associations in Chittagong and Gazipur.[82] A 2005 investigation by the *Daily Star,* the popular Bangladeshi English language paper, discovered that over 30 militant Islamist organizations have established networks throughout the country since 1989 with the goal of establishing an Islamic state.[83] Many activists are former veterans of the Soviet-Afghan war or have received training elsewhere, at camps in either Bangladesh or Libya in the 1980s and the 1990s.[84] These attacks finally prompted the government and the security services to act, arresting senior militant leaders in March 2006.[85] Like Indonesia, this indicates that the central issue is one of firmness in enforcing the law.

The state has also been increasingly ineffective in ensuring the provision of education and social services to alleviate the country's grinding poverty and high illiteracy rates. According to 2005 figures, approximately 70 million Bangladeshis live below the poverty line, 30 million are unemployed or underemployed, and 90 million have no access to health care.[86] Where the state has retrenched, Islamist groups, funded often by external inputs from neo-Salafi and Wahabi groups in the Middle East, have moved in to fill the void. The state has been unable to monitor those Islamist groups who do supplement the state. While the government in the late 1970s set up a Madrasa Education Board in the Ministry of Education to monitor the madrasa system and ensure that the curriculum was at par with that of secular education, this has not been rigorously pursued.[87]

State investment in public education has been particularly poor. If one examines the UNDP's Human Development Index for public expenditure on education, Bangladesh spends less on education, both per capita and as a percentage of government expenditure, than any country studied here, save Yemen.[88] "Most of the unsolved problems that Bangladesh has been facing with increased difficulty are rooted in the leadership's inability to understand the role of education and training as perhaps the most effective agent of change and advancement in society."[89] While the government has invested more in education and health care in the 1999 budget, the existing infrastructure remains woefully inadequate.[90] According to Sumit Ganguly,

> The most compelling, proximate cause of the emergence of militant Islam in Bangladesh is the state's failure to address endemic problems of unemployment, poverty, environmental degradation and the political order. As a result, large segments of the population have little faith in the efficacy of state institutions. In such a political milieu, religious groups and organizations, which provide basic social services, assume an important role. Furthermore, they underscore the state's inability to perform the quotidian tasks of maintaining public order, providing essential social services, generating employment and pursuing public works.[91]

Where the state has failed to provide for education and social services, most notably in rural areas, a combination of secular NGOs and Islamist groups have stepped in to supplement, and in some cases, supplant the state. Jamaat-i-Islami has increased its popularity in the rural areas by its provision of social services through its network of schools, health clinics, and charities.[92] Likewise, due to the massive inputs from Middle Eastern countries, service-oriented Islamist organizations have proliferated throughout Bangladesh, filling the void left by the state in the provision of education.

Official statistics indicate that there are 9,000 madrasas registered with the government, another 8,000 private madrasas under the control of the Bangladesh Qawmi Madrasa Education Board, and thousands more that fall outside the state's monitoring purview.[93] The number of students in madrasas has increased by 818 percent over the past 20 years, compared with a 317 percent increase in public secondary schools.[94]

However, secular groups have also been quite successful in providing education and social welfare in the rural areas. The Bangladesh Rural Advancement Committee has established a network of 73,000 education centers throughout Bangladesh, where 2.6 million adults and children attend.[95] There has been considerable conflict between the secular and Islamist organizations, for the Islamist groups allege that the secular NGOs are attempting to undermine Islam by empowering women.[96] This has impeded the ability of secular groups to provide these needed services successfully and has ceded more of the sphere of influence to Islamist groups.[97]

External forces intervention has been on the rise in Bangladesh due to Afghan veterans, spillover effects from Burma's insurgencies, and the presence of al Qaeda-affiliated organizations, particularly in the Southeast, where the state is not in full control. There is substantial evidence of terrorist activity in the Bangladesh, particularly among the Rohingya refugees. Al Qaeda has recruited Burmese Rohingyas and Bangladeshi militants as mine sweepers and porters in Afghanistan.[98] The umbrella group the Jihad Movement of Bangladesh and its influential subsidiary, Harkat ul-Jihad-al-Islami (HuJI), are headed by former Afghan veterans.[99] Fazlul Rahman, leader of the Jihad Movement of Bangladesh, was a signatory to the official declaration of jihad against the United States on February 23, 1998, together with bin Laden, Ayman Al-Zawahiri (leader of the Jihad Group in Egypt), and Sheikh Mir Hamzah (Jamiat-ul-Ulema-e-Pakistan).[100] Thus, Islamist militant groups in Bangladesh are well connected to international terrorist organizations through which they can receive training and funding for their own internal activities.

In sum, over the past two decades, opportunities for political participation in Bangladesh have been greater than any other case presented in this chapter. Islamist movements, some of which seek to eventually transform the state into an Islamic state, have reacted strategically and are utilizing those channels to work toward their goals. Bangladesh also has the most vibrant civil society in this chapter that lobbies on a wide variety of issues from corruption to women's rights to sharia. However, the state has taken insufficient measures to discourage violence. By retrenching in the provision of social services, it has enabled radical movements to make legitimacy gains at the state's expense. By turning a blind eye to radical violence against religious minorities, women, secular movements, journalists, and members of the judiciary, it has allowed militants to act with impunity. One challenge in Bangladesh is that the two most influential Islamist parties, the Jamaat-i-Islami and the IOJ, have ties to the radical movements and their members have participated in bombings. As a result, the government was reluctant to target the radical movements until the violence grew to such a degree that action became imperative. One cause for greater optimism is that once the government chose to act, it did so, which shows that the problem is not a lack of capacity as in Yemen, but the need for a firm political will.

## Yemen

Since the unification of North and South Yemen into the Republic of Yemen in 1990, Yemen has become quite open, when compared with other states on the Arabian peninsula. Yet, it has had the same president, Ali Abdallah Salih, since 1978, and Salih has sought to centralize a great deal of power in the executive. However, despite the powerful executive, there is also room for mobilization. Civil society groups, political parties, and interest groups have proliferated throughout the country.[101] The Yemeni government has been careful to ensure that political institutions exist to channel popular mobilization. In April 1991, less than a year after unification, Yemen voters approved a constitutional referendum calling for a collective presidency, an elected parliament with considerable power vis-à-vis the executive, and local elected councils.[102]

Yemen has had three multiparty elections—in 1993, 1997, and 2003. The Islamist Islah party is an active participant in party politics. Islah has understood the importance of institutional channels since its inception.

> Islah first established a formal structure within the party including eight administrative divisions of headquarters office, an executive committee and a consultative council. They routinized operations, organized public events to expand visibility and prepared for national elections. Within this routinization was the formulation of official party positions on a variety of social, political, economic and religious issues.[103]

Due to this institutionalization and routinization, Islah could effectively channel the demands of Islamist groups and incorporate various Islamic sectors into its party through these channels. For example, many of the Afghan veterans who returned to Yemen joined Islah, thus reducing the proportion that sought extra-institutional and often violent means to change the political system.[104]

Islah also has a history of alliances with majority and minority parties in parliament. In the 1993 multiparty elections, it formed a coalition government with the Congress Party and the Yemeni Socialist Party. After its alliance with the Congress Party fell apart, it joined an alliance with a group of smaller opposition parties. In 2005, Islah joined the Yemeni Socialist Party, the Popular Nasirist Unity Organization, and two Zaydi parties, al Haqq and the Union of Popular Forces, in an opposition alliance—the Joint Meeting Parties (JMP). As in Malaysia, this coalition brings parties committed to sharia together with secular parties. Yet, it has endured. In 2006, the JMP showed its metal when it nominated Faysal bin Shamalan, member of parliament and former oil minister, known for his honesty, as its candidate for president to oppose longtime President Ali Abdallah Salih.[105] These alliance-building opportunities have been key to the institutionalization of the Islah party within the political system.

Despite the existence of channels for participation, Yemen has experienced more violent Islamist mobilization than any other case in this book. This is due to the shortcomings in its capacities to provide public goods. Yemen is a weak and fragile state. Violence is endemic to both rural and urban areas, brought about by a combination of factors, including poverty, sectarianism, rapid population growth, and uneven distribution of resources.[106] The government has never had a monopoly over the use of force. Yemen is a country with a heavily armed population dispersed over remote and inaccessible areas; the state is often unable to extend its authority to rural areas; and the country's borders are porous.[107] The state has been unable to penetrate entire regions of the country to provide education and social welfare services, particularly the northern and eastern governorates, which are particularly remote and have strong traditions of tribal autonomy. A lack of central authority combined with the decay of tribal legal norms, most notably in the Zaydi heartlands, has led to an increased climate of lawlessness in these areas.[108] The ensuing political vacuum caused by the insufficient reach of the state's authority and the decline of tribal authority has led to increasing Islamist militancy, greater intervention by external forces, and more violence in these regions.

It is clear that the Yemeni government has had great difficulty in preventing violence. Between 1998 and 2002, radical Islamist groups were responsible for numerous violent incidents. The Aden-Abyan Islamic Army conducted repeated attacks on domestic and foreign targets in Yemen, including assaults on Yemeni socialists prior to the 1993 parliamentary elections; several bomb attacks around Aden in the late 1990s; the kidnapping of 16 Western tourists on December 28, 1998; and the attacks on the British Council in Saana and the *USS Cole* in Aden in 2000.[109] The

Yemeni Islamic Jihad militants have been held responsible for the assassination of Jarallah Omar, the deputy secretary general of the Yemeni Socialist Party, and the killing of three American aid workers at a Baptist hospital in Jiblah in 2002. In 2003, however, the government negotiated a truce with Qa'idat al-Jihad fi al-Yemen (Base of Jihad in Yemen), an umbrella group that includes the Aden-Abyan Islamic Army as well as al Qaeda sympathizers.[110] Since then, radical Salafi violence from al Qaeda-affiliated local sources has decreased, but a prison break of 23 terror suspects in 2006 shows the weakness of the security apparatus.[111]

Although violence by some radical Salafi movements has decreased since the 2003 truce, the state still faces rising frustrations in the South and rebellions in the North. One notable example is the al Huthi uprising in the northern governorate of Saada. Since 2004, the Yemeni security services and allied tribal forces have repeatedly clashed with the Believing Youth, a radical Islamist student movement, whose members were originally follow-ers of Hussein al Huthi, a Zaydi cleric and former member of parliament from the Hizb al Haqq party.[112] This is problematic in itself, for it shows that some political leaders are willing to support the use of violence to effect change. Since 2004, the conflict has spread to encompass the area tribes, pitting those bought and paid for by the military against those loyal to the al Huthis.[113] Here too, we see the presence of another disturbing trend—the military arming certain tribes to take action against the al Huthis. As in Indonesia with Laskar Jihad, this has only exacerbated the conflict taking place. What was once a small rebellion of a few thousand students has now become a veritable guerilla war.[114]

Not only is the state's reach of authority insufficient, but the state security services are also inconsistent and often overly repressive. This has harmed the state's credibility, especially in the South, where the state's ineffectiveness has been greatest. Southern Yemenis seethe under the watchful eye of the security services, which have functioned as a quasi-occupation force ever since the South lost its bid for secession from the North in the mid 1990s.[115] While they may be well entrenched, they are not a professionalized security apparatus.[116] This ineffectiveness combined with the repressive treatment of southerners has contributed to the emergence of some radical Islamist groups, particularly the Aden-Abyan Islamic Army, whose name indicates southern roots. In the Saada revolt, which incidentally is taking place in a traditional Salih stronghold, the military responded by deploying over 20,000 soldiers, attacking civilian targets using heavy weaponry and shelling indiscriminately. [117] This has only created sympathy for the rebels in other parts of Yemen, particularly in the South, but also among elements within the security apparatus. This is evidenced by the fact that in January 2006, two leaders of the rebellion escaped from a maximum security prison, which could not have occurred had it not been for assistance from inside.[118]

Yemen is perhaps the least effective provider of education and welfare in this book. Its terrain has made certain tribal and rural areas inaccessible to the state. Thus, while the Yemeni government may provide a measure of education and social welfare to its population, these services go only as far as the paved roads do.[119] In accessible areas, the state has nationalized and centralized the provision of education, as well as improved utilities, electricity, and infrastructure. Within this span of territory, "these services remain physical conduits of a national system whose hub is Sanaa."[120] However, these services do not penetrate into the remote tribal areas where they are most needed and where the perception of the government as effective is most necessary. The situation is not improving. Yemen struggles, with a high rate of unemployment as well as 3.9 percent population growth and 75 percent female illiteracy.[121]

The Yemeni case is a clear example of where the state's inability to provide sufficient education and welfare in rural and remote tribal areas has led puritan and radical Islamist movements to make inroads at the state's expense. In some cases, the Salih regime has even encouraged the primacy of neo-Salafi and Wahabi groups in these areas and the proliferation of these religious institutes to counter the influence of the left.[122] Many of these "scientific institutes," as they are called, are concentrated in the southern highlands, as well as the northern and eastern governorates where the state is unable to penetrate.[123] While Wahabi clerics gained key positions teaching the state's curriculum in state schools, Afghan veterans also opened their own private religious institutes in the rural and tribal areas and used them to propagate their ideology.[124] In the northern Zaydi-dominated governorates, the proliferation of these Wahabi institutes has eroded the influence of the traditional Zaydi private schools.[125]

Islamist groups often supplant the state in the provision of social welfare services. There are more community and Islamic charity groups in Yemen than in the rest of the Arabian peninsula combined.[126] Islah has been especially effective in providing hospitals, religious education, and vocational training and in installing water tanks, while other groups concentrate on other areas. The Salafi Al-Hikma society donates money to mosques, schools, and health care centers; Hujariyya undertakes unfinished development projects; other groups provide medical services or assist particular occupational groups.[127] These groups gain legitimacy at the state's expense

Recently, the international financial institutions have pushed Yemen to privatize many of these social services. This will allow the Islamic social service sector to take on an even greater role in the provision of social welfare and may enable them to supplant the state. While Islamist groups already do so in the remote regions, it may be disastrous to erode this element of the state's credibility and effectiveness in the currently accessible areas. According to Sheila Carapico, "Alienation of public services from the state may further alienate people from a polity whose legitimacy rested tenuously on its material relevance to every day life."[128]

Yemen has had a significant problem with intervention by external forces—Saudi funders, Afghan veteran militias, and international terrorism. Thousands of Yemenis fought in Afghanistan, and when they returned, many supported and fought for the northern side in the civil war in 1994.[129] While some were rewarded for this with ministerial posts, another group joined Islah, a third group sought to operate independently and received government aid, and a fourth group took up arms against the state, forming the Islamic Jihad Movement and the Aden-Abyan Islamic Army.[130]

Recently, it has been alleged that the Aden-Abyan Islamic Army has financial and organizational ties to al Qaeda, while the Yemeni Islamic Jihad Movement had relations with Osama bin Laden in the past.[131] The inability of the Yemeni state to maintain law and order within its territories has allowed al Qaeda to use Yemen as a recruitment and staging area.[132] However, it is very important to note that the Yemeni government has not offered direct support to al Qaeda as Afghanistan and Sudan did in the 1990s; moreover, al Qaeda has been unable to set up large bases in Yemen.[133] Thus, while Yemen's state capacity is exceptionally weak, it is not at par with failed states like Afghanistan and Sudan.

Another source of external force intervention and destabilization has been the influence of Wahabi funders and the Saudi state itself. Historically, the Saudi kingdom has preferred a weak and divided Yemen over which they could exert a strong influence.[134] Militant Islam arose in Yemen as a result of substantial Saudi funding of Yemeni madrasas or "scientific institutes," as they were termed, and from Wahabi proselytizing in the Yemen Arab Republic in the 1970s and the 1980s, and in the republic following unification.[135] Both the Afghan veteran phenomenon and the Saudi-Wahabi influence has had the effect of exacerbating violent mobilization by radical Islamist groups in Yemen today.

In sum, Yemen provides opportunities for political participation to a greater degree than other Arabian peninsular states, including Kuwait. In doing so, it encourages Islamist groups to mobilize peacefully through political parties, alliance building, and civil society. However, the state is not successful in discouraging violence. Yemen is approaching failed state status. There are entire regions of the country where state authority does not dominate, and the state's provision of public goods goes only as far as the paved roads. As a result, radical Islamist groups have made inroads at the state's expense. External forces intervention is among the highest in all cases in this book. In Yemen, while many Islamist groups utilize peaceful strategies, numerous radical militias and insurgent groups exploit the state's weaknesses for their own ends.

## Conclusion

This brief comparative analysis indicates that the theoretical framework put forth in this book has broader applicability to the larger Muslim world beyond, given certain qualifications. Kuwait offers some channels for political inclusion, which are reasonably institutionalized, while maintaining effective capacity in both law and order and education and social welfare. This system, although not as open as Bangladesh or Yemen, does provide political access for various streams of Islam from Shias to Salafis to the Muslim Brotherhood. Despite its proximity to Iraq, the war has not spilled over to the degree that it has in Turkey, and intervention by al Qaeda has been minimal. Of the cases examined in this chapter, Kuwait comes closest to approximating an effective participatory state.

In a second group of cases, Yemen and Bangladesh possessed institutionalized channels for political participation to a greater extent than Kuwait, but the state could not provide education and welfare services or ensure effective reach of authority. Despite high levels of Islamist mobilization through the peaceful channels, violence is also a frequent tactic. In these cases, the existence of lawless areas where state authority has not penetrated has enabled radical groups and terrorist groups to thrive. In these states, the inability to provide education and social welfare has allowed Islamist groups to move in to fill the void, gaining recruits in the process. In both Bangladesh and Yemen, the state's inability to provide comprehensive education has enabled radical groups, aided by funding from neo-Salafi and Wahabi groups, to open hundreds of radical madrasas. Intervention by external forces has been especially high in these countries—Salafi and Wahabi funders subsidize orthodox Islamic schools and social welfare organizations; Afghan veterans establish militant organizations in the lawless areas; and al Qaeda and other terrorist organizations conduct activities in these areas.

Finally, like New Order Indonesia, Bahrain shows shortcomings of effective authoritarianism. In refusing to establish even channels for political participation on the Kuwaiti model, there was little way for the Shia majority to express their grievances or have their voices heard. When petitioning did not lead to greater political and socioeconomic reform, disgruntled Shias and like-minded Sunnis, liberals, and leftists took to the streets. The security services did not delineate between movements advocating greater socioeconomic equality and those that utilized violence. Bahrain in the mid-1990s reeled under arson attacks and bombings. Although the security services had been viewed to that point as effective, they could do little to stop the violence. Retrenchment in social services contributed to tensions. While the government provided education and health care, there was no social safety net for unemployed Shias. The government of Bahrain has continued to treat Shias with suspicion despite the fact that violence is rare in Bahrain today. While elections are held for parliament, districts are gerrymandered to favor Sunni candidates. Despite this fact, Shia are working through the political system. However, should this discrimination continue, rising frustrations may lead to a rejection of these channels.

These brief cases have affirmed that those states that possess both effective capacity and institutionalized channels are better able to encourage Islamist groups to adopt peaceful strategies and eschew violent ones, compared with states that only have one or the other. When states retrench in providing public goods, radical Islamist movements can utilize those opportunities to make legitimacy gains at the states' expense. However, radicalism can also be sparked by political exclusion, mounting frustration at continuing marginalization, even if capacity is reasonably effective.

# CHAPTER 7

# Conclusion: Patterns of Mobilization

In the aftermath of September 11, 2001, interest in the Muslim world increased exponentially. A large portion of the discussion on the Muslim world is devoted to radical Islamism and terrorism, in particular in Iraq, Afghanistan, Pakistan, and Israel. This research trend is both interesting and necessary. However, it marginalizes the positive developments that have been taking place in the Muslim world since the late 1980s. We cannot fully understand why some countries face violence unless we analyze how others prevent and avoid it. It is not sufficient to examine what went wrong; we must also investigate what went right. This book has endeavored to unpack the reasons for the variation in Islamist mobilization. It asked why some states have had comparatively greater success in encouraging Islamist groups to adopt peaceful mobilization strategies than others.

The key message of this book is that the state matters, but not just any state. A participatory state with effective capacities can influence Islamist groups to employ peaceful and systemic mobilization strategies and to eschew violence. This is a marked departure from many studies on political Islam which view the state as either an authoritarian and repressive actor or a weak and powerless one, often rightly so. However, numerous states within the Muslim world do not fall into either of these categories. Some provide incentives that influence the mobilization strategies Islamist groups adopt. This book lays out a framework of three conditions that can be generalizable across the larger Islamic world. First, states encourage Islamist groups to employ peaceful mobilization strategies and to eschew violence by (1) establishing institutionalized channels for political participation, (2) ensuring law and order in the territories within their borders so that no lawless areas emerge where the state is not the dominant authority, and (3) providing social services to gain credibility and to prevent radical Islamist groups from making legitimacy gains in these areas at the state's expense.

**Table 7.1** The variation in Islamist mobilization

|  | Turkey | New Order Indonesia (1967–1998) | Indonesia (1998–Present) | Malaysia |
|---|---|---|---|---|
| **Institutionalized channels for participation** | Yes | No | Yes | Yes |
| **Effective state capacity** | Mixed | Yes | No | Yes |
| (1) Effective Provision of Social Services | Yes | Yes | No | Yes |
| (2) Reach of Authority | Mixed | Yes | No | Yes |
| **External forces** | Mixed | No | Yes | No |
| **Result: Domination of peaceful Islamist mobilization** | Mixed | N/A | No | Yes |

From Table 7.1, we can discern three cases: Malaysia, Turkey, and post–New Order Indonesia where the state permitted participation and peaceful mobilization was the dominant mode of political engagement. In contrast, New Order Indonesia acts as a disconfirming case. It constrained all Islamist mobilization because the state feared it could be a rallying point for political opposition. In both instances, Islamist groups reacted strategically to adapt to the circumstances and arenas available for activity.

The three participation cases validate the contention that institutionalized channels for participation are necessary to ensure peaceful Islamist mobilization. In each case, when the state gave Islamist groups the opportunity to work toward their goals through institutionalized channels, the vast majority reacted strategically and did so. In Turkey, a moderate Islamist party, the Justice and Development Party (AKP), has governed the country since 2002, and the Refah Party led the governing coalition from 1995 to 1997. In post–New Order Indonesia, as democratic institutions began to consolidate, Islamist organizations began utilizing them more extensively. In 2004, following the turnover of 70 percent of the legislature, Islamist organizations began lobbying in earnest, holding hearings, submitting petitions, and writing alternative drafts of legislation. There are numerous parties representing various streams of Islam, and Islamist organizations have engaged with them to promote sharia-inspired legislation at the district and provincial levels.

In Malaysia, the Malaysian Islamic Party (PAS) works as both party and pressure group to move the country in a more Islamic direction. It pushes for the incremental adoption of sharia-based policies in the states where it has a presence or where it governs. Furthermore, following the co-option of the Malaysian Islamic Youth Movement (ABIM) in 1982, there was a marked increase in the volume of legislation pertaining to Muslim issues, Islamic institution building, and sharia. Islamist groups are reacting strategically to the political space available for mobilization and are forming umbrella coalitions to leverage their influence, lobbying and holding hearings.

In contrast, the government of New Order Indonesia pursued policies of institutional marginalization for the majority of its rule because it feared the power of political Islam as an oppositional force. Islamist groups had to react strategically to this political climate. Many politico-Islamist groups went underground and sought refuge in study circles where they isolated themselves from others that did not share their perspective. Many of the radical groups active in Indonesia today have their roots in the underground movements and study circles of this period. The New Order claimed that it restricted Islamist participation to ensure stability and security. However, the New Order was unable to prevent violent mobilization; it was only able to temporarily limit the oppositional power of political Islam. Violent mobilization continued in Indonesia at a low hum throughout Suharto's tenure. These policies actually contributed to the explosion in violent mobilization that followed Suharto's resignation.

If we compare New Order Indonesia with Malaysia, the contrast becomes clear. Both are states that prioritized security and stability. However, in permitting Islamist groups to mobilize through institutional channels, the Malaysian state encouraged engagement as the acceptable way to work for goal attainment. In marginalizing Islamist groups and constraining them from legitimate political channels, the New Order alienated that segment of the population. While many Islamist movements focused on *dakwah* (Islamic propagation), some communities began to see violence as a legitimate means of dissent. The variation in institutionalized participation has been illustrated in Figure 7.1.

**Figure 7.1** Variation in participation.

It is not sufficient for a state to encourage peaceful mobilization strategies; it must also take steps to discourage violent ones. This book contends that the best way to do this is for the state to be as a positive provider of public goods. It should maintain law and order throughout its territories and offer a measure of education and social welfare. This enables the state to gain legitimacy from the provision of these services, and cuts off an important avenue for radical Islamist recruitment, popularity, legitimacy, and activity. Here too, there has been variation across cases. The Malaysian government has been most effective in its ability to ensure law and order, education, and poverty relief. There are no lawless areas where communal conflicts fester. There are no regions where the state lacks a monopoly in the use of force. The Malaysian police force is adept at infiltrating and monitoring "deviant" groups, and the state tends to use the force of law against radical groups rather than brute force. Likewise, the Malaysian state has gained tremendous legitimacy from its ability to raise the standard of living of Malay Muslims and provide them with education and employment opportunities through the New Economic Policy, the National Education Policy, and subsequent economic development programs. Islamist violence has been exceptionally rare in Malaysia, with fewer than a dozen notable incidents since 1975.

While New Order Indonesia was not as successful as Malaysia in ensuring law and order, the two should be grouped together, for New Order Indonesia was also reasonably effective in these capacities. Like Malaysia, the Indonesian state gained credibility from its role in providing education, welfare, and poverty relief, thus raising the standard of living for a majority of Indonesians, reducing poverty from 60 percent in 1965 to 16 percent in 1996, and raising literacy rates.[1] While Indonesia was not as effective as Malaysia in preventing groups from undertaking violent acts, the security services were adept at identifying the perpetrators and holding them accountable. Likewise, there were no lawless areas where state authority could not penetrate. However, the state in Indonesia does not and has never had a monopoly in the use of force. In New Order Indonesia, violent Islamist mobilization was relatively low compared with Turkey and contemporary Indonesia. However, church burnings increased exponentially during this period. Moreover, there were periodic violent incidents every few years, which the state was never quite able to prevent.

Turkey's capacity has improved over time. As in Malaysia and New Order Indonesia, the state in Turkey today is a major provider of primary and secondary education. It has a substantial degree of control over the curriculum at Islamic schools and effectively monitors them to a degree at par with Malaysia. Turkey's law and order capacity has been mixed due to conflicts in the 1960s and 1970s, largely between leftists and ultranationalists, and in the 1990s, due to the unrest in the Southeast. The Marxist terrorist group the Kurdish Workers

Party (PKK) fought a low-intensity secessionist war, and radical Islamist groups emerged in response to the PKK threat with Iranian assistance. When the state lost control over security in the Southeast, violent Islamist mobilization increased significantly nationwide as radical groups employed strategies of violence, including assassinations and murders. However, following the restoration of order in the Southeast and the subsequent arrest of the members and leaders of the two main radical Islamist organizations, Hizballah and the Great East Islamic Raiders Front, violent mobilization decreased substantially.

Indonesia has faced the most challenges since its democratic transition began. The Indonesian state has attempted to provide education and poverty relief, but many of its programs have faced problems in implementation due to corruption. Since the transition began, law and order has been Indonesia's greatest challenge. In 1999, the state was unable to cope with the outbreak of multiple communal conflicts in four provinces near simultaneously. After 18 months of unabated conflict, radical Islamist groups traveled to the provinces of Maluku and Central Sulawesi with the stated goal of "protecting Muslims." They also had the secondary agenda of proving to Indonesian Muslims the supremacy of Islam and sharia vis-à-vis the "secular" state system. Their actions served to further inflame the conflicts. The state was only able to reestablish its supremacy in these areas in 2002. However, since then, violent Islamist mobilization in Maluku and Central Sulawesi has decreased dramatically. Indonesia's capacity has improved substantially since 2003, with the increasing capabilities of the police. However, vigilante violence is still a problem, particularly where religious minorities are concerned. Despite obvious improvements, it remains weaker than Malaysia, Turkey, and New Order Indonesia (see Figure 7.2).

Finally, this book predicted that external forces would play an intervening role when state capacity was weak. This has proven to be the case. On a sliding scale of aligned with capacity (see Figure 7.2), intervention by external forces was greatest in Indonesia post–New Order, followed by Turkey. Suharto resigned in 1998, when the international terror networks were not

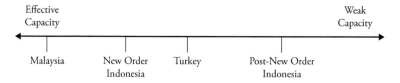

**Figure 7.2** Variation in capacity.

fully operational in their international scope of activities. However, even in Malaysia, intervention has been minimal, for they have been unable to make inroads due to the strength of state capacity.

These results clearly show the powerful relationship between participation and capacity. Effective participatory states have the lowest instances of violence. It is not sufficient to simply have an effective security apparatus and provide social services. Neither is it sufficient to be a weak state that enables participation. Both elements are needed. Islamist groups react strategically and utilize those channels through which they can make the greatest gains. In the Malaysian case, this is clearly the path of institutionalized participation. Likewise, the variation in the Turkish case also shows the importance of capacity. The majority of Islamist groups in Turkey work toward their goals through the political system. Violence only increases when the state loses control of the Southeast and radical movements exploit state lapses. Even Indonesia has seen this variation. Violent Islamist mobilization has decreased, as the police force has grown more effective. After the state reestablished security in Maluku and Central Sulawesi and negotiated cease fire agreements, many radical Islamist and Christian militias put down their weapons.

The participation-capacity link is not unique to these four cases. Islamist mobilization in Kuwait, Bahrain, Yemen, and Bangladesh has followed similar trajectories, despite the variation in these nations' histories and the extent of their political liberalization. Currently, Malaysia, Turkey, and Kuwait provide institutionalized channels for participation while maintaining effective capacities. In each case, violent Islamist mobilization is rare and intervention by external forces is low. In each effective participatory state, Islamist groups choose to utilize the channels for participation available to them within the political system, and violence is rare. Bahrain can be grouped with New Order Indonesia as an effective authoritarian state, for both limited channels for participation while providing public goods for the population. These two states illuminate the shortcomings of the effective authoritarian model.

Yemen and Bangladesh can be grouped into the category of ineffective participatory states together with post-New Order Indonesia, although both are in *far* worse straits than Indonesia. Both states provide various channels for political participation, and Islamist groups react strategically and mobilize through political parties, organizations, and social movements. However, both states have extremely high rates of violent mobilization. This is due to significant lapses in both law and order and social services. In Bangladesh, the state could not control the northwestern and southeastern regions, while in Yemen, the state could not exert authority over the northern and eastern governorates. Thus, there were large swaths of the country where the state had ceded the sphere of social service provision to various Islamist groups. Bangladesh has significantly retrenched in the provision of education and health care. Both secular and Islamist organizations have struggled to provide social services in lieu of the state. As a result of the state's lapses in both instances, radical movements have made inroads at the states expense aided by Wahabi funders. Al Qaeda and Afghan veteran movements have also exploited state lapses.

## Broader Implications

This book has several broad implications for debates over Islam and democracy and for state-Islamist group relations. First, the problem for Muslim states in becoming democratic is not rooted in Islam or the Islamic worldview. Like all religions, Islam has elements that are supportive of democratization and liberalization, such as the concepts of *ijma* (consensus), *shura* (consultation), and *ijtihad* (independent reasoning), and other elements that are not. Some claim that the Islamic worldview impedes political liberalization. It has not impeded Indonesia and Turkey from transitioning to democracy or Bangladesh, and Kuwait from liberalizing in the 1990s or Malaysia from becoming more open. These successes are real and tangible.

Islamist parties, especially, have worked in a highly pragmatic manner to achieve incremental yet substantial victories. For example, PAS has reaped significant gains by engaging in the political system and through its pressure and presence has reshaped the face and fabric of Malay Muslim society. Without PAS pressure, it is unlikely that the BN coalition would have taken on Islamization and shariatization policies to the extent that it did. When PAS engages in the system, it wins victories for its cause of Islamization without having to lead the government. It impacts national and local agendas.

Even hard-line Islamist groups have been willing to engage in the political system. In Indonesia, both Dewan Dawkah Islamiyah Indonesia (DDII) and Hizbut Tahrir have joined the Tim Penanggulangan Terorisme (Anti-Terrorism Team, TPT), a state-civil society initiative to counter the influence of terrorist groups and to educate Indonesian Muslims about the true meaning of jihad, as a fundamentally defensive, rather than an offensive course of action. In these efforts, they have worked with mainstream organizations like Nahdlatul Ulama and Muhammadiyah as well as the state fatwa body, the Indonesian Ulama Council (MUI). Islamist organizations have partnered with Islamist parties like the Prosperous Justice Party (PKS), United Development Party (PPP), and Crescent and Star Party (PBB) at the local level to support sharia-inspired legislation to improve Islamic educational opportunities, to ensure Muslim dress is in accordance with provisions on *aurat* (modesty), and to mandate time off for prayers and Koran reading. In the public sphere, the more conservative Islamist groups are compelled to engage in debates and arguments with progressive and mainstream Islamic organizations. *The problems of political development in the Muslim world are not rooted in Islam. They are a matter of opportunities. The vast majority of groups across the politico-Islamic spectrum are engaging through systemic channels.*

## Engagement as a Force for Political Moderation

In Indonesia, Malaysia, and Turkey, we have seen that when Islamist parties join the legislature, they moderate their ideology as well as short- and medium-term goals over time. The domestic goals of AKP in Turkey have been far more moderate and incremental compared with the Refah Party, which governed Turkey from 1995 to 1997, or the National Salvation Party, which participated in coalition governments in the 1970s. Through its moderation and clean government image, it has appealed to a wide array of Muslims who have become disgruntled with corruption in the center-right parties. This is one of the most democratic nations in the Muslim world and it is led by a moderate Islamist party, which has stepped carefully. While its foreign policy has grown closer to the nations of the Middle East, it has also taken care not to adopt domestic policies that either alienate secular or moderate Muslim voters or alarm the military.

In Indonesia, one has also seen the moderation on the part of the popular Islamist party, the Prosperous Justice Party (PKS). According to Dr. Azyumardi Azra,"If you look at the national level, PKS is becoming more accommodative. They became a partner in the SBY [Susilo Bambang Yudonyono] governing coalition. At the Kabupaten (district) level, they're forging coalitions with secular and Christian parties. They're adjusting themselves to the day to day of politics."[2] In Malaysia, PAS has also realized the importance of moderating its message to deemphasize strict formalist sharia in order to appeal to a wider array of voters. It made significant gains in 1999, both nationally and at the state level when it partnered with the Chinese Democratic Action Party (DAP) and the Keadilan Party to form the Barisan Alterantif. Yet, it was thrown out of office in 2004 in Terengganu for focusing too heavily on passing the Islamic criminal code to the detriment of other more pressing concerns. This taught PAS a valuable lesson about the importance of party moderation and incremental victories. In 2008, it put these lessons into practice adopting a universalist message with cross-religious appeal and forming a coalition with the DAP and the People's Justice Party (PKR). *Islamist parties are moderating as they make gains in elections, as they enter local and national legislatures, and as they form alliances.*

*They begin to work on a more diverse array of issues and seek incremental rather than immediate change.*

## The State as a Positive Actor

What is most notable about this book is the role it attributes to the state. It shows how the state can actively discourage violent Islamist mobilization by behaving in a manner that lends it legitimacy. First, the state should keep law and order within their territories, so that the populace is ensured stability and security, and radical Islamist groups know they cannot act with impunity. Second, the state should act as a provider, helping to improve popular well-being by offering social services.

Turkey, Malaysia, and New Order Indonesia have also succeeded in gaining credibility by being dominant providers of education and poverty relief. New Order Indonesia and Malaysia succeeded in drastically reducing poverty rates. In Malaysia, Muslims have been major beneficiaries of the New Economic Policy, the National Education Policy, and subsequent economic development policies and as such have been more willing to engage with the state in offering supplemental services rather than compete against the state. Indonesia, Malaysia, and Turkey have taken dominant roles in standardizing, improving, and extending public education. In 2002, the Indonesian MPR amended the constitution to require the state allocate 20 percent of the national and provincial budgets to education and in 2005, the DPR enacted a law to make primary and junior secondary education free. As the delivery mechanisms for these programs are improved and expanded throughout the 33 provinces, the state is posed to reap substantial legitimacy gains.

The states in Turkey and Malaysia also play leading roles in developing and funding Islamic education programs to ensure that a pro-system Islam is taught in religious schools and to show their investment in Islamic issues. Both states gained legitimacy as a result of their role in education, impeding the ability of radical Islamist groups from making inroads. In Indonesia, *pesantren* run by the mainstream Nahdlatul Ulama organization have traditionally maintained a significant degree of independence, and as a result, the state has been unable to specify the curriculum for *pesantren* as it does madrasas or regulate *pesantren* to the same degree as Islamic schools in Malaysia or Turkey.[3] However, it has reached out to the *pesantren* to provide them with supplemental study materials. Moreover, the state has improved efforts in recent years to identify and monitor radical *pesantren*, most notably those within the Ngruki network, which have been linked to the Bali bombings. Together with the state, the dominant role of Nahdlatul Ulama (NU) and Muhammadiyah in the provision of Islamic education has impeded the ability of radical Islamist groups to make significant inroads in the crucial area of education and gain ready recruits as a result. *Effective capacity simultaneously improves perceptions of the state's legitimacy and impedes radical Islamist groups from gaining recruits and popularity. The state's effectiveness will cause radical Islamist groups to be more reticent in employing violence; if the state is viewed widely as legitimate and effective, they will not be able to make significant gains through violence.*

## Problems of Capacity

This book has contended that when states permit lawless areas to emerge either as a result of rising communal conflict or general weakness, radical Islamist groups will take advantage of this opportunity to make inroads. However, it is not always a simple matter of the state retrenching and Islamist groups supplanting, like a tug-of-war. Instead, the issue is complicated by the tendency of elements in the security services who make Faustian alliances, in which they arm radical groups to take actions against those groups perceived as a greater threat. This has the effect of further exacerbating the conflict, for radical groups believe they can act with a large measure of impunity. When the police or the military tries to reestablish their authority, they are met with radical groups with revolutionary aims who conduct violent acts with military-issued weapons. In addition, if radical groups have military patrons, it becomes more difficult for the security apparatus to effectively crack down on their activities.

In examining the cases where the state has lost capacity, military-radical alliances of varying strength were established in Indonesia, Turkey, Bangladesh, and Yemen. In each of these cases, this move empowered radical Islamist groups and exacerbated the violence in the affected regions. Laskar Jihad was highly effective in its village razing operations due to the military training and weapons they received from certain allies in the security services. Violence in Maluku and Poso rose significantly following the introduction of Laskar Jihad. The military-radical alliance caused President Abdurrahman Wahid to be seen as weak for his inability to stop Laskar Jihad from leaving for Maluku and subsequently hindered efforts to bring Laskar Jihad leaders to justice and to establish a workable peace. They only abandoned violence after their supporters within the military withdrew support, following the 2002 Bali Bombings.

Likewise, in Turkey, there is compelling evidence that elements of the military at the very least turned a blind eye to Hizballah's activities in the Southeast region because they viewed the Kurdish Workers Party as a greater threat to national stability. This empowered Hizballah and led to great troubles for the security services, which, following the reestablishment of control over the Southeast, had to identify and arrest Hizballah members who had fled to and were conducting operations in Istanbul and Ankara. In effect, *retrenchment in a state's capacity to provide law and order is often inflamed by the establishment of military-radical alliances. This empowers radical groups to commit violent acts, for they now have attained a measure of impunity. It also impedes the ability of the state to enforce the law against such groups.*

### Should States Just Repress Radical Islamist Groups?

This book has also shown that the provision of law and order does not necessitate the frequent use of violent repression by the state. In fact, brute force repression may contribute to alienation and the strategic response of violent mobilization. The contrasting cases of Malaysia and New Order Indonesia showed two states with divergent repressive apparatuses. In Malaysia, the state relied on the force of law to crack down on radical Islamist groups rather than brute force. When the police employed violent force at Memali in 1985, which resulted in the death of 14 Islamists and four policemen, there was a serious political backlash. As Dr. Noraini Othman explains, "Memali showed the state's willingness to use force against radical Islamists. Yet this could not be the rule. It cost UMNO and UMNO learned a lesson. The key is that you have the capacity to use force but using it is a sign of weakness. UMNO lost credibility with this act [the violent repression at Memali]."[4] When radical Islamists from the Al Ma'unah group staged an arms heist in 2000, the state reacted differently and took measures to minimize casualties.[5] They arrested the Al Ma'unah members and brought them to trial.

New Order Indonesia utilized brute force repression more frequently than Malaysia, yet its violent mobilization rates were much higher. There are strong parallels between the 2000 Al Ma'unah incident in Malaysia and the 1989 Lampung incident in Indonesia on the surface. It is interesting to analyze the Indonesian state's choice of reaction at Lampung. Like Al Ma'unah, there was evidence that the Lampung commune was stockpiling weapons. Rather than taking measures to minimize casualties while still enforcing the law, the military stormed the compound, killing over 100 Islamists, including women and children. The Malaysian authorities move to minimize casualties and use the force of law against the Al Ma'unah militants served them better in the long-term than the New Order strategy of brute force. Despite the number of casualties at Lampung, the state's response did not eliminate violent Islamist mobilization. If anything, it radicalized the remaining commune members and other hard-line Islamists.

The adverse consequences of brute force repression can also be seen in the response to another incident: the military's repression of the Tanjung Priok demonstrators in September 1984, where 63 Muslims were killed and hundreds injured. The state's violent repression empowered underground radical groups to take action in response. In the following weeks, Jakarta was wracked by fires and bombings. The violence culminated in the bombing of the Borobodur temple in Yogyakarta. Moreover, clashes between the armed forces and incensed Muslims occurred, most notably for this story, at the Lampung commune in 1989.

Thus, Dr. Othman's statement about the state bears further analysis. The capacity of the state to use brute force may often be sufficient to discourage violent acts. This shows radical Islamist groups that they cannot act with impunity and that there would be consequences for acts of violence and the planning of violence. *Repression by force of law is likely to be accepted by Islamist organizations, and it will have an impact on how groups mobilize. However, brute force repression resorting in hundreds of deaths only serves to further alienate Islamists and contributes to their radicalization.*

### External Forces Don't Operate the Same Everywhere

If one examines cases where external forces (Afghan veterans, international terrorist groups, spillover effects from wars, revolutionary neighbors) have had the most significant impacts, they have all been countries where the state has lapsed in its ability to ensure law and order within its borders. These include not only Indonesia but also Turkey, Algeria, Yemen, Bangladesh, Pakistan, Afghanistan, Sudan, Yemen, and many other countries. Al Qaeda and Jemaah Islamiyah (JI) were more likely to set up training camps in the Southern Philippines or Indonesia, where state authority was weak compared with Malaysia, where they could be identified and quickly closed. In 2002, JI moved its main base of operations in Indonesia from Malaysia. When Indonesia began to reassert its authority over its territories and target JI cells, the group began to reassess it strategy. It has not conducted another major attack since 2005.

Even in the event of war in a neighboring country, a state's effective capacity can limit the spillover effects. For example, Pakistan's inability to exert control over the Northwest Frontier led to the proliferation of thousands of radical madrasas on their border with Afghanistan and enabled Pakistan to become the transit point for tens of thousands of young militants during the Soviet-Afghan War. By contrast, Malaysia has not experienced significant spillover effects from the Thai secessionist conflict, even in Kelantan, which is governed by the PAS. The provinces bordering Thailand—Kelantan, Terengganu, and Perlis are not facing increased violence or instability. This shows us that *effective state capacity can reduce the impact of external forces.*

## Theoretical Propositions

The theory developed in this book can be used as a framework to inform analyses of other cases outside the four cases of Indonesia during and post–New Order, Malaysia, and Turkey and the four brief cases of Bangladesh, Bahrain, Yemen, and Kuwait. However, it is also possible that one can use this framework to examine other cases, including those outside the genre of political Islam, experiencing other forms of ideologically driven mobilization. The results of this thesis are summarized in four theoretical propositions.

Proposition 1: The state matters. States, through their institutions, policies, and capacities influence the mobilization strategies that Islamist groups choose.

Proposition 2: When states permit participation *and* possess the capacity to enforce law and order and provide for education and welfare, Islamist groups react strategically. They will overwhelmingly utilize peaceful and democratic channels for mobilization. Incidents of violent mobilization by radical Islamist groups will be rare.

Proposition 3: When states permit participation, but cannot ensure law and order and education and welfare, most Islamist groups will still employ peaceful strategies. However, radical Islamist groups will be emboldened by the states lapses. These radical groups will attempt to replace the state in these areas and gain legitimacy and popularity in the process. Many radical groups will employ strategies of violence and intimidation as they work for their goals. External forces will intervene, providing funding, training and weapons and exacerbating the violence already taking place.

Proposition 4: if states curtail opportunities for participation through institutionalized channels, but they maintain control over public goods, this will constrain all mobilization. While violent mobilization may decline temporarily, it will never fully diminish. Islamist groups will go underground and wait for a more auspicious time (due to state lapses or openings) to emerge and push for their goals. When this occurs, it is likely that violence will increase significantly.

In sum, the central message of this book is that the state can influence Islamist group mobilization strategies in a positive manner. However, not all states can do this equally well. A participatory state with effective capacities will be best able to encourage Islamist groups to employ peaceful and systemic strategies and to eschew violent ones. States that lack either institutions of participation or effective capacity will be fundamentally impaired in their ability to make an impact. Authoritarian states with limited participation will constrain mobilization, driving Islamist groups underground, where they can become alienated, isolated and radicalized. Participatory states with weak capacities will provide radical Islamist groups with opportunities to make inroads by using violence and by supplanting the state in the provision of necessary public goods like law and order and education. States can make a positive impact, and they can influence Islamist groups to engage with the state to work toward their goals.

# Epilogue

In contrast to the unpredictability that has marked the Arab uprisings in 2011, the past two years in Turkey, Indonesia, and Malaysia has brought a significant degree of continuity. As democracy begins to consolidate in Turkey and Indonesia and as the renegotiation of the political space persists in Malaysia, Islamist parties and social movements continue to react strategically and utilize formal and informal political channels to work toward their goals. Most notable, in 2011, the Justice and Development Party (AKP) was reelected to a third term as the dominant party in the Grand National Assembly, a victory that has had widespread reverberations across the Muslim world for Islamist parties that would also like to achieve similar success in their home countries. In Malaysia, the ramifications of the 2008 elections, where, for the first time in history, the National Front (BN) lost its two-thirds parliamentary majority are still ongoing, as the Malaysian Islamic Party (PAS) and its opposition partners (as well as other civil society groups) are reshaping the boundaries of Malaysia's political space. In Indonesia, the 2009 elections saw a declining vote for Islamist parties amid the continued efforts at the mainstreaming of political Islam by nationalist parties. At the same time, Islamist parties again joined the governing coalition of Susilo Bambang Yudhoyono and participated in legislative, electoral, and issue-based alliances to work toward their goals. Of the three countries, only Indonesia remains shockingly unwilling or perhaps unable to consistently enforce the rule of law against radical Islamist vigilante militias and, in recent months, has experienced a spate of small-scale terror attacks.

## Greater Space for Political Islam in Turkey amid State-Specified Boundaries

After narrowly avoiding closure by the Constitutional Court in 2008 on the charge of anti-secular activities for lifting the headscarf ban, the AKP was reelected in Turkey in 2011 with 50 percent of the vote amid 87 percent voter turnout.[1] Due to a shift in voting behavior away from the smaller

**Table Ep. 1**   Legislative election results

|                                        | 2007   |       | 2009   |       |
| -------------------------------------- | ------ | ----- | ------ | ----- |
| Political Party                        | Votes% | Seats | Votes% | Seats |
| Justice and Development Party (AKP)     | 46.58  | 341   | 50     | 326   |
| Republican People's Party (CHP)         | 20.88  | 112   | 26     | 135   |
| National Movement Party (MHP)           | 14.47  | 70    | 13     | 53    |
| Peace and Democracy Party (BDP)*        | –      | –     | 6      | 36    |
| Felicity Party (SP)**                   | 2      | –     | 2.5    | –     |

*candidates ran as independents to circumvent the 10% electoral threshold.
**did not pass the electoral threshold. Heymi Bahtiar, "The Real Winners and Losers of Turkey's July 2007 Elections." *Middle East Review of International Affairs.* Volume 11, No.3 Article 7/9 (September 2007): 2, "AK Party Sweeps Polls for Third Single Term in Power." *Today's Zaman.*

parties and toward those parties most likely to surmount the 10 percent electoral threshold, the 4 percent increase in AKP votes vis-à-vis 2007 actually resulted in a decline in Assembly seats (see table Ep.1).

The AKP victory is significant for several reasons. First, it points to a consolidation of center-right support around the AKP and away from other alternatives such as the Motherland Party (ANAP), the True Path Party (DYP), and the Felicity Party (SP). Second, that the AKP was victorious in all provinces apart from those on the coast, on the European side, and in the Southeast indicates the party has truly become an Islamically-oriented catchall party, bridging the boundaries of age, class, region, and ideological orientation. At the same time, it has retained the votes of its core base in the Islamic conservative entrepreneurial and middle classes, who are comfortable both with conservative religious values and the secular orientation of the Turkish constitution.[2]

Finally, the party's second reelection makes it unique among Islamically-oriented parties in the Muslim world for its ability to win. The original AKP victory in 2002 occurred at a moment when the established parties faced criticism for poor governance, corruption, and economic distress, which triggered a measure of protest voting in favor of an Islamic alternative.[3] The first and second reelections of the AKP in 2007 and 2011 as the dominant party in government indicates a clear move beyond protest voting toward a consolidation of support based on the legitimate achievements of the party in the arenas of economic growth, good governance, anti-corruption foreign policy, and democratic reform. This provides instruction for other Islamist parties about the importance of understanding one's constituency, successfully adapting to the constraints that exist within one's political system, and diversifying one's agenda to emphasize universal themes.

It is also important to note that, in the 2007–2011 term, the AKP successful survived iterated attempts to limit its governing authority. In 2007, elements in the military threatened to intervene, if Abdullah Gul was elected president, and in 2008, the AKP faced proscription for lifting the ban on headscarves in universities. Yet, Gul was elected president and the AKP narrowly avoided closure by the Constitutional Court by a 6:11 vote, one vote shy of the seven needed for closure. While these events clearly showed the AKP that it was important to remain aware of the religious red lines in a Kemalist republic, the survival of the party also showed the extent to which the space for political Islam in the Turkish republic has increased.

## The Decline of Islamist Parties and the Mainstreaming of Political Islam in Indonesia

The past two years in Indonesia have also been remarkably consistent, both in terms of participation and capacity. Islamist parties and social movements continue to engage in what is arguably the most open and democratic political system in the Muslim world. In 2009, Indonesians participated in another round of presidential and legislative elections, which were largely deemed free and fair by international observers, although some administrative problems did arise in remote regions. In these elections, the share of the vote for all Islamist and pluralist Islamic parties declined, apart from that of the Prosperous Justice Party (PKS). Notably, the Islamist United Development Party's (PPP) vote share decreased from 10.72 percent in 1999, to 8.15 percent in 2004 to 5.32 percent in 2009. The pluralist Islamic National Mandate Party (PAN) and National Awakening Party (PKB) saw their respective shares of the vote decline from 7.12 percent and 12.66 percent in 1999 to 6.44 and 10.57 percent in 2004 to a low of 6.01 and 4.94 percent in 2009. The Islamist Star and Crescent Party (PBB) and Reform and Star Party (PBR) did not even pass the newly established 2.5 percent electoral threshold in 2009. (For a complete breakdown, see table Ep.2).

It would be a mistake to interpret the declining share of the vote for Islamist parties as a rejection of Islamic values or political Islam. Instead, this outcome is the result of the interaction of several of factors. First, voters perceive the nationalist parties, notably Democrat and Golkar, as better able to provide for their needs than Islamist parties. Evidence supporting this contention can be derived from the results of two surveys in 2008 and 2009 conducted by the Indonesian Survey Institute (LSI) that asked respondents which party had "the best programs for the people" and which parties

**Table Ep. 2** Indonesia's election results compared: People's Representative Assembly (DPR).

| Party | Votes 1999 | Seats 1999 | Votes 2004 | Seats 2004 | Votes 2009 | Seats 2009 | Pancasila / Islamist |
|---|---|---|---|---|---|---|---|
| Indonesian Democratic Party-Struggle (PDI-P) | 33.73 | 153 | 18.53 | 109 | 14.0 | 93 | PS |
| Golkar | 22.46 | 120 | 21.58 | 128 | 14.5 | 106 | PS |
| Democrat Party (PD) | —* | — | 7.45 | 57 | 20.85 | 150 | PS |
| Greater Indonesia Movement Party (Gerindra) | — | — | — | — | 4.45 | 27 | PS |
| People's Conscience Party (Hanura) | — | — | — | — | 3.77 | 18 | PS |
| National Awakening Party (PKB) | 12.66 | 51 | 10.57 | 52 | 4.94 | 28 | PS |
| National Mandate Party (PAN) | 7.12 | 45 | 6.44 | 52 | 6.01 | 48 | PS |
| Prosperous Justice Party (PKS) | 1.52 | 7 | 7.34 | 45 | 7.88 | 57 | IS |
| United Development Party (PPP) | 10.72 | 58 | 8.15 | 58 | 5.32 | 38 | IS |
| Reform Star Party (PBR) | — | — | 2.4 | 13 | 1.2 | —** | IS |
| Star and Crescent Party (PBB) | 1.94 | 13 | 2.62 | 11 | 1.8 | —** | IS |
| Other parties | 9.85 | | 14.92 | | 15.28 | | |
| Total | 100 | | 100 | | 84.72 | | |

*The Democrat and the PBR did not exist in 1999, Gerindra and Hanura did not exist in 1999 or 2004;

**In 2009, an electoral threshold of 2.5% was implemented. No party receiving less than 2.5% of the vote obtains seats in the DPR.

*Source:* Compiled from Leo Suryadinata. *Elections and Politics in Indonesia* (Singapore: ISEAS, 2002) 103 and R. William Liddle and Saiful Mujani, "Indonesia in 2004: The Rise of Susilo Bambang Yudhoyono." *Asian Survey* Vol 45. Issue 1 (2005):120; Stephen Sherlock, "Consolidation and Change: the Indonesian parliament after the 2004 elections." *Center for Democratic Institutions.* July 2004: 5–6; Web site of the People's Representative Assembly (DPR),<www.dpr.go.id>; Web site of the Indonesian Election Commission (KPU) http://mediacenter.kpu.go.id/images/mediacenter/berita/SUARA_KPU/ HASIL_PENGHITUNGAN_SUARA_SAH.pdf.

"cared the most about the people."[4] In these surveys, Democrat was viewed as having the best programs and caring the most about the people by 24 percent and 22 percent of respondents, respectively, compared to 11 and 10 percent, respectively, for the nationalist Golkar.[5] By contrast, the PKS averaged 5 percent on both measures; the PPP ranked lower still with 2 percent on both measures; PAN and PKB averaged between 2 and 3 percent on both measures; and PBB and PBR were not listed.[6] Thus, it is clear that Islamically-oriented parties have been less successful in communicating their policy initiatives on themes with universal appeal and their community welfare activities, compared to their nationalist competitors.

A second key factor explaining the outcome of the 2009 elections has been the increasing shift to the politico-religious center by the nationalist parties in order to appeal to new segments of the voting public. For nationalist parties, these efforts have included co-opting popular Islamic legislation such as the controversial 2008 Anti-Pornography Bill, especially in the run up to an election; establishing Islamic wings that hold devotional events; and running religiously themed campaign ads. Most successful in this regard has been Democrat, which Marcus Meitzner classifies as a "nationalist-religious catchall party."[7] The Democrat Party formed the Nurussalam Dhikir (The Light of Peace Council), which has organized collective devotional events, including recitation of the divine names and supplications and aphorisms from sections of the Koran and Hadith.[8] In the 2009 campaign, the Democrat Party also ran campaign ads honoring the birthday of the prophet Muhammad with party leaders in Islamic dress stating that Islamic values were an important component of Democrats' anti-corruption campaign.[9] The co-optation of moderate, popular Islamic legislation and public displays of party piety, together with the nationalist perception advantage on economic programs has enabled nationalist parties, most notably the Democrat Party, to curry favor with some voters, who had previously supported the Islamically-oriented parties.

Most Islamically-oriented parties have also faced significant internal challenges, which have impeded their ability to project a competent image. Greg Fealy notes that many of the ministers from the 2004–2009 Cabinet from Islamist parties, most notably M. S. Kaban from the PBB, Minister of Cooperatives Suryadharma Ali from the PPP, and public housing minister, Yusuf Asy'ari from the PKS were disappointingly ineffectual.[10] The PPP and the PKB also are deeply embroiled in internal party conflicts. For the PPP, this conflict is simultaneously ideological, personal, and generational, which impedes the party's ability to compete effectively. First, as the PPP is the result of the forced amalgamation of traditionalist and modernist parties in 1973, the party has been unable to formulate a coherent ideology or party program to appeal to both segments of its base. Moreover, within these streams are personal factions that have competed for influence and dominance within the party for over three decades. In 2002, such personality clashes resulted in popular preacher Zainuddin MZ defecting from the party with his followers to establish the PBR. More recently, serious conflicts emerged between PPP Chairman, Suryadharma Ali and the Chairman of the Supervisory Board, Bachtiar Chamsyah, over the future direction of the party with both leaders blaming the other for the party's poor performance in the 2009 elections.[11] The party has also lost its hold on pious young Muslims between 17 and 30 over the past decade due to its unwillingness to accommodate their political aspirations.[12] As a result of these challenges, pious Muslim youth have shifted their support over the past decade to the PKS, a party that affords them more opportunities for upward mobility within the party and that markets itself as a youth-oriented party.[13]

It is arguable that no party has been more affected by internal conflict than PKB. The PKB had gone through four party chairmen between 2004 and 2009. Legal battles between the late former president and party founder, Abdurrahman Wahid, and other party officials, many of whom were members of his family, led to the estrangement of Wahid from the party.[14] These iterated conflicts led to the departure of influential *kyai;* the weakening of the party's base among rural Javanese Muslims; and a decline of support from a height of 12.66 percent in 1999 to 4.94 percent in 2009, as voters left the PKB for Democrat and PKS. A 2010 Supreme Court ruling against Wahid's faction, led by his daughter, Yenny, following the death of Wahid in December 2009, lead to Yenny's decision to fully break from PKB to form the National Prosperity Party (PKBN) in 2011 to contest the 2014 election.[15]

This then begs the question of why the PKS out-performed other Islamist and pluralist Islamic parties. While the votes of all Islamically-oriented parties declined, PKS's remained relatively constant with the total vote percentage increasing from 7.34 to 7.88 percent and the total number of votes decreasing by 119,065.[16] The maintenance of PKS support can most likely be attributed to a combination of factors. First, according to a survey conducted by the Center for Strategic and International Studies, the party has a higher voter loyalty rate compared to its competitors, with 75 percent of PKS supporters remaining loyal to the party in iterated elections.[17] Second, the PKS is consolidating the support of those voters seeking a political role for Islam. According to an internal PKS survey, 75.2 percent of respondents said their strongest reason for choosing the party was its Islamic image.[18] Third, the PKS has a devoted network of cadre that conducts year-round activities and marshalls support for the party around election time. The party holds regular community welfare activities micro-targeting segments of the population, including agricultural training workshops for farmers, maternal and infant health and nutrition programs for mothers, and microfinance programs for entrepreneurs. Together these programs constitute the PKS soft campaign and help the party to make inroads into new communities by creating a positive perception of the PKS as a "caring" party. Finally, the PKS balances the Islamic and the universal in its campaign messaging. In national campaigns, the party adopts universalist messaging, focusing on issues with widespread appeal like clean government. At the same time, individual candidates adopt Islamic messaging or coloring in districts where doing so may prove beneficial, for example, hosting an Islamic singing group, passing out prayer attire, or extolling voters to choose devout candidates.[19]

However, in the weeks prior to the 2009 elections, Mohammed Razikun, Head of the Campaign Winning Team, projected the party would attain 12 percent of the vote, which begs the question of why the PKS did not do better.[20] The PKS has sought to project an image of being an inclusive party, by joining the governing coalition of President Susilo Bambang Yudhoyono in 2005 and remaining in it over the protests of its core base; declaring the party "open" in 2008 and inviting non-Muslims to join; and running campaign ads showing women without headscarves. Each of these actions disappointed the party's core base, which saw them as yet another compromise in the pursuit of power. However, when the PKS made news, it was most often on morality issues or for controversial public statements by leading figures such as the call for the banning of Jaipongan folk dancing on the grounds of being too sexy by West Java Governor Ahmed Heryawan. These inconsistencies raised questions among voters. Moreover, when several PKS parliamentarians were implicated in corruption scandals, in the run up to the 2009 elections, it tarnished the party's clean image and led some former supporters to view the PKS as no different than any other party. As the 2009 election results indicated that the PKS is consolidating the support of voters seeking a political role for Islam, the party faces a difficult decision as to whether it will return to its roots or whether it will commit to courting the center.[21] As the party has been coping with iterated scandals and coalitional infighting over the past two years, no clear trajectory has become apparent.

Despite the decline in the share of the vote for Islamist parties, there is no question that they remain salient and relevant, as does political Islam. First, PKS, PPP, PKB, and PAN are all members of the governing coalition of Susilo Bambang Yudhoyono and thus run ministries, influence policy, and control patronage streams. They lead district and provincial-level governments often in coalition with other parties; the PBB and the PBR are also represented in these coalitions. Moreover, the shift to the politico-religious center by the nationalist parties has led to the blurring of boundaries between the Islamic parties and the nationalist parties; Islamic themes, symbolism, and messaging are no longer the exclusive purview of the Islamic parties.[22] For those Islamist movements that seek to make policy more reflective of Islamic values or that favor an incremental approach toward a more Islamic society, the channels through which to work for those goals are richly varied.

There is some concern, however, regarding the General Election Bill, which includes an effort by the major nationalist parties to increase the electoral threshold from 2.5 percent (currently supported by PKS, PKB, PAN, and PPP as well as smaller nationalist parties) to either 4 percent (favored by the Democrat Party) or 5 percent (supported by Golkar and PDI-P).[23] If the declining trend in Islamist party support continues, this bill could have adverse effects for those parties sitting close to or at 4–5 percent, most notably the PKB and the PPP, two parties that represent the interests of traditionalist Muslims. The infighting that plagued the PPP during the Suharto era shows that the diverse streams of Islam cannot be accommodated into a single party. Thus, consolidation behind the PKS is not a realistic or viable option. Fearing an inevitable increase in the electoral threshold, the PPP engaged briefly in talks with smaller traditionalist-oriented Islamist parties, most notably the PBR, which broke away from the PPP in 2002, and the Ulama National Awakening Party (PKNU) about a merger, but no agreement was reached in time for the July 2011 deadline for certification.[24] The implementation of a high 4–5 percent electoral threshold would at once make the system less representative, less participatory, and less democratic. If that occurs, one consequence would likely be fewer choices for those voters seeking a political role for Islam.

## Challenges of Law and Order in Indonesia

Although Indonesia stands apart from Malaysia and Turkey for the extent to which Islamist parties and social movements can participate freely and openly through formal political channels, it also diverges from them in its shortcomings in the enforcement of the rule of law. Indeed, great strides have been made since the transition period. Notably, the communal conflicts in Maluku and Central Sulawesi have long been resolved. However, over the past two years, religiously motivated attacks by radical Islamist vigilante groups and coalitions, including the Islamic Community Forum (FUI), the Islamic Defenders Front (FPI), the Movement against Illegal Sects and Non-Believers (GAPAS), and the Indonesian Mujahideen Council (MMI) have increased.[25] In 2010, NGOs that monitor religious freedom violations in Indonesia cited over 200 incidents, most of which occurred in West Java and Jakarta.[26] Between January and September 2010, over 30 attacks against churches took place and attacks on Ahmadiyah also spiked.[27] In one incident, in February 2011, a mob of 1,500 attacked 20 Ahmadiyah members in the Cikeusek district of Banten, killing three and seriously wounding five.[28] In another notable example, several hundred FUI members attacked an open-air worship service held by the Batak Christian Protestant Church on church land in Bekasi, West Java, injuring 20 people, most of whom were women.[29] Radical Islamists often justify the need for vigilante attacks by what they see as creeping Christianization, a term they use to refer to both undue Christian influence in society and efforts by Christians to proselytize among Muslims.[30]

While many Muslim leaders have spoken out against vigilante attacks, some government officials have given the impression of endorsing the violence.[31] The governor of Jakarta, the Minister of Religious Affairs, and the National Police Chief have all appeared at FPI events, with the police chief seeming to welcome FPI as a partner in maintaining law and order in Jakarta.[32] The International Crisis Group contends that Christian-Muslim tensions in Indonesia are rising due, in part, to the government's failure to effectively prosecute those who incite mob violence or those groups that attack or intimidate religious minorities.[33] In fact, some officials have taken to blaming the targets of the violence for bringing it on themselves. Suryadharma Ali, the Minister for Religious Affairs, has used this logic with regard to Ahmadiyah; if they did not hold "deviant" views, they would not be attacked.[34] However, in taking up those positions, they tacitly grant legitimacy to those radical militias that take the law into their own hands and embolden them to push the boundaries of acceptable behavior.

It is perhaps then not surprising that terrorist attacks have also steeply increased over the past two years, although it must be noted that police effectiveness has improved since the first Bali Bombings in 2002. Densus 88, the police anti-terror branch, enhanced its capacities both under the tenures of Brigadier General Suryadharma and General Tito Karnavian. Careful intelligence gathering led to major arrests, the sum total of which had structurally weakened Jemaah Islamiyah (JI), KOMPAK, Ring Banten, and other groups linked to terrorism. The arrests that occurred following the bombing of the Marriot and Ritz Carlton hotels in Jakarta in 2009, masterminded by Noordin Top's breakaway faction of JI, as well as those that followed the discovery of a pan-jihadi training camp in Aceh in 2010 constrained the ability of jihadis to operate. Jihadi groups, however, have reacted strategically and altered tactics, prioritizing strengthening their base; shifting from large-scale attacks to assassinations of individuals or targeted attacks on the police or churches; and organizing via small groups.[35] It is important to note that JI and its affiliates were already quite decentralized prior to these arrests. In this current stage of devolution, many small groups emerging from radical study circles possess only a tangential link to the structural JI.[36] In other instances, youths are being radicalized via the Internet with no direction from JI or its affiliates other than ideological inspiration. Two such small-scale attacks were recently thwarted by the police: a plot to blow up a Catholic Church and arms depot on Good Friday and another plot to poison police officers.[37] The police have been particular targets in this round of terror attacks, several of which have been linked to Jemaah Ansharut Tauhid (JAT), a new radical Islamist movement formed by Abu Bakar Ba'asyir[38] in 2008.[39] The suicide bombing at the Cirebon police mosque in April 2011 and the assassination of two police officers in Palu, Central Sulawesi the following month were both linked to members of JAT.

Much as the state has been inconsistent in enforcing the rule of law against radical Islamist vigilante militias, it has yet to commit the necessary funds, resources, and manpower to the development of a whole scale counter-terrorism strategy, including deradicalization and counter-radicalization initiatives. The programs that do exist are ad hoc and underfunded. Tito Karnavian, the former head of Densus 88 and the current deputy head of the National Anti-Terrorism Bureau (BNPT) notes that serious weaknesses exist within Indonesian prisons that enable jihadi groups to recruit and radicalize new members.[40] For example, senior jihadi leaders are not held in separate cells or sections of the prison. Instead, they are mixed with the general prison population and allowed to hold religious study sessions, which enable them to radicalize attendees.[41] The police are indeed quite effective in investigating and arresting the perpetrators of attacks and have improved their prevention capacities. Yet, prevention activities cannot be left to the police alone, as true prevention includes grassroots counter-radicalization efforts. The police together with the BNPT need to work on efforts to reform corrupt prisons to prevent prison radicalization; to improve the police's capacity to monitor newly released prisoners; and to assist newly released prisoners to reintegrate into society. In this regard as well as on societal counter-radicalization, the BNPT could take lessons from its counterparts in Malaysia and Saudi Arabia, both of which have active programs targeting prevention, disengagement and deradicalization, and aftercare.

## Redrawing the Political Boundaries in Malaysia

The past two years in Malaysia have seen consistency in effective capacity in both law and order and the provision of social services. However, political change in Malaysia has been more dynamic than its Indonesian or Turkish counterparts. Islamist PAS continues to work with its partners in the Pakatan Rakyat (People's Coalition-PR), the secular Democratic Action Party (DAP), and the multi-ethnic People's Justice Party (PKR). Islamist NGOs engage with a wide variety of partners on varied issues including efforts to repeal the Internal Security Act, to push for electoral reform and in so doing to expand Malaysia's political space. PAS and UMNO continue to utilize Islamic frames of reference to different ends. As PAS, the PKR, and the DAP attempt to position themselves as a viable alternative to the ruling National Front coalition (BN), so too does the United Malays National Organization (UMNO) attempt to position itself as the true defender of Malay Muslim interests in order to prevent the opposition from further eroding BN support. At the outset, we must recall that ethnic and religious identity is often conflated in Malaysia. The Constitution stipulates that a key characteristic of belonging to the Malay ethnic group is defining oneself as Muslim. Thus, UMNO is resisting the renegotiation of space by drawing upon ethno-religious themes, while PAS and its partners in the PR are pushing for its expansion by transcending those very sectarian constructs.

To restate briefly, in the 2008 elections, PAS, the PKR, and the DAP succeeded in depriving the BN of its two-thirds majority for the first time in history. These parties, together known as the Pakatan Rakyat (PR) coalition, won control of five states: Kelantan, Selangor, Perak, Kedah, and Penang, 82 seats in the national legislature, and 196 seats at the state level.[42] Of these, PAS won 23 and 83, respectively.[43] In the 2008 electoral campaign, PAS and its partners emphasized universal themes, including good governance, equal opportunities across ethnic groups, environmental conservation, balanced development, civil liberties, and combating corruption.[44]

The 2008 election also served to highlight the extent to which electoral activism outside the established parties has increased.[45] For example, BERSIH campaigned for free and fair elections; the abolition of postal voting; equal media access; and the use of indelible ink to mark the fingers of those who voted.[46] The Women's Candidacy Initiative (WCI), an advocate for greater women's participation in politics, put forth an independent candidate for parliament.[47] The Defenders of Islam issued a manifesto demanding stricter enforcement of sharia, and even normally apolitical Christian churches hosted debates.[48] The sum total of these changes indicated greater efforts at political engagement across ethno-religious groups and that the traditional sectarian boundaries that defined Malaysian politics were blurring. Further evidence of this new reality occurred when the PR went on to defeat BN candidates in the next seven out of nine by-elections, with PAS winning four of them.

In reaction to its veritable hemorrhaging of seats and to the reconfiguration of the Malaysian political space, UMNO drew upon the familiar themes of Malay identity and Islam under threat to rally Muslim support to the party, as the defender of Malay Muslim interests.[49] The most notable example of this behavior was the effort by the Ministry for Home Affairs to ban the *Herald,* a Catholic weekly, from using Allah[50] to denote God in its Malay language edition, contending that the word "Allah" belonged to Muslims exclusively. The Allah issue evoked controversy on two grounds. On the one hand, it reignited concerns over declining Malay ethno-religious dominance. On the other hand, the ban ignored the reality that Malay Christians had long referred to God as Allah in their worship. In addition to inflaming Muslim anxieties, the government had another goal in igniting the Allah controversy. It sought to force PAS to take a stance, surmising that the Islamist party would throw its support behind the ban, given its history of taking hard-line stances on Islamic issues to compete with UMNO on religious grounds. Such a move would have not only harmed PAS's relations with its PR allies, but also proven antithetical to its long-term political interests, which increasingly rely on non-Muslim support.[51] To the government's dismay, PAS leaders came together on a common position in favor of Christians' right to use Allah to denote God.

After the ban was overturned by High Court Judge Lau Bee Lau, amid rancorous protests and heightened rhetoric on the part of UMNO, eight churches were attacked, followed by several Muslim prayer halls.[52] In the aftermath, 120 civil society groups from various faiths and sectors joined together to condemn the violence.[53] PAS leaders severely condemned the attacks. President Hadi Awang stated, "Even in war, Muslims are forbidden from desecrating houses of worship, what more now when we are living in peace. I don't know if these people [the perpetrators] perform prayers."[54] UMNO's efforts to resist the renegotiation of political space by drawing on ethno-religious themes have continued. In a recent incident, Perkasa, an UMNO-affiliated Malay chauvinist NGO, again sought to ignite Malay fears of Islam under threat by calling for a jihad against Christians, if evidence is found that Christians are attempting to usurp Islam's official status. PAS vice president Husam Musa condemned Perkasa, chastising the movement for "using religious issues for one-sided political reasons" and contending that "Perkasa does not follow true Islamic teachings and is not qualified to talk about *jihad,* which must be clean and pure."[55]

What we are seeing is a reorientation of PAS toward the realization that their interests are not best served through a perpetual Islamization race with UMNO, where each party tries to out-Islamize the other. This is not to say that the party is abandoning its Islamist agenda. The party consistently uses

Islamic frames of reference in their decision-making; ulama play an important role in the party; and PAS still takes up positions on issues of vice, morality, and even occasionally *hudud* and *qisas*.[56] They are, however, becoming more strategic over *which* issues they choose to take up so as to not alienate their PR allies and potential non-Muslim and moderate Muslim voters. This is not to say the party has completely resolved its internal divisions between purists, who would hold fast to the party's raison d'etre and mainstreamers, who understand that the party must cooperate with its PR partners and compromise fundamental sacred cows, if it wishes to make significant electoral gains. However, the influence of mainstreamers has been increasing since the 2008 elections.

According to Bridget Welsh, "what distinguishes PAS from UMNO today is that those willing to engage in reform have taken the party's helm, while, in contrast, the dialogue and direction from UMNO and its Perkasa allies remain locked in a time warp of radical ideas of the 70s, whose time has long passed."[57] Indeed, PAS's 2011 Annual Congress has seemingly reinforced the hand of the mainstream faction within the party, with Mohammed Sabu ousting two ulama candidates, including two-term incumbent Nasharuddin Mat Isa to secure the Deputy President position, while Husam Musa won one of the four vice-presidential positions. PAS mainstreamers comprise a majority on the Central Committee as well.[58] While the party continues to face deep suspicion from non-Muslims and more secular Malays who view the election of the mainstreamers as evidence of a moderation of strategy rather than a fundamental ideological change, it is important to note that PAS is a dynamic learning party that is cognizant of the fact that it cannot win nationally without its PR partners and without non-Muslim support. Moreover, it can make inroads into non-Muslim voters, if it projects an inclusive image and emphasizes issues with a broad appeal across the races and religions. Should the party swing hard-line, it would lose all it had built. The party leaders recognize that with the BN's share of seats plunging to 63 percent and its overall popular vote dipping to 51 percent, its chance of taking power in coalition with the PKR and the DAP in the next election are better than at any other point in history. As stated by PAS Treasurer Hatta Ramli, "[We have] to be careful. We have to honor our friendships. We need to put forth a national image, the image of a government in waiting."[59]

The government's reticence to accept the changing dynamics of Malaysian political space extends beyond party politics to civil society as well. The BERSIH 2.0 rally, held on July 9, 2011 is an example of the state's missteps in this regard. BERSIH, the Malay word for clean, is an umbrella comprising human rights groups, media watchdogs, women's rights organizations, Islamic organizations, and representatives of all parties.[60] Some 62 organizations are included under the BERSIH banner.[61] The rally was envisioned as an event that would both engage in politics and be above it, calling upon the government to undertake reforms so that elections would be free and fair.[62] After announcing it would hold a rally on July 9, BERSIH was the target of a campaign of fear and intimidation by the Ministry for Home Affairs, which refused to grant the permit to hold the rally. In the weeks leading up to the rally, 223 people were brought into the police for questioning in connection with BERSIH 2.0; the Ministry for Home Affairs gazetted BERSIH as an illegal organization; and 91 individuals, many of whom were affiliated with or members of the BERSIH steering committee, were placed on restriction orders, barring them from certain parts of Kuala Lumpur on July 9.[63] BERSIH was accused of being beholden to foreign powers and of having communist leanings. Perkasa and UMNO Youth threatened counter-rallies. Government officials cited concerns of instability and a few made allusions to the 1969 race riots. In spite of the increasingly tense atmosphere, a broad cross section of Malaysian society turned out for the rally: Malays, Chinese, Indians; Muslims and non-Muslims; middle class, rich, and poor; old and young. In total, BERSIH contended that 50,000 Malaysians came out for the rally despite police roadblocks, of which, 20,000 were estimated to come from PAS.[64] Despite the peaceful nature of the protest, the police responded with excessive force, arresting between 1,600 and 1,700 participants, firing tear gas into the crowds, and turning water cannons on yellow-shirted protestors.

The government's heavy-handed reaction was widely condemned both domestically and internationally. According to Marina Mahathir, had the government not made such a big issue out of the BERSIH 2.0 rally, it could have avoided such fallout.[65] Had the government permitted the rally or even allowed their members to join, they could have co-opted the rally as a symbol of Prime Minister Najib Razak's "1 Malaysia" United campaign. Instead, the crackdown has turned what would have otherwise been considered a moderately successful rally into a grand emblem of all that is wrong with the current system. Namely, it highlighted the failure of the rhetoric of fear and division in an increasingly open Malaysian polity. The results of the 2008 elections underscored that the political space in Malaysia is changing. Malaysians, Islamist and secular, Muslim and non-Muslim are increasingly demanding more than oppositionism and are working together to achieve it

In sum, in examining state-Islamist group relations in Turkey, Indonesia, and Malaysia over the past three years, several common trends have emerged. First, while Turkey and Malaysia maintained effective capacity, Indonesia still faces significant challenges in the sphere of law and order, particularly in dealing with radical Islamist vigilante coalitions and small-scale terrorism. Second, in all cases, the space for Islamist mobilization is increasing and the boundaries between what is considered the secular or nationalist domain and what is deemed the religious sphere is blurring. While in Turkey, such mobilization is still constrained by Kemalism, the second re-election of the AKP indicates a broader Turkish-Islamic synthesis is taking root that is reflective of both the secular constitution and an increasingly devout polity. In Indonesia, that the Democrat and Golkar parties are moving to the politico-religious center indicates that Islamic values and symbols are not the sole purview of Islamist parties. In Malaysia, while the renegotiation of the political space has become a veritable political tug-of-war between the opposition and allied civil society groups and UMNO and its allied NGOs, there is no doubt that fundamental changes are taking place. Lest we see the government's position as static, it should be noted that in September 2011, PM Najib promised reforms to several repressive laws, most notably the ISA.

Finally, Islamist parties are also shifting to the center and, in Malaysia and Indonesia, partnering with other parties that do not share their ideological goals, including nationalist and Christian parties in Indonesia and secular and multi-ethnic parties in Malaysia[66] in order to portray themselves as inclusive and make inroads into new groups of voters. In the case of the AKP, this moderation is the culmination of 30 years of political learning and has enabled the party to transform itself into an Islamically oriented catchall party and to win re-election twice. For PAS and the PKS, there is an ongoing struggle within both parties over the extent to which they should moderate. At this point, PAS seems to be committing to a shift to the center to a greater degree than the PKS, in large part, due to the incentives such a shift would bring, notably, inroads into non-Muslim constituencies and the possibilities of substantial electoral gains in the next national elections in 2012.

There are important lessons that Egypt, Tunisia, and other Arab states can glean from the experiences of Indonesia, Malaysia, and Turkey. While this study has sought to address the relationship between the state and varied Islamist movements, its findings also have implications beyond religious movements per se. The grievances that fueled the uprisings in Tunisia and Egypt in 2010 and 2011 were both rooted in failures of state capacity in providing for the people and the lack of opportunities to seek redress through the formal political process. It is no surprise that Kuwait, a state that is both effective and participatory, has been able to avoid the violence that has marked Yemen and Bahrain. While we run the risk of oversimplification to reduce the diverse Arab uprisings to failures of participation and capacity, the salience of two issues also cannot be ignored, for they go to the core of a regime's legitimacy.

# Glossary

## Turkey

Diyanet Isleri Baskanligi: Directorate of Religious Affairs

*Gecekondu:* Turkish slums

*Imam-hatip:* Turkish Islamic schools

*Naksibendi:* Turkish Sufi *tarikat.* Tends to be more politically active.

*Neo-Nurcus:* Followers of Fetullah Gulen. Also referred to as the Fetullah Gulen movement.

*Nurcu:* Turkish Sufi *tarikat.* Followers of Said-i-Nursi.

*Tarikat:* Sufi brotherhoods

*Suleymanci:* Turkish Sufi *tarikat.* It tends to avoid political activism.

## Malaysia

*Dakwah songsang:* Deviant Islamic propagation

*Pakatan Rakyat:* People's Pact. The 2008 opposition coalition comprised the Malaysian Islamic Party (PAS), the Democratic Action Party, and the People's Justice Party. It governs the states of Kelantan, Selanghor, Kedah, Perak, and Penang.

*Sekolah Bantuan:* PAS-affiliated schools that combine the government's mandated curriculum with that of Al Azhar University.

*Sekolah Agama Negeri:* State religious schools

*Sekolah Agama Persekutan:* Federal religious schools

*Sekolah Agama Rakyat:* Community religious schools

*Sekolah Agama Swasta:* Private religious schools

*Semangat '46:* Spirit of 46, a breakaway faction of the United Malays National Organization (UMNO) that formed a new political party and contested the 1990 and 1995 elections before rejoining UMNO in 1998.

## Indonesia

*azas tunggal:* Sole foundation

*Bintang:* Star

*dwi fungsi:* Under the Suharto regime, the idea that the military should have a dual function, its traditional security role and a political role.

*Kembali ke kittah 1926:* Return to the 1926 charter. When Nahdlatul Ulama withdrew from formal politics in 1984, it stated it would return to the 1926 charter, as a mass organization that provided Islamic education and social services to its members.

*Kyai:* The headmaster and head teacher of an Islamic boarding school

Madrasa: In Indonesia, madrasas are Islamic day schools.

*Pancasila:* Five principles—social justice, belief in one god, humanitarianism, unity in diversity, and democracy through deliberation and consensus. The unifying national ideology of Indonesia.

*Pembaruan:* Islamic renewal movement

*Pengajian:* Teaching sessions.

*Pesantren:* Indonesian Islamic boarding schools

*Preman:* Thug gangs

*Proporsionalisme:* Proportionality—the call by Indonesian Muslims during the late New Order period for greater proportionality in government hiring practices to ensure better representation for Muslims.

*Rakyat:* Common people (term used also in Malaysia)

*Reformasi:* The term for democratic reform movements that occurred in both Indonesia and Malaysia during the financial crisis period in the late 1990s.

*Santri:* Students at a *pesantren.* Also can be used to refer to orthodox Muslims.

SARA *(suku, agama, ras, antar-golongan)* laws: Prohibit discussion on contentious race, religion, intercommunal, and ethnic issues.

*Transmigrasi:* Transmigration. In Indonesia, it refers to the movement of peoples from the island of Java and other crowded islands to more sparsely populated islands. The transmigration policy had the effect of inflaming tensions between the new arrivals and the indigenous peoples.

*Undang-Undang Keormasan:* Mass Organizations Law. According to it, all organizations had to adopt Pancasila as their sole foundation.

## General Terms

*Ahmadiyah:* Sect of Islam considered heretical by some conservative groups for believing that there was an additional prophet after Prophet Muhammad. This sect has faced discrimination in several countries referred to in this book, including Indonesia, Malaysia, and Bangladesh.

*al-dawlah al-Islamiyyah:* Islamic state

*Alevis:* Sect of Shiism popular in Turkey and Syria

*Amar ma'aruf nahi munkar:* To encourage the good and discourage the bad. This term is used by mainstream Islamist groups to categorize their general mission of promoting moral and ethical behavior among Muslims. However, it is also a frequent justification by radical Islamists for attacking gambling dens and outlets selling alcohol.

*Aqidah:* Faith

*Dakwah:* Literal translation from Arabic "the call." The term "Dakwah" or "Dawa" refers to Islamic movements that seek to convert non-Muslims to the Islamic faith and to persuade Muslims to become more observant.

*Deobandi:* Islamic reformist sect founded in India in 1866. The Deobandis emphasize correct ritual and personal behavior practice of Islam. They have a thriving network of madrasas throughout Pakistan.

*Din:* "Religion," especially in practice. See *Islam ad-din.*

Fatwa *(Turkish-Fetwa):* A proclamation or determination on matters of Islamic law

*Fiqh:* Islamic jurisprudence

Hajj: One of the five pillars of faith. A pilgrimage to Mecca that Muslims must take once in a lifetime.

*Halqah:* Small religious study circles

*Hudud:* Islamic criminal code

*Ijma:* Consensus

*Ijtihad:* Independent reasoning

Intifada: An uprising (lit-shaking off). This term usually refers to mass protest movements in the West Bank and Gaza. It has also been used to refer to the Bahraini protest movement.

*Islam ad din:* Islam as a way of life—one of the key ideas of the *dakwah* movement.

*Jemaah Islamiyah*: This term literally translates to Islamic community; in this book, it is used to refer to the terrorist group active in Southeast Asia. It is discussed in chapters 3–6.

Jihad: Struggle. In the West, it is often used to refer to Islamic holy war. However, it may also refer to a struggle to purge oneself of one's sinful habits/characteristics. Finally, jihad, understood correctly, is always defensive.

*Ka'bah:* The Kabah is a holy site in Islam and part of the Hajj ritual pilgrimage. It is a large obsidian block that Muslims circumambulate.

*Kadi:* Muslim judges

*Khutba* (also hudba): The sermon preached at Friday prayers.

Madrasa: Islamic boarding school (in Indonesia, a madrasa is a day school). In Turkey, *imam-hatip* school. For Islamic boarding school in the Indonesian context, see *pesantren.*

*Majelis al Shura:* Consultative Council

*Maktab:* A school for children to learn to read and recite the Koran. This is typically a supplement to public school or day school.

*Matam:* Shia social welfare providers in Bahrain

Mujihideen: One who fights in a jihad

*Mutazelites:* A sect of Islamic jurisprudence that believes in rationalist analysis

*Qisas:* Part of Islamic criminal code

*Salafi:* Salafis also seek to return Islam to its pure roots. They believe that the true sources of Islam are the Koran, the Hadith, and the consensuses reached by scholars during the first three generations after Prophet Muhammad's death. They shun modern interpretations.

Sharia: Islamic law

Shia (also Shiite): Sect of Islam that differs from the Sunnis over who should have led Muslims after the death of Prophet Mohammad. Shias are a majority in Bahrain, Iran, and Iraq. Significant Shia minorities exist in Kuwait, Saudi Arabia, Lebanon, and Pakistan.

*Shura:* Consultation

Sunni: Popular name for Muslim majority sect also known as *Ahl al-Sunna Wa'l-Jama'ah.*

*Tafsir:* Explanation, interpretation, commentary. Term used to refer to the Koran.

*Tarikat:* Turkish Sufi brotherhoods

Ulama: Religious scholars

*Umma:* The Islamic community

*Usroh:* Lit. family. This term is used to describe Islamist study circles in various parts of the Muslim world.

*Ustaz:* Religious teachers

Wahabi: Puritanical reform movement led by Muhammad Ibn Abd al-Wahhab in the Arabian peninsula in the eighteenth century.

*Waqfs:* Islamic foundations or charities. Often used to refer to foundations by land grant.

*Zakat:* One of the five pillars of faith in Islam—annual contribution to the poor or less fortunate.

*Zaydi:* Sect of Shiism popular in Yemen

# Notes

## Chapter 1

1. Singer, Peter Warren, "Pakistan's Madrassahs: Ensuring a System of Education, Not Jihad." Brookings analysis paper, no. 14 (November 2001), 3.
2. External Forces, see Said, Edward, "The Clash of Ignorance," *Nation*, October 22, 2001, thenation.com/do/20011022/said, and Schwartz, Stephen, *The Two Faces of Islam* (New York: Anchor Books, 2003); *Militant Islam in Southeast Asia: Crucible of Terror* (Boulder: Lynne Rienner, 2003), 18.

   Exclusion-Repression Nexus, see Hafez, Mohammed, "From Marginalization to Massacres: A Political Process Explanation of GIA Violence in Algeria," in *Islamic Activism: A Social Movement Theory Approach,* ed. Quintan Wiktorowicz (Bloomington: Indiana University Press, 2004), 37–60, and Hafez, Mohammed, *Why Muslims Rebel: Repression and Resistance in the Islamic World* (Boulder: Lynne Rienner, 2003).

   Backlash against modernization, see Ansari, Hamied, "The Islamic Militants in Egyptian Politics," *International Journal of Middle East Studies* 16 (1984): 123–144; Dekmejian, R. Hrair, *Islam in Revolution: Fundamentalism in the Arab World* (Syracuse: Syracuse University Press, 1995); and Kepel, Gilles, *Jihad: The Trail of Political Islam* (Cambridge: Belknap, 2002).
3. See Mishal, Saul, and Sela, Avraham, *The Palestinian Hamas: Vision, Violence and Coexistence* (New York: Columbia University Press, 2006); Wiktorowicz, Quintan, *The Management of Islamic Activism: Salafis, the Muslim Brotherhood, and State Power in Jordan* (New York: State University of New York Press, 2001); *God Willing: The Politics of Islamism in Bangladesh* (Lanham: Rowman and Littlefield, 2004); Sidel, John, *Riots, Pogroms, Jihad: Religious Violence in Indonesia* (Ithaca: Cornell University Press, 2006); Ramage, Doug, *Politics in Indonesia: Democracy, Islam and the Ideology of Tolerance* (London: Routledge, 1997); and Effendy, Bahtiar, *Islam and the State in Indonesia* (Athens: Ohio University Press, 2003).
4. See Lewis, Bernard, "The Revolt of Islam," *New Yorker*, November 19, 2001, 56, and Huntington, Samuel, "Clash of Civilizations," *Foreign Affairs* 72, no. 3 (Summer 1993): 32.
5. Inglehart, Ron, and Norris, Pippa, "The True Clash of Civilizations," *Foreign Policy Magazine* (March/April 2003): 66.

6. Esposito, John L., and Piscatori, James P., "Democratization and Islam," *Middle East Journal* 45, no. 3 (Summer 1991): 428.

7. Scholars may cite any of the following verses from the Koran to support conceptions of *shura* and social justice.

   Those who hearken to their Lord, and establish regular prayer; who (conduct) their affairs by mutual consultation; who spend out of what we bestow on them for sustenance (42: 38).

   It is part of the Mercy of Allah that thou dost deal gently with them. Wert thou severe or harsh-hearted, they would have broken away from about thee: so pass over (their faults), and ask for (Allah's) forgiveness for them; and consult them in affairs (of moment). Then, when thou hast Taken a decision put thy trust in Allah. For Allah loves those who put their trust (in Him) (3:159).

   To thee we sent the Scripture in truth, confirming the scripture that came before it, and guarding it in safety: so judge between them by what Allah hath revealed, and follow not their vain desires, diverging from the Truth that hath come to thee. To each among you have we prescribed a law and an open way. If Allah had so willed, He would have made you a single people, but (His plan is) to test you in what He hath given you: so strive as in a race in all virtues. The goal of you all is to Allah. It is He that will show you the truth of the matters in which ye dispute (5:48).

8. See McAdam, Doug, Tarrow, Sidney, and Tilly, Charles, *Dynamics of Contention* (Cambridge: Cambridge University Press, 2001); Schwedler, Jillian, *Faith in Moderation: Islamist Parties in Jordan and Yemen* (Cambridge: Cambridge University Press, 2007); Hafez, *Why Muslims Rebel: Repression and Resistance in the Islamic World*; Abootalebi, Ali Reza, *Islam and Democracy: State-Society Relations in Developing Countries 1980–1994* (New York: Garland, 2000); Ghadbian, Najib, "Political Islam and Violence," *New Political Science* 22, no. 1 (2000): 77–88; Ibrahim, Anwar, "Who Hijacked Islam," *Time Asia,* November 8, 2004; Tarrow, Sidney, *Power in Movement: Social Movements and Contentious Politics* (Cambridge: Cambridge University Press, 1998); and Nasr, Vali, "The Rise of Muslim Democracy," *Journal of Democracy* 16.2 (2005): 13–27.

9. Huntington, Samuel, *Political Order and Changing Societies* (New Haven: Yale University Press, 1969), and Sartori, Giovanni, *Parties and Party Systems: A Framework for Analysis* (New York: Cambridge University Press, 1976).

10. Huntington, *Political Order and Changing Societies.*

11. Snyder, Jack, *From Voting to Violence* (New York: W.W Norton and Company, 2000), 37–38.

12. Abootalebi, Ali Reza, "Islam, Islamists and Democracy," *Middle East Review of International Affairs* 3, no. 1 (1999): 20.

13. Ghadbian, "Political Islam and Violence," 77.

14. Ibrahim, Anwar, "Who Hijacked Islam," *Time Asia,* November 8, 2004, http://www.time.com/time/world/article/0,8599,178470,00.html (accessed on April 24, 2005).
15. Goodwin, Jeff, *No Other Way Out: States and Revolutionary Movements* (London: Cambridge University Press, 2001), 290.
16. Hafez, *Why Muslims Rebel,* 15.
17. Sidel, *Riots, Pogroms, Jihad,* 102.
18. Wiktorowicz, *Islamic Activism,* 8–9.
19. Schwartz, *The Two Faces of Islam,* 180.
20. Ibid.
21. Kepel, *Jihad;* Dekmejian, *Islam in Revolution;* and Lewis, "The Revolt of Islam," 56.
22. Kepel, *Jihad,* 66–67, and Dekmejian, *Islam in Revolution,* 33.
23. Sivan, Emanuel, "Why Radical Muslims Aren't Taking Over Governments," *Middle East Review of International Affairs* 2, no. 2 (1997): 2.
24. Sivan, Emanuel, "The Clash within Islam," *Survival* 45, no. 1 (Spring 2003): 28.
25. Hafez, *Why Muslims Rebel,* 10–11.

## Chapter 2

1. The Turkish state extended its control over the religious sphere, in part, because of its historic tradition of doing so. Under the Seljuks and even under the Ottomans, religion never became the dominant source of state authority; instead, there was a partial separation between religion and worldly affairs. Islam had a strong social impact, but no political authority. Furthermore, Islamist groups and institutions had a strong tradition of obedience to political authority (from interviews with Professor Tufan Buzpinar, Istanbul, Turkey, August 18, 2005, and Professor Nuri Tinaz, Istanbul, Turkey, August 24, 2005).
2. Sayari, Sabri, "The Changing Party System," in *Politics, Parties and Elections in Turkey,* eds. Sabri Sayari and Yilmaz Esmer (Boulder: Lynne Rienner, 2002), 22.
3. Ozbudun, Ergun, *Contemporary Turkish Politics* (Boulder: Lynne Rienner, 2000), 83.
4. Yavuz, Hakan, *Islamic Political Identity in Turkey* (Oxford: Oxford University Press, 2003), 213.
5. Ibid.
6. Toprak, Binnaz, "The State, Politics and Religion in Turkey," in *State, Democracy and the Military: Turkey in the 1980s,* eds. Metin Heper and Ahmet Evin (Boulder: Westview Press, 1988), 125.
7. Yesilada, Birol. A, "The Virtue Party," *Turkish Politics* 10, no. 33 (2002): 65.
8. Toprak, "The State, Politics and Religion in Turkey," 124.
9. White, Jenny. B, *Islamist Mobilization in Turkey: A Study in Vernacular Politics* (Seattle: University of Washington Press, 2002), 114–115.
10. Yesilada, "The Virtue Party," 67.

11. Sakallioglu, Umit Cizre, "Parameters and Strategies of Islam-State Interaction in Republican Turkey," *International Journal of Middle East Studies* 28 (1996): 243.
12. Pope, Nicole, and Pope, Hugh, *Turkey Unveiled* (New York: The Overlook Press, 1998), 318.
13. Atacan, Fulya, "Explaining Religious Politics at the Crossroad: AKP-SP," *Turkish Studies* 6, no. 2 (June 2005): 188.
14. Ibid., 195.
15. Yavuz, *Islamic Political Identity in Turkey*, 66.
16. Zubaida, Sami, "Turkish Islam and National Identity," *Middle East Report* (April–June 1996): 11.
17. Yesilada, "The Virtue Party," 70.
18. White, *Islamist Mobilization in Turkey*, 180.
19. Interview, Professor Tufan Buzpinar, August 18, 2005.
20. Narli, Nilufer, "The Rise of the Islamist Movement in Turkey," *Middle East Review of International Affairs* 3, no. 33 (September 1999): 42.
21. Ibid.
22. Ozbudun, *Contemporary Turkish Politics*, 85.
23. Howe, Marvine, *Turkey Today* (Boulder: Westview Press, 2000), 29, and White, *Islamist Mobilization in Turkey*, 120.
24. White, *Islamist Mobilization in Turkey*, 11.
25. The February 28th process or "soft coup" constituted a widespread crackdown on Islamist leaders. Recep Tayyip Erdogan was thrown into prison after reading a poem by Turkish nationalist Ziya Golkap. Foundations and newspapers sympathetic to the Islamists were all closed. The military boycotted Islamist businesses. Professors accused of reactionary views were barred from university posts of dean or rector. Mango, Andrew, *The Turks Today* (New York: The Overlook Press, 2004), 97.
26. Howe, *Turkey Today*, 183–184.
27. Onis, Ziya, "The Political Economy of Islam and Democracy in Turkey: From the Welfare Party to the AKP." Draft paper (May 2005), 8.
28. Guens-Ayata, Ayse, and Sencer, Ayata, "Ethnic and Religious Bases of Voting," in *Politics, Parties and Elections in Turkey*, eds. Sabri Sayari and Yilmaz Esmer (Boulder: Lynne Rienner, 2002), 148.
29. Ibid.
30. Interview, Professor Tufan Buzpinar, Fatih University, Istanbul, Turkey, August 21, 2005.
31. Ibid.
32. Interview, Ismail Safi, vice president AKP, Ankara, Turkey, August 17, 2005.
33. Ibid., August 18, 2005.
34. Yavuz, *Islamic Political Identity in Turkey*, 257.
35. Ibid.
36. Ibid.
37. Ibid.

38. Cagaptay, Soner, "The November 2002 Elections and Turkey's New Political Era," *Middle East Review of International Affairs* 6, no. 4 (December 2002): 42.

39. Bahar, Heymi, "The Real Winners and Losers of Turkey's July 2007 Elections," *Middle East Review of International Affairs* 11, no. 3 (September 2007): 69.

40. Ibid.

41. Ibid.

42. Zubaida, "Turkish Islam and National Identity," 11.

43. Onis, "The Political Economy of Islam and Democracy in Turkey: From the Welfare Party to the AKP," 5.

44. Yesilada, "The Virtue Party," 73.

45. Zubaida, "Turkish Islam and National Identity," 11.

46. Yavuz, *Islamic Political Identity in Turkey*, 141.

47. Vertigans, Stephen, *Islamic Roots and Resurgence in Turkey* (London: Praeger, 2003), 73.

48. Yesilada, "The Virtue Party," 71.

49. Ibid., 73

50. Atacan, "Explaining Religious Politics at the Crossroad: AKP-SP," 190, and Yesilada, "The Virtue Party," 65.

51. Yavuz, *Islamic Political Identity in Turkey*, 143.

52. Atacan, "Explaining Religious Politics at the Crossroad," 188.

53. Ibid.

54. Ibid., 196.

55. Interview, Professor Tufan Buzpinar, August 21, 2005.

56. Ibid., August 16, 2006.

57. Mango, Andrew, *The Turks Today*, 76.

58. Ibid.

59. Ibid.

60. Ibid., 128.

61. Aras, Bulent, and Gokhan, Bacik, "The Mystery of Turkish Hizballah," *Middle East Policy* 9, no 2 (June 2002): 150.

62. Ibid.

63. Pope and Pope, *Turkey Unveiled*, 327.

64. Aras and Bacik, "The Mystery of Turkish Hizballah," 148.

65. Ibid., 153.

66. Ibid.

67. Ibid.

68. In the early 1990s, Ugur Mumcu, a noted investigative reporter, was murdered by car bombing; Bahriye Ucok, a prominent secular Islamic scholar, who asserted that covering one's hair was not compulsory under the Koran, was killed by a package bomb; Muammer Askoy, president of the Turkish Law Society, was murdered; and churches were bombed. In 1994, the IBDA-C was responsible for five bombings in cities around Turkey and 90 smaller incidents. Turkish Hizballah was held responsible for over 400 murders.

Information cited from Karmon, Ely, "Radical Islamic Political Groups in Turkey," *Middle East Review of International Affairs* 1, no. 4 (1997), http://meria.idc.ac.il/journal/1997/issue4/jv1n4az.html (accessed on October 27, 2005), and Howe, *Turkey Today,* 49–51.

69. Karmon, "Radical Islamic Political Groups in Turkey."
70. Ibid.
71. Howe, *Turkey Today,* 51.
72. Lesser, Ian, "Turkey: 'Recessed' Islamic Politics and Convergence with the West," in *The Muslim World After 9/11,* eds. Angel Rabasa, Cheryl Benard, Peter Chalk, C. Christine Fair, Theodore Karasik, Rollie Lal, Ian Lesser, and David Thaler (Arlington: Rand, 2004), 195.
73. Nugent, John Jr, "The Defeat of Turkish Hizballah as a Model for Counter-Terrorism Strategy," *Middle East Review of International Affairs* 8, no. 1 (March 2004): 72.
74. Aras and Bacik, "The Mystery of Turkish Hizballah," 147.
75. Vertigans, *Islamic Roots and Resurgence in Turkey,* 73.
76. Interview, Ali Bardakoglu, president, Directorate of Religious Affairs, Ankara, Turkey, August 17, 2005.
77. Tank, Pinar, "Political Islam in Turkey: A State of Controlled Secularity," *Turkish Studies* 6, no. 1, 8.
78. Yavuz, *Islamic Political Identity in Turkey,* 125, and Vertigans, *Islamic Roots and Resurgence in Turkey,* 94.
79. Yavuz, *Islamic Political Identity in Turkey,* 125.
80. Ibid., 126–127.
81. Ibid., 125.
82. Ibid.
83. Aras, Bulent, and Caha, Omer, "*Fetullah Gulen* and his Liberal 'Turkish Islam' Movement," *Middle East Review of International Affairs* 4, no. 4 (December 2000): 34
84. Tank, "Political Islam in Turkey," 5, and Toprak, "The State, Politics and Religion in Turkey," 122.
85. Tank, "Political Islam in Turkey," 5.
86. Sakallioglu, "Parameters and Strategies of Islam-State Interaction in Republican Turkey," 256.
87. Tank, "Political Islam in Turkey," 5.
88. Interview, Professor Ihsan Dagi, Middle East Technical University, Ankara, Turkey, August 16, 2005.
89. Ibid.
90. Yavuz, *Islamic Political Identity in Turkey,* 127–128.
91. Interview, Professor Ihsan Dagi, August 16, 2005.
92. Ibid.
93. Heper, Metin, "The Justice and Development Party Government and the Military in Turkey," *Turkish Studies* (June 2005): 225.
94. Ibid.

95. Interview, Professor Ihsan Dagi, August 16, 2005.
96. Heper, "The Justice and Development Party Government and the Military in Turkey," 225, and Tank, "Political Islam in Turkey," 15.
97. Tank, "Political Islam in Turkey," 15.
98. Aras and Caha, "*Fetullah Gulen* and his Liberal 'Turkish Islam' Movement," 33.
99. Karmon, "Radical Islamic Political Groups in Turkey."
100. Ibid.
101. Ibid.
102. Howe, *Turkey Today,* 50.
103. Ibid, 48.
104. Ibid.
105. "Turkish Kurds in Iraq: We Want Peace, They Say," *The Economist,* August 31, 2006.
106. Ibid.
107. "Turkey and Europe: The Way Ahead," *International Crisis Group Europe Report,* no. 184 (August 17, 2007): 14. According to the International Crisis Group, Turkish government officials are divided as to how many active PKK fighters are based in Iraq and how many reside in Turkey. Prime Minister Erdogan has stated that he believes that the majority of PKK fighters reside in Turkey itself, but this is disputed by the army. The latest figure given by the Turkish land forces commander, Ilter Basbug, at a news conference in June 2007 was 1,800–1,900 inside Turkey and 5,150–5,650 inside northern Iraq. Prior to that, the official number of PKK fighters in Turkey was 500. According to the International Herald Tribune, "Attacks Put Turkey in a Bind Over Kurdish Rebels," May 24, 2007. Turkish military sources say that 3,800 are based over the border in Iraq, while 2,300 operate inside Turkey.
108. Ibid.
109. Wright, Robin, and Abramowitz, Michael, "US Warns Iraq to Halt Rebel Raids on Turkey," *Washington Post,* October 23, 2007, A01, and "Attacks Put Turkey in a Bind over Rebel Kurds," *International Herald Tribune,* May 24, 2007, http://www.iht.com/articles/2007/5/24/news/turkey.php (accessed on November 2, 2008).
110. "Turkish Kurds in Iraq: We Want Peace, They Say," August 31, 2006.

## Chapter 3

1. Fealy, Greg, and Platzdach, Bernhard, "The Masyumi Legacy: Between Islamist Idealism and Political Exigency," *Studia Islamika* 12, no.1 (2005): 81. This does not imply that all of these organizations were closely tied to Masyumi. Some were closer than others. For example, the HMI had members in both NU and Masyumi. However, the streams of thought were present, and members of these organizations tended to support Masyumi.
2. "Seorang Besar Dengan Banyak Teman," *Tempo Laporan Khusus 100 Tahun Mohammad Natsir, Tempo Edisi* (July 14–20, 2008): 83.

3. Van Bruinessen, Martin, "Genealogies of Islamic Radicalism in Post-Suharto Indonesia," *Southeast Asia Research* 10, no. 2 (2002): 118.

4. International Crisis Group, "Al-Qaeda in Southeast Asia: The Case of the Ngruki Network," Indonesia Briefing, Jakarta/Brussels, August 8, 2002, 6.

5. Interview, longtime Indonesian observer, Jakarta, Indonesia, March 2006.

6. Hefner, Robert, *Civil Islam* (Princeton: Princeton University Press, 2000), 98–99.

7. Juoro, Umar, "Indonesia," in *Political Party Systems and Democratic Development in East and Southeast Asia, vol. 1. Southeast Asia,* eds. Wolfgang Sachsenroder and Ulrike Frings (Aldershot: Ashgate, 1998), 214.

8. Liddle, R. William, "The Islamic Turn in Indonesia: A Political Explanation," *Journal of Asian Studies* 55, no. 3 (1996): 621.

9. Interview, Irwan Abdullah, director of the Graduate School at Gadjah Mada University, Yogyakarta, Indonesia, April 2006.

10. Umar "Indonesia," 198.

11. Interview, Husnan Bey, editor of *Majalah Pakar—the Newspaper of the United Development Party,* Jakarta, Indonesia, May 2006.

12. Effendy, Bahtiar, *Islam and the State in Indonesia* (Singapore: Institute of Southeast Asian Studies, 2003), 49.

13. Sukarno established *Pancasila* as the unifying national ideology of the Indonesian nation. It comprised five principles: belief in one god, social justice, unity in diversity, humanitarianism, and democracy through deliberation and consensus.

14. The Kabah is a holy site in Islam and part of the Hajj ritual pilgrimage. It is a large obsidian block that Muslims circumambulate.

15. Barton, Greg, *Jemaah Islamiyah: Radical Islamism in Indonesia* (Singapore: Ridge Books, 2005), 89.

16. Effendy, *Islam and the State in Indonesia,* 51.

17. SARA-*suku, agama, ras, antar-golongan.*

18. Van Bruinessen, Martin, "Islamic State or State Islam? Fifty Years of State-Islam Relations in Indonesia, in Ingrid Wessel (Hrsg.), *Indonesien am Ende des 20. Jahrhunderts* (Hamburg: Abera-Verlag, 1996), 19–34.

19. It is important to note that Muslim interests do not necessarily imply political interests. A major Muslim interest in Indonesia at that time was upward mobility and the inclusion of more orthodox Muslims in the bureaucracy, which was seen as being dominated by Christians and secularists. Other issues slowly pushed over 20 plus years were the establishment of an Islamic bank and the equalization of the Islamic court system with the civil courts. One could then argue that Muslims could achieve their goals through institutional channels, but these policies were enacted after Suharto's change of heart. Thus, it was not successful mobilization, but a shift in Suharto's mind-set with regard to Muslim activists and his strategy for rallying votes for another term in office.

20. Interview, Bahtiar Effendy, professor of political science, UIN-Syarif Hidyatullah, Jakarta, Indonesia, May 2006.

21. Porter, Donald, *Managing Politics and Islam in Indonesia* (London: Routledge, 2002), 76.

22. Hamayotsu, Kikue, "Islam and Nation Building in Southeast Asia: Malaysia and Indonesia in Comparative Perspective," *Pacific Affairs* 75, no. 3 (Fall 2002): 371.

23. In the 1970s and 1980s, the Suharto regime had overwhelmingly promoted secular Muslims and Christians into the upper levels of the bureaucracy. This was also true of cabinet appointment and promotions in the military. The bias in recruitment and promotion added to Muslim perceptions of being marginalized and aggrieved. The term *proportionalisme* became a buzzword to imply that since a majority of Indonesians were Muslims, this should be reflected in the leadership of the agencies and organs of state.

24. Hefner, *Civil Islam*, 121.

25. Ibid.

26. Interview, Doug Ramage, country representative, and Robin Bush, assistant country representative, The Asia Foundation, Jakarta, Indonesia, March 2006.

27. Effendy, *Islam and the State in Indonesia,* 130.

28. Abdurrahman Wahid, former chairman of Nahdlatul Ulama and former president of Indonesia, quoted in Ramage, Douglas, *Politics in Indonesia: Democracy, Islam and the Ideology of Tolerance* (London: Routledge, 1995), 56.

29. Interview, Bahtiar Effendy, May 2006.

30. "Generator Lapangan Dakwah," *Tempo Laporan Khusus 100 Tahun Mohammad Natsir. Tempo Edisi* (July 14–20, 2008): 104–105.

31. Collins, Elizabeth Fuller, "*Dakwah* and Democracy: The Significance of Partai Keadilan and Hizbut Tahrir" (2004). Forthcoming, http://www.classics.ohiou.edu/faculty/collins (accessed on July 3, 2006), 5.

32. Hefner, *Civil Islam*, 109.

33. Interview, Ahmad Syafi'i Ma'arif, chairman of Muhammadiyah from 2000 to 2005, Jakarta, Indonesia, May 2006.

34. Hefner, *Civil Islam*, 109.

35. International Crisis Group. "Al Qaeda in Southeast Asia: The Case of the 'Ngruki Network' in Indonesia." ICG Indonesia Briefing, August 8, 2002, 10.

36. Amnesty International, "Indonesia: Imprisonment of Usroh Activists in Central Java." Report, October 1986, 2.

37. Van Bruinessen, Martin, "The Violent Fringes of Indonesia's Radical Islam." Background information after the Bali Bombing of October 2002. Extended version of article published in ISIM Newsletter11 (December 2002): 9, www.let.uu.nl/~martin.vanbruinessen/personal/publications/violent_fringe.htm (accessed on July 30, 2006). Machmudi, Yon, "Islamizing Indonesia" (PhD diss., Australia National University, 2006), 118.

38. Machmudi, Yon, "Islamizing Indonesia," 118.

39. Schwarz, Adam, *A Nation in Waiting: Indonesia's Search for Stability* (NSW: Allen & Unwin, 2004), 174.

40. Van Bruinessen, Martin, "Post-Muslim Engagements with Civil Society and Democratization" (paper presented at the Third International Conference and Workshop, "Indonesia in Transition." *Universitas Indonesia,* Depok, August 24–28, 2006).

41. Ibid.

42. Interview, Mutammimul Ula, member of the DPR from the Prosperous Justice Party, Jakarta, Indonesia, April 2006.
43. Barton, *Jemaah Islamiyah: Radical Islamism in Indonesia,* 89.
44. Interview, Ismail Yusanto, founding member of Hizbut Tahrir Indonesia, Jakarta, Indonesia, March 2006.
45. Van Bruinessen "Genealogies of Islamic Radicalism in Post-Suharto Indonesia," 128.
46. "Indonesia: The Imprisonment of Usroh Activists in Central Java," *Amnesty International Report,* October 1988, 1.
47. Amnesty International, "Indonesia: Imprisonment of Usroh Activists in Central Java." Report, October 1986, summary introduction page.
48. Van Bruinessen, Martin, "The Violent Fringes of Indonesia's Radical Islam."
49. Interview, Bahtiar Effendy, May 2006.
50. Schwarz, *A Nation in Waiting: Indonesia's Search for Stability,* 38.
51. Robinson, Richard, and Hadiz, Vedi R, *Reorganizing Power in Indonesia* (London: Routledge, 2004), 115.
52. Liddle, "The Islamic Turn in Indonesia: A Political Explanation," 625.
53. Hefner, *Civil Islam,* 139.
54. Interview, Bahtiar Effendy, May 2006, and interview, Fadli Zon, former member of Golkar, former member of ICMI, and founding member of *Partai Bulan Bintang,* Jakarta, Indonesia, April 2006.
55. Barton, *Jemaah Islamiyah,* 46.
56. Hefner, *Civil Islam,* 10.
57. Ibid., 167.
58. Ibid., 203. To facilitate cooptation, the Golkar Strategy Bureau and affiliated think tanks such as the Institute for Policy Studies published anti-Chinese, anti-Christian, and anti-Semitic propaganda to recast the Suharto regime as the victim of international conspiracy and to discredit the fledgling democracy movement. This propaganda revised Indonesian history to attribute the decades long marginalization of Muslim interests to an all powerful Jesuit extremist group with support from the Chinese and certain elements of the military
59. Interview, Fadli Zon, founding member of the PBB and member of the KISDI, Jakarta, Indonesia, April 2006.
60. Many Indonesia observers agree that the state was quite adept at keeping law and order in the territories within its borders, save the two peripheral provinces of Aceh and East Timor, where ongoing secessionist conflicts flared up intermittently throughout the New Order regime. However, neither conflict was overtly religious in nature. East Timor was an ethnic secessionist conflict, while Aceh was largely a conflict over resources and historical promises of autonomy. The Acehnese, like the majority of Indonesians, are Muslim. While East Timor was majority Catholic, religious rights were not a primary issue for the secessionists. Since religion was not a key issue in either secessionist conflict, it did not cause an increase in violent Islamist mobilization. Thus, these conflicts will not be examined in this book.

61. O'Rourke, Kevin, *Reformasi: The Struggle for Power in Post-Suharto Indonesia* (Crows Nest: Allen and Unwin, 2002), 9.
62. Ibid.
63. Interview, General Saurip Kadi, Jakarta, Indonesia, May 2006.
64. Ibid.
65. Interview, Doug Ramage and Robin Bush, March 2006.
66. "Indonesia: Rethinking Internal Security Strategy," *Crisis Group Asia Report*, no. 90 (December 20, 2004): 2.
67. Collins, Elizabeth Fuller, "Indonesia: A Violent Culture," *Asian Survey* vol. 42, no. 4 (July–August 2002): 584.
68. Interview, longtime Indonesia observer, international NGO, Jakarta, Indonesia, March 2006.
69. Barton, *Jemaah Islamiyah*, 48.
70. Van Bruinessen, Martin, "The Violent Fringes of Indonesia's Radical Islam," 6.
71. "Al Qaeda in Southeast Asia: The Case of the 'Ngruki Network' in Indonesia," *International Crisis Group Indonesia Briefing*, August 8, 2002, 8.
72. Ibid, 9.
73. Conboy, Ken, *The Second Front: Inside Asia's Most Dangerous Terrorist Network* (Jakarta: Equinox, 2006), 153.
74. Ibid.
75. Ibid.
76. Suryadinata, Leo, *Elections and Politics in Indonesia* (Singapore: Institute for Southeast Asian Studies, 2002), 60.
77. Interview, Endy Bayuni, editor-in-chief, *Jakarta Post*, Jakarta, Indonesia, March 2006.
78. Schwarz, *A Nation in Waiting*, 331.
79. Barton, *Jemaah Islamiyah*, 50–51.
80. Sidel, John, *Riots, Pogroms, Jihad: Religious Violence in Indonesia* (Ithaca: Cornell University Press, 2006), 55.
81. Ibid., 56, and Aspinall *Opposing Suharto: Compromise, Resistance, and Regime Change in Indonesia* (Stanford: Stanford University Press, 2005), 66.
82. Friend, Theodore, *Indonesian Destinies* (Cambridge: Belknap Press, 2003), 190.
83. Sidel, *Riots, Pogroms, Jihad*, 56.
84. Bresnan, John, *Managing Indonesia: The Modern Political Economy* (New York: Columbia University Press, 1993), 223–224.
85. Sidel, *Riots, Pogroms, Jihad*, 56.
86. Collins, "Indonesia: A Violent Culture," 584, 593.
87. Hefner, *Civil Islam*, 190.
88. Collins, "Indonesia," 2002, 592.
89. Hefner, *Civil Islam*, 192.
90. Ibid.
91. Ibid.
92. Interview, Kevin O'Rourke, author of the *Reformasi: Struggle for Power in Post-Suharto Indonesia*, Jakarta, Indonesia, April 2006.
93. Hefner, *Civil Islam*, 192.

94. Sidel, *Riots, Pogroms, Jihad*, 84.
95. Bertrand, Jacques, *Nationalism and Ethnic Conflict in Indonesia* (United Kingdom: Cambridge University Press, 2004), 101, and Sidel, *Riots, Pogroms, Jihad*, 84.
96. Hefner, *Civil Islam*, 192.
97. Ibid.
98. Liddle, R. William, *Leadership and Culture in Indonesian Politics* (Sidney: ASAA Southeast Asia Publication Series of Allen and Unwin, 1996), 6.
99. Ibid.
100. UN Human Development Report Statistics. Country sheet, http://hdr.undp.org/statistics/data/countries.cfm?c=IDN (accessed on July 24, 2006).
101. "Survey Indonesia: Time to Deliver," *The Economist*, http://www.economist.com/surveys/displayStory.cfm?story_id=3444238 (accessed on December 9, 2004).
102. Friend, *Indonesian Destinies*, 139.
103. Ibid., 147–148.
104. "Making the New Indonesia Work for the Poor." *The World Bank*. November 2006, 10.
105. Ibid., 146.
106. Ibid.
107. Interview, Dr. Din Syamsuddin, chairman of Muhammadiyah, Jakarta, Indonesia, March 2006, and interview, Mariah Ulfah, head of the Fatayat Welfare Foundation, Fatayat Woman's Wing of NU, Jakarta, Indonesia, April 2006.
108. Interview, Mariah Ulfah, April 2006.
109. Ibid.
110. Porter, *Managing Politics and Islam in Indonesia*, 55.
111. Pohl, Florian, "*Pesantren* and Global Integration" (paper presented at informal talk held at the Center for Religion and Cross-Cultural Studies, Yogyakarta, Indonesia, May 6, 2006, 4).
112. Thomas, Murray R, "The Islamic Revival and Indonesian Education," *Asian Survey* 28, no. 9 (September 1998): 903.
113. Ibid.
114. Hefner, Robert, "Islamization and Democratization in Indonesia," in *Southeast Asia in the New International Era*, eds. Robert Hefner and Patricia Horavitch (Honolulu: University of Hawaii Press 1997), 88, and Van Bruinessen, Martin, "Traditionalist and Islamist *Pesantren* in Contemporary Indonesia (paper presented at the ISIM workshop on "The Madrasa in Asia," Leiden, Netherlands, May 23–24, 2004, 6).
115. Statistics provided by Education Management Information Systems (EMIS). Yunanto, S., and Badrudin, Harun, "Terminology, History, and Categorization," in *Islamic Education in South and Southeast Asia: Diversity, Problems and Strategy*, eds. S. Yunanto et al (Jakarta: Ridep Institute, 2007), 30. Other organizations such as the DDII, the LDI, and Persis also ran smaller networks of Islamic boarding schools, to supplement state efforts. However, these groups account for .43 percent, .18 percent, and.50 percent, respectively, and thus do not play a significant supplemental role compared to NU or Muhammadiyah.

116. Feillard, Andree, "Traditionalist Islam and the State in Indonesia: The Road to Legitimacy and Renewal," in *Islam and the Era of Nation-States,* eds. Robert Hefner and Patricia Horavitch (Honolulu: University of Hawaii Press, 1997), 141–142.
117. Porter, *Managing Politics and Islam in Indonesia,* 113.
118. Van Bruinessen, "The Violent Fringes of Indonesia's Radical Islam," 4.
119. Pohl, *"Pesantren* and Global Integration," 3.
120. Ibid.
121. Abdul Mukti, head of Pemuda Muhammadiyah, Jakarta, Indonesia, March 2006. Indonesians are considered "youth" until their early 40s.
122. Ahmad Syafi'i Ma'arif, former chairman of Muhammadiyah, Jakarta, Indonesia, May 2006.
123. Pincus, John and Rizal, Ramli, Rizal, "Indonesia: From Showcase to Basket Case." *Cambridge Journal of Economics* (1998) 22, p728.

## Chapter 4

1. "Making the New Indonesia Work for the Poor." *The World Bank.* Jakarta (2006), 20.
2. Suryadinata, Leo, *Elections and Politics in Indonesia* (Singapore: Institute for Southeast Asian Studies, 2002), 75.
3. The inclusion of PAN is the result of conversations with Dr. Saiful Mujani. PAN is indirectly linked with Masyumi, for many Muhammadiyah members belonged to Masyumi. As the former head of Muhammadiyah, Amien Rais could count on that indirect linkage. Mujani, who comes from a Masyumi family in Banten, noted that this historical Masyumi connection was one reason why he chose to vote for PAN in 1999. The other reason was the perception of PAN as a party of intellectuals, given the active participation of scholars like Goenawan Mohamad and Emil Salim in its founding.
4. Other exclusive Islamist parties including the Indonesian Islamic Union Party 1905 and the Indonesian Political Party Masyumi failed to cross the electoral threshold in either the 1999 or the 2004 elections.
5. Azra, Azyumardi, "Islam and Indonesian Transition to Democracy," in *Indonesia, Islam and Democracy: Dynamics in a World Context* (Jakarta: Equinox Forthcoming. Pre-published manuscript), 17.
6. Ananta, Aris, Arifin, Evi Nurvidya, and Suryadinata, Leo, *Emerging Democracy in Indonesia* (Singapore: ISEAS, 2005), 12, and interview, Fadli Zon, founding member of the PBB and member of the KISDI, Jakarta, Indonesia, April 2006.
7. Ibid.
8. Ananta, Arifin, and Suryadinata, *Emerging Democracy in Indonesia,* 12.
9. Interview, Mutammimul Ula, founding member of PK(S), Jakarta, Indonesia, April 2006. Collins, Elizabeth Fuller, "Dakwah and Democracy: The Significance of Partai Keadilan and Hizbut Tahrir." Forthcoming, http://www.classics.ohiou.edu/faculty/Collins (2004), 2.

"Hidayat Nur Wahid, chairman of PK, tried to position the party as a centrist Islamic party that occupied the middle ground between radical Islamist groups that reject democracy and Muslim organizations committed to democracy. In his view, Salafi groups are on the extreme left because they reject democracy as un-Islamic and are open to the use of violence. Next is Hizbut Tahrir which also views democracy as un-Islamic but rejects violence. Next are the old Masyumi activists and those who support the Jakarta charter and would impose Islamic law on Muslims. To the right of PK are . . . Muhammadiyah and NU, who reject the slogan 'Islam is the solution' but struggle for a better society through democratic means."

10. Ananta, Arifin, and Suryadinata, *Emerging Democracy in Indonesia*, 12.
11. First three columns of table 4.1. The 1999 election results first appeared in Chapter 5, "Old Rivalries, Blurred Identities," *Elections and Politics in Indonesia* by Leo Suryadinata, 103. Reproduced with the kind permission of the publisher, Institute of Southeast Asian Studies, Singapore, http://bookshop.iseas.edu.sg.
12. The Jakarta charter was a seven word phrase that was submitted for inclusion in the 1945 Constitution. At that time, the Constitution said all Indonesians should believe in one god. The Jakarta charter added, with the obligation of Muslims to obey sharia. Sukarno removed it before the Constitution was ratified, amid protests by secular Muslims and Christian groups.
13. Interview, senior member of parliament, Partai Keadilan Sejahtera, Jakarta, Indonesia, February 2006.
14. Van Zorge, Heffernan, and Associates, "Creeping *Sharia* ?" *Van Zorge Report on Indonesia* VIII/8 (May 9, 2006): 6.
15. Harsanto, Damar, "Thousands Rally for Education Bill," *Jakarta Post,* June 11, 2003.
16. Ananta, Aris, and Arifin, Evi Nurvidya, "Indonesia's Education Bill Opens Pandora's Box," *Straits Times,* October 6, 2003.
17. Hari, Kurniawan, "House Passes Education Bill," *Jakarta Post,* June 12, 2003.
18. Harsanto, Damar, "Thousands Rally for Education Bill," *Jakarta Post,* June 11, 2003.
19. Ibid.
20. Ananta and Arifin, "Indonesia's Education Bill Opens Pandora's Box." The Cipayang Forum comprises members of the HMI; Pergerakan Mahasiswa Islam Indonesia (Indonesian Muslim Students Movement, PMII); Gerakan Mahasiswa Kristen Indonesia (Indonesian Protestant Students Movement); and Perhimpunan Mahasiswa Katolik republic Indonesia (Association of the Republic of Indonesia's Catholic Students).
21. Hari, Kurniawan, "House Passes Education Bill," and Unidjaja, Fabiola Desy, "Megawati Eats Her Words, Signs Education Law," *Jakarta Post,* July 17, 2003.
22. Civil society aggressively mobilized for and against RUU-APP, lobbying, participating in hearings, holding seminars, and organizing mass demonstrations. A coalition of progressive Muslims organizations and women's organizations,

including the National Coalition for Women, the Liberal Islam Network, the Fatayat wing of NU, Rahima, and Apik, successfully lobbied DPR members against the bill and participated in hearings on the bill. Demonstration banners proclaimed, "Indonesia is not America but it also is not Saudi Arabia." The pro-bill coalition included the Indonesian Ulama Council, Gerakan Tarbiyah, Muhammadiyah, Hizbut Tahrir, Forum Betawi Rempug, Mer-C, DDII, Muslima Peduli Ummat, and the PBNU and Muslimat wings of NU, but not the Young NU or Fatayat wings. The pro-bill factions claimed the bill was necessary to protect women from sexual exploitation, while the anti-bill faction contended it was creeping Arabization.

23. Barton, Greg, "Theodicy, Theocracy and the Individual: The Challenge of Political and Jihadi Islamism to Pluralism and Liberal Democracy in Asia" (prepared for the Conference on Political Legitimacy in Islamic Asia, organized by ARI, NUS, April 25–26, 2005, 14).

24. Interview, Husnan Bey, editor-in-chief of *Majalah Pakar*, the PPP magazine, Jakarta, Indonesia, May 2006.

25. Barton "Theodicy, Theocracy and the Individual: The Challenge of Political and Jihadi Islamism to Pluralism and Liberal Democracy in Asia," 14.

26. Interview, Dr. Saiful Mujani, professor at UIN-Syarif Hidyatullah and research director of the Freedom Institute, Jakarta Indonesia, April 2006.

27. Ibid.

28. Ibid.

29. Interview, Hj.Yoyoh Yusroh, member of Commission 8 of the DPR for the Prosperous Justice Party, Jakarta, Indonesia, April 2006.

30. Interview, Muhammad Kaththath, head of Hizbut Tahrir, Jakarta, Indonesia, April 2006.

31. Van Zorge, "Creeping *Sharia* ?" 10.

32. Ibid.

33. Ibid.

34. Interview, Doug Ramage, country representative, and Robin Bush, assistant country representative, The Asia Foundation, Jakarta, Indonesia, March 2006.

35. The law and order concern was brought up repeatedly in interviews with scholars, politicians, journalists, NGO leaders, and international NGO leaders in response to the question, what is the greatest challenge for Indonesia today?

36. Interview, Azyumardi Azra, professor of history and former rector, UIN Syarif Hidyatullah, Jakarta, Indonesia, March 2006.

37. International Crisis Group, "Indonesia: The Search for Peace in Maluku," *Asia Report*, no. 31 (February 8, 2002): 1.

38. Bertrand, Jacques, *Nationalism and Ethnic Conflict in Indonesia* (Cambridge: Cambridge University Press), 118; Van Klinken, Gerry, "The Maluku Wars: Bringing Society Back In," *Indonesia* 71 (2001): 18; International Crisis Group, "Indonesia: The Search for Peace in Maluku," 1; Azra, Azyumardi, "Communal Riots in Recent Indonesia," in *Indonesia, Islam and Democracy: Dynamics in a World Context* (Jakarta: Equinox Forthcoming, 2006), 87–88.

39. International Crisis Group, "Indonesia: The Search for Peace in Maluku," 1.
40. Van Klinken, "The Maluku Wars," 9.
41. Interview, Badrus Sholeh, a researcher on social conflicts at the Center for Peace Studies at the Institute for Social and Economic Research, Education and Information (LP3ES), Jakarta, Indonesia, March 2006.
42. Ibid., 3
43. Van Klinken, "The Maluku Wars," 9.
44. Bertrand, *Nationalism and Ethnic Conflict in Indonesia,* 126.
45. International Crisis Group, "Indonesia," 4.
46. Ibid., 5
47. Azca, Muhammad Najib, "Security Forces in Ambon: From the National to the Local," in *Violence in Between: Conflict and Security in Archipelagic Southeast Asia,* ed. Damien Kingsbury (Singapore: ISEAS, 2006), 241.
48. Interview, Endy Bayuni, editor-in-chief, *Jakarta Post,* Jakarta, Indonesia, March 2006; interview, Badrus Sholeh, March 2006; and Hefner, Robert, "Muslim Democrats and Islamist Violence," in *Remaking Muslim Politics,* ed. Robert Hefner (Princeton: Princeton University Press, 2005), 288.
49. Interview, Indonesian army general, Jakarta, Indonesia, May 2006.
50. Yunanto, Sri, "The Logic behind the Growth of Militant Islamic Movements," in *Militant Islamic Movements in Indonesia and Southeast Asia,* eds. S. Yunanto et al (Jakarta: Friedrich-Ebert Stiftung; Ridep Institute, 2003), 125.
51. Interview, Endy Bayuni, March 2006.
52. Bertrand, *Nationalism and Ethnic Conflict in Indonesia,* 132.
53. International Crisis Group, "Indonesia," 3.
54. Ibid, 1.
55. Interview, Azyumardi Azra, Rektor UIN Syarif Hidayatullah, Ciputat, Indonesia, March 2003.
56. Hefner, "Muslim Democrats and Islamist Violence," 288.
57. International Crisis Group, 13. Sidel, John. *Riots, Pogroms, Jihad* (Ithaca: Cornell University Press, 2006), 208.
58. International Crisis Group, "Indonesia," 13.
59. Bertrand, *Nationalism and Ethnic Conflict in Indonesia,* 133.
60. Ibid.
61. Ibid.
62. Sidel, *Riots, Pogroms, Jihad: Religious Violence in Indonesia,* 156.
63. Human Rights Watch, "Breakdown: Four Years of Communal Conflict in Central Sulawesi." Report 14, no 9, 2002, 2.
64. Aragon, Lorraine, "Communal Violence in Poso, Central Sulawesi: Where People Eat Fish and Fish Eat People," *Indonesia* 72 (October 2001): 48.
65. Sidel, *Riots, Pogroms, Jihad,* 62, and Aragon "Communal Violence in Poso, Central Sulawesi: Where People Eat Fish and Fish Eat People," 49.
66. Sidel, *Riots, Pogroms, Jihad,* 162.
67. Interview, Badrus Sholeh, researcher on social conflicts at the Center for Peace Studies at the Institute for Social and Economic Research, Education and Information (LP3ES), Jakarta, Indonesia, February 2006.

68. Interview, regional representative from Central Sulawesi, Jakarta, Indonesia, March 2006.
69. Human Rights Watch, "Breakdown: Four Years of Communal Conflict in Central Sulawesi," 2.
70. Ibid., 41.
71. Ibid., 11.
72. International Crisis Group, "Indonesia Backgrounder: Jihad in Central Sulawesi." *ICG Asia Report,* no. 74 (February 3, 2004): 2.
73. International Crisis Group, "Jihad di Indonesia: Poso di Ujung Tanduk". *Asia Report,* no. 127 (November 24, 2007): 3.
74. Ibid., 30.
75. Rabasa and Haseman, *The Military and Democracy in Indonesia: Challenges, Politics and Power,* 95.
76. Interview, Central Sulawesi expert, international NGO, Jakarta, Indonesia, March 2006.
77. Interview, Central Sulawesi observer, international NGO, Jakarta, Indonesia, March 2006, "Indonesia Flashpoints: Sulawesi, http://news.bbc.co.uk/2/hi/asia-pacific/3812737.stm (June 28, 2004), and "Another Killed in Poso Blast," *Jakarta Post,* September 10, 2006.
78. International Crisis Group, "Indonesia: Tackling Radicalism in Poso," *Asia Policy Briefing,* no. 75 (January 22, 2008): 1.
79. Ibid.
80. Ibid.
81. Ibid.
82. Ibid.
83. International Crisis Group, "Indonesia: Rethinking Internal Security Strategy," *Asia Report,* no. 90 (December 20, 2004): 7.
84. "Clamping Down on Cults," *Van Zorge Report* X/1 (January 2008): 1.
85. International Crisis Group, "Indonesia: implications of the Ahmadiyah Decree," *Asia Briefing,* no. 78 (July 7, 2008): 5.
86. Ibid.
87. Ibid.
88. Indraswari, "Numbers Speak in Inter-Religious Relations," *Jakarta Post,* January 22, 2008.
89. "Four Arrested in Attack on Ahmadiyah," *Jakarta Post,* Jakarta, Malang, Semarang, February 7, 2006, and Suwarni, Yuli Tri, "W. Java Police Back Closure of Churches," *Jakarta Post,* February 26, 2006.
90. International Crisis Group, "Indonesia: Implications for the Ahmadiyah Decree," 3, and Sufa, Theresia, "Thousands Besiege Ahmadiyah Complex," *Jakarta Post,* July 16, 2005.
91. Ibid.
92. Sufa, Theresia, "Bogor Disperses Ahmadiyah, Sends Followers Home. *Jakarta Post,* July 17, 2005, and Suryana, A'an, "Ahmadiyah Fighs Back—In a Civilized Way," *Jakarta Post,* September 30, 2005.
93. "Cianjur 'bans' Ahmadiyah," *Jakarta Post,* September 29, 2005.

94. "Ahmadiyah Can Worship, Kalla Says," *Jakarta Post,* June 11, 2008.

95. Interview, Khoirul Roes Soetardjo, chairman of the Islamic Defender's Front (FPI) Solo area and secretary general of the Islamic Paramilitary Group (Laskar Umat Islam), Solo, Indonesia, July 2008.

96. International Crisis Group, "Indonesia: Implications for the Ahmadiyah Decree," 8.

97. "Anti-Ahmadiyah Campaign Escalating," *Jakarta Post,* June 21, 2008.

98. International Crisis Group, "Indonesia: Implications for the Ahmadiyah Decree," 8.

99. Khouw, Ida Indawati, "Guntur Refuses to Belong to the Silent Majority," *Jakarta Post,* November 2, 2008.

100. International Crisis Group, "Indonesia: Implications for the Ahmadiyah Decree," 14.

101. Ibid.

102. Ibid. ICG notes that the survey was conducted over telephone, which indicates that the respondents were members of the middle class.

103. Interview, Azyumardi Azra, professor of history and former Rektor UIN Syarif Hidayatullah, Ciputat, Indonesia, March 2003.

104. Ibid.

105. Interview, Khoirul Roes Soetardjo, July 2008.

106. United Nations Development Program-Bappenas-Indonesian Bureau of Statistics, "Towards a New Consensus: Democracy and Human Development in Indonesia," *Indonesia Human Development Report 2001,* 11Ja.

107. Perdana, Ari, "Poverty Alleviation and Social Insurance Policy: Past Lessons and Future Challenges," *The Indonesian Quarterly* 32, no. 3 (2004): 269.

108. "Making the New Indonesia Work for the Poor." *The World Bank.* Jakarta (2006), 17

109. *Social Safety New: Providing Hope to Indonesia's Underprivileged.* Jakarta: Badan Perencanaan Pembangunan Nasional (BAPPENAS) (2004), 14, and Schwarz, Adam, *A Nation in Waiting: Indonesia's Search for Stability* (NSW: Allen & Unwin, 2004), 409.

110. Perdana, Ari, "Poverty Alleviation and Social Insurance Policy: Past Lessons and Future Challenges," 270.

111. Ibid.

112. Hendytio, Medelina, "The State's Role in Social Development," *The Indonesian Quarterly* 32, no. 3 (2004): 293.

113. Sawitri, Adisti Sukma, "Government Told to Fix Health Care Scheme," *Jakarta Post,* September 21, 2007.

114. Ibid.

115. Interview, Kevin O'Rourke, author of *Reformasi,* Jakarta, Indonesia, April 2006.

116. Interview, Dr. Din Syamsuddin, chairman of Muhammadiyah, Jakarta, Indonesia, March 2003.

117. *Hasil-Hasil Muktamar XXX Nahdlatul Ulama* 21–26 November 1999, Pondok Pesantren Hidayatul Mubtadi'in Lirboyo Kediri Jawa Timur. P55 (results of

the 30th NU Congress November 21–26 1999, Pesantren Hidaytul Pesantren Hidayatul Mubtadi'in, Kediri Jawa Timur) 55.

118. Interview, Syafi'i Ma'arif, chairman of Muhammadiyah from 1999 to 2004, on the phone from West Sumatra, July 2008.

119. Interview, Rachmat, leader of Al-Islam pesantren, Solo, Central Java, Indonesia, May 2006.

120. Human Rights Watch, "Breakdown," 33.

121. Schwarz, *A Nation in Waiting: Indonesia's Search for Stability,* 409.

122. Van Zorge, Heffernan, and Associates, "Grade Point Average," *Van Zorge Report on Indonesia"* VIII/18 (July 12, 2006): 6.

123. The Indonesian Constitution states, "The state should allocate a minimum of 20 percent from the national budget and regional budget to education expenditures" (Article 31–34). In 2002, the Indonesian Constitution was amended to say that "the state prioritizes a budget for education of at least 20 percent from the national budget and regional budgets to fulfill the needs of providing national education."

124. "Indikator Pendidikan di Indonesia 2006/2007." *Departemen Pendidikan Nasional Badan Penelitian dan Pengembagan Pusat Statistik Pendidikan* (2007), 15.

125. "EFA Mid Decade Assessment Indonesia." EFA Secretariat, Ministry of National Education, Republic of Indonesia (2007), 71.

126. Ibid, 73., Kepulaun Bangka Belitung, Sulawesi Barat, Irian Jaya Barat, Gorontalo, Papua, and Nusa Tenggara Timur.

127. Khalik, Abdul, "State Still Fails to Provide Free Basic Education," *Jakarta Post,* July 17, 2005.

128. Ibid.

129. "EFA Mid Decade Assessment Indonesia," 73.

130. Mujani, Saiful, "Macro Condition, Policy and Electoral Attitudes on the Eve of the 2009 Election: Public Opinion Trends."

131. Yunanto, Sri, and Badrudin, Harun, "Terminology, History and Categorization," in *Islamic Education in South and Southeast Asia: Diversity, Problems and Strategy,* ed. Sri Yunanto (Jakarta: The Ridep Institute, 2006), 30.

132. Suparto, "Reforming *Pesantren:* While Reform of Islamic Education is Necessary, Secularization is Not," *Inside Indonesia* (2004): 1.

133. Interview, Jahja Umar, director general of Islamic Education, Ministry of Religious Affairs, Jakarta, Indonesia, May 2006.

134. Interview, Kyai Hj. Mutasim Billah, leader of Pesantren Sunan Pandanaran, Jakarta, Indonesia, Bahasa Indonesia, April 2006.

135. Ibid.

136. Interview, two teachers from Al-Mujihideen *pesantren,* Solo, Indonesia, May 2006, and interview, Wahyuddin, head of the Al-Mu'mim-Ngruki *pesantren,* Ngruki village, Solo, Indonesia, May 2006.

137. Interview, Ali Usman, head of the Ngruki Alumni Network, Solo, Indonesia, Bahasa Indonesia, May 2006.

138. Interview, Badrus Sholeh, researcher on social conflicts at the Center for Peace Studies at the Institute for Social and Economic Research, Education and Information (LP3ES), Jakarta, Indonesia, May 2006.
139. Barton, Greg. *Jemmah Islamiyah: Radical Islamism in Indonesia* (Singapore: Ridge Books, 2005), 55, Conboy, Ken. *The Second Front: Inside Asia's Most Dangerous Terrorist Network* (Jakarta: Equinox, 2006), 99. Afghan veterans include Hambali, the former head of Mantiqi 1, comprising Malaysia and Singapore; Ali Gufron (alias Muklas), subsequent head of Mantiqi 1; Fathur Rahman al-Ghozi, mastermind behind the Philippine Embassy bombing; and Imam Samudra, sentenced to death for his role in the 2002 Bali bombing, among many others.
140. Conboy, *The Second Front: Inside Asia's Most Dangerous Terrorist Network*, 95.
141. Interview, Nasir Abas, former head of Mantiqi 3, Jakarta, Indonesia, March 2006. Mantiqis are regions. There are four mantiqis: Malaysia and Singapore are Mantiqi 1, the fund-raising region; Sumatra and Java are Mantiqi 2, the recruiting region; Mantiqi 3 is Eastern Malaysia, Sulawesi, and the Southern Philippines, the training region; Mantiqi 4, Australia and Papua, never became viable as an administrative unit.
142. Ibid.
143. Conboy, *The Second Front*, 110.
144. "Indonesia: Jemaah Islamiyah's Current Status," *International Crisis Group Asia Briefing*, no.63, May 3, 2007, 1.
145. Interview, Bahtiar Effendy, professor of political science at the UIN Syarif Hidayatullah, Ciputat, Indonesia, April 2006.
146. "Two Years of Party Performance: A Public Evaluation." Lembaga Survey Indonesia (LSI) National Survey Findings, March 2006.

## Chapter 5

1. Hussein, Syed Ahmad, "Muslim Politics and the Discourse on Democracy," in *Democracy in Malaysia: Discourse and Practices*, eds. Francis Loh Kok Wah and Khoo Boo Tiek (NSW: Curzon, 2002), 75.
2. Interview, Dr. Chandra Muzaffar, head of JUST, former leader of Keadilan, JUST headquarters, Kuala Lumpur, Malaysia, February 2006.
3. Interview, Professor Dato Shamsul Amri Bahruddin, National University of Malaysia (UKM), Bangi, Malaysia, January 2006.
4. Interview, Datuk Shahrir Samad, backbencher in UMNO, Kuala Lumpur, Malaysia, February 2006.
5. Interview, Shahran Kasim, former secretary general of ABIM, ABIM headquarters, Gombak, Malaysia, February 2006, and Shamsul, AB, "Identity Construction, Nation Formation and Islamic Revivalism in Malaysia," in *Islam in the Era of Nation States*, eds: Robert Hefner and Patricia Horavitch (Honolulu: Hawaii University Press, 1997), 212.
6. Ibid.

7. Camroux, David, "State Responses to Islamic Resurgence in Malaysia: Accommodation, Cooptation and Confrontation," *Asian Survey* 36, no. 9 (1996): 859.

8. Nasr, Seyyed Vali Reza, *Islamic Leviathan* (Oxford: Oxford University Press, 2001), 125.

   Two nationwide committees were formed to guide Islamic policy making: *Badan Perundingan Islam* (Islamic Consultative Board), to recommend Islamic Policies, and *Lembaga Bersama Penyelarasan Kegiatan Islam-Malaysia* (Joint Committee on Management and Implementation of Islamic Activities-Malaysia), to monitor implementation of all decisions and programs that the government had agreed to establish according to Islamic tenets. New national-level committees were formed to contend with various aspects of Islamization: National Council for Islamic Affairs, Board for the Promotion of Muslim Welfare-Malaysia, Consultative Council, National Board for the Implementation of Civil and Sharia Laws-Malaysia, and Advisory Board for Islamic Education and Curriculum.

9. Compiled from Mutalib, Hussin, *Islam and Ethnicity in Malay Politics* (Oxford: Oxford University Press, 1990), 106–141; Nasr, *Islamic Leviathan,* 126; Faruqi, Shahad Saleem, "The Malaysian Constitution, the Islamic State and the Hudud Laws," in *Islam in Southeast Asia: Political, Social and Strategic Challenges for the 21st Century,* eds. KS Nathan and Mohammad Hashim Kamali (Singapore: ISEAS, 2005), 260–263; Nair, Shanti, *Islam in Malay Foreign Policy* (New York: Routledge, 1997), 101; and Riddell, Peter, "Islamization, Civil Society and Religious Minorities in Malaysia," in *Islam in Southeast Asia,* 165.

10. Milne, RS, and Diane Mauzy, "The Mahathir Administration in Malaysia: Discipline through Islam," *Pacific Affairs* 56, no. 4. (1983–1984): 637.

11. Interview, Shahran Kasim, February 2006.

12. Ibid.

13. Camroux, "State Responses to Islamic Resurgence in Malaysia: Accommodation, Cooptation and Confrontation," 859.

14. Interview, Shahran Kasim, February 2006.

15. Interview, Yusri Mohamad, president of ABIM, ABIM headquarters, Gombak, Malaysia, February 2006.

16. Interview, Professor Noraini Othman and Professor Clive Kessler, Kuala Lumpur, Malaysia, January 2006.

17. Interview, Professor Dato Shamsul Amri Bahruddin, National University of Malaysia (UKM), Bangi, Malaysia, January 2006.

18. Ibid.

19. Abdullah, Kamarulnizam, *The Politics of Islam in Contemporary Malaysia* (Bangi: Penerbit Universiti Kebangsaan Malaysia, 2003), 133.

20. Interview, PAS leader, Kuala Lumpur, Malaysia, February 2006.

21. Ibid. Interview, PAS party leader, Kelantan, Kota Bahru, Malaysia, February 2006.

22. Interview, Dr. Chandra Muzaffar, head of JUST, former leader of Keadilan, JUST headquarters, Kuala Lumpur, Malaysia, February 2006.

23. Interview, Dr. Noraini Othman, professor of sociology and religion at the Universitas Kebangsaan Malaysia, and Dr. Clive Kessler, professor emeritus of sociology and anthropology at New South Wales University, Kuala Lumpur, Malaysia, February 2006.

24. Interview, Dzulkielfy Ahmad, member of parliament for Kuala Selanghor and former head of PAS research wing, Kuala Lumpur, Malaysia, February 2006.

25. Ibid.

26. Interview, Dr. Chandra Muzaffar, February 2006.

27. Interview, Zaid Kamaruddin, president of Jemmah Islah Malaysia, Kuala Lumpur, Malaysia, February 2006.

28. Ibid. Interview, PAS leader, February 2006.

29. Interview, Zainah Anwar, executive director, Sisters in Islam, Petaling Jaya, Malaysia, February 2006.

30. Ibid.

31. Ibid.

32. Ibid.

33. Ibid.

34. Ibid.

35. Interview, Professor Dato Shamsul Amri Baharuddin, January 2006.

36. Crouch, Harold, *Government and Society in Malaysia* (New South Wales: Talisman, 1996), 76.

37. Professor Dato Osman Bakar, ISTAC, Kuala Lumpur, Malaysia, January 2006.

38. Statistics compiled from Crouch, Harold, *Government and Politics of Malaysia* (Singapore: Talisman, 1996), 75; Ung-Ho Chin, James, "Malaysia: The Barisan Nasional Supremacy," in *How Asia Votes,* eds. John Fuh-Sheng Hsieh and David Newman (Washington, D.C.: CQ Press), 226; Loh, Francis, "Understanding the 2004 Election Results: Looking beyond the Pak Lah Factor," *Aliran Monthly* 3 (2004); Koshy, Shaila, "BN loses 12 percentage points in the popular vote," *Malaysia Star,* March 11, 2008. *In 1974, PAS was part of the BN coalition. It was expelled in 1977. **Semangat 46 was an UMNO faction that separated and formed its own faction in 1987, contested the 1990 and 1995 elections, and rejoined UMNO in 1998. ***DAP is a Chinese party. Whereas the Malaysian Chinese Association joined the BN coalition, DAP has stayed in the opposition.

39. Compiled from Crouch, *Government and Society of Malaysia,* 75; Ung-Ho Chin, James, "Malaysia: The Barisan Nasional Supremacy,", 226; "Election Results," *Malaysia Star;* and "Malaysia Decides 2008," *Malaysia Star,* March 10, 2008, http//thestar.com.my/election/story.asp?file=/2008/3/11/election 20 08/20080311150101&sec=election 2008 (accessed on November 25, 2008).

40. Abuza, Zachary, *Militant Islam in Southeast Asia: Crucible of Terror* (Boulder: Lynne Rienner, 2003), 57.

41. Ibid., 55.

42. Liow, Joseph, "Exigency or Expediency? Contextualizing Political Islam and the PAS challenge in Malaysian Politics," *Third World Quarterly* 25, no. 2 (2004): 368.

43. Martinez, Patricia, "Mahathir, Islam and the New Malay Dilemma," in *Mahathir's Administration Performance and Crisis in Governance,* eds. Ho Khai Leong and James Chin (Singapore: Times Books International, 2001), 243.

44. Ibid.

45. Ibid.

46. Ibid.

47. Ibid.

48. Nair, *Islam in Malaysia's Foreign Policy,* 27.

49. Ibid.

50. Welsh, Bridget, "Real Change? Elections in the Reformasi Era," in *The State of Malaysia: Ethnicity, Equity and Reform,* ed. Edmund Terence Gomez (New York: Routledge/Curzon, 2004), 133.

51. Tiek, Khoo Boo, *Beyond Mahathir: Malaysian Politics and its Discontents* (London: Zed Books, 2003), 82.

52. "Repressive Laws," *Human Rights Watch,* http:/www.hrw.org/campaigns/malaysia/2000/laws.htm (accessed on September 10, 2006).

53. Ibid.

54. Ibid.

55. As quoted in Crouch, *Government and Society in Malaysia,* 79.

56. Ibid., 93.

57. Milne and Mauzy, "The Mahathir Administration in Malaysia: Discipline through Islam," 87.

58. Barraclough, Simon. "The Dynamics of Coercion in the Malaysian Political Process," *Modern Asian Studies* 19, no.4 (1985): 800.

59. Ibid.

60. Interview, Dr. Noraini Othman and Dr. Clive Kessler, Kuala Lumpur, Malaysia, January 2006.

61. Barraclough, "The Dynamics of Coercion in the Malaysian Political Process," 800.

62. Hilley, John, *Malaysia: Mahathirism, Hegemony and the New Opposition* (London: Zed Books, 2001), 171, and Kamarudin, Raja Petra, "Someone is Watching," *Malaysia Today,* March 6, 2006, www.malaysia-today.net/loonyMY/2006/03/someone-is-watching (accessed on September 8, 2006).

63. Ibid.

64. Nair, *Islam in Malaysia's Foreign Policy,* 30.

65. Hussein, Syed Ahmad, "Muslim Politics and the Discourse on Democracy," in *Democracy in Malaysia,* eds. Francis Lok Kok Wah and Khoo Boo Tiek (New South Wales: Routledge/Curzon, 2002), 92.

66. Nair, *Islam in Malaysia's Foreign Policy,* 150.

67. Following the Islamic revolution in Iran, Malaysian Islamists adopted the Iranian model as the possible Islamic state system for Malaysia, given that Iran permits non-Muslims to practice their faith and is far more tolerant of pluralism compared with the Wahabi model.

68. Milne and Mauzy, "The Mahathir Administration in Malaysia," 87.
69. Abdullah, *The Politics of Islam in Contemporary Malaysia*, 170–171.
70. Ibid, 172.
71. Crouch 1996, 81.
72. Ibid.
73. Ibid.
74. Ten members of the Keadilan party would also be imprisoned under the ISA in April 2001.
75. "Aliran's ISA Watch," *Aliran Online*, http://www.aliran.com/oldsite/monthly/2001/3e.htm (accessed on March 15, 2009). In 2005, of the remaining 28 people detained under the ISA, 22 were currency counterfeiters, while 13 were imprisoned for document falsification. In 2006, these numbers were similar, with 22 detained for currency counterfeiting and 14 for document falsification.
76. Ibid. In December 2008, another ten people were detained under the ISA for document falsification.
77. Abdullah, *The Politics of Islam in Contemporary Malaysia*, 197.
78. Ibid.
79. Milne and Mauzy, "The Mahathir Administration in Malaysia," 87.
80. Abdullah, *The Politics of Islam in Contemporary Malaysia*, 199.
81. Interview, Dr. Noraini Othman and Dr. Clive Kessler, January 2006.
82. Interview, professor at University of Malaya, Kelantan Campus, Kota Bahru, Kelantan, Malaysia, February 2006.
83. Ibid.
84. Interview, Dr. Noraini Othman and Dr. Clive Kessler, January 2006.
85. "Death Penalty for Three Malaysians," *BBC News,* December, 28 2001, http://news.bbc.co.uk/2/hi/asia-pacific/1731503.stm (accessed on September 22, 2006).
86. Crisp, Penny, and Santha, Oorjitham, "How Can This Happen? Cults are Nothing New, but Raids on the Army Demand Some Answers," *Asiaweek* 26, no. 28 (July 21, 2000).
87. Ibid.
88. Shome, Anthony, *Malay Political Leadership* (New York: Routledge/Curzon, 2002), 193.
89. "Death Penalty for Three Malaysians," *BBC News,* December 28, 2001.
90. Interview, Tan Sri Ahmad Sarji, head of IKIM, Kuala Lumpur, Malaysia, February 2006.
91. Abuza, *Militant Islam in Southeast Asia: Crucible of Terror,* 50.
92. Interview, Dr. Patricia Martinez, senior research fellow for religion and culture, head of intercultural studies, Asia-Europe Institute, University of Malaya, Petaling Jaya, Malaysia, January 2006.
93. Nasr, *Islamic Leviathan,* 71.
94. Ibid.
95. Abdullah, *The Politics of Islam in Contemporary Malaysia*, 57, and Shamsul, "Identity Construction, Nation Formation and Islamic Revivalism in Malaysia," 252.

96. Shamsul, "Identity Construction, Nation Formation and Islamic Revivalism in Malaysia," 253.
97. Ibid.
98. Interview, Tan Sri Ahmad Sarji, February 2006.
99. Interview, Samsuddin Bin Mat Daud, the secretary of legislative affairs for PAS-Kelantan, Kota Bahru, Kelantan, Malaysia, February 2006.
100. Interview, official from the Ministry of Women, Youth, and Sports; name withheld upon request. Kota Bahru, Kelantan, February 2006.
101. Interview, Saifuddin Mohamed Arrif, secretary general-PERKIM, Kuala Lumpur, Malaysia, January 2006.
102. Ibid.
103. Ibid. Funding also comes from zakat donations.
104. Interview, Zaid Kamaruddin, president of Jemmah Islah Malaysia, Kuala Lumpur, Malaysia, February 2006.
105. Abdullah, *The Politics of Islam in Contemporary Malaysia*, 96.
106. Interview, Shahran Kasim, former secretary general of ABIM, ABIM headquarters, Gombak, Malaysia, February 2006.
107. Ibid.
108. Abdullah, *The Politics of Islam in Contemporary Malaysia*, 109.
109. Ibid.
110. Nasr, *Islamic Leviathan,* 84.
111. Daud, Wan Mohd Nor Wan, *The Concept of Knowledge in Islam and its Implications for Education in a Developing Country* (London: Mansell, 1989), 97.
112. Interview, Jagdeesh Gul, Ministry of Education, Putra Jaya, Malaysia, February 2006.
113. Hamid, Ahmad Fauzi Abdul, "The Strategy of Islamic Education in Malaysia: An Islamic Movement's Experience," in *Islamic Education in South and Southeast Asia,* ed. S. Yunanto et al (Jakarta: Ridep Institute, 2005), 173.
114. Interview, Jagdeesh Gul, February 2006.
115. Interview, Abdul Halim Bin Mohd Naam, assistant director, Curriculum Division, Department of Islam and Moral Education, JAPIM, Kuala Lumpur, Malaysia, February 2006.
116. Hamid, "The Strategy of Islamic Education in Malaysia," 175.
117. Hashim, Rosnani, *Educational Dualism in Malaysia: Implications for Theory and Practice* (South-East Asian Social Science Monographs) (Oxford: Oxford University Press, 1996), 8.
118. Interview, Dr. Rosnani Hashim, professor at the International Islamic University of Malaysia, Gombak, Malaysia, February 2006.
119. Abuza, *Militant Islam in Southeast Asia,* 57.
120. Interview, PAS official in the Ministry of Education, Kelantan, February 2006. The PAS-run state administration allocates 40 million ringgit to cover the remaining expenses.
121. Ibid.
122. Interview, Abdul Halim Bin Mohd Naam, February 2006.

123. Interview, Professor Dato Osman Bakar, January 2006.
124. Interview, Zaid Kamaruddin, February 2006.
125. Abdullah, *The Politics of Islam in Contemporary Malaysia*, 95.
126. Ibid.
127. Ibid, 108.
128. Ibid.
129. Interview, Dr. Rosnani Hashim, February 2006.
130. Ibid.
131. Interview, Professor Dato Osman Bakar, January 2006.
132. Interview, Abdul Halim Bin Mohd Naam, February 2006.
133. Hashim, *Educational Dualism in Malaysia: Implications for Theory and Practice*, 221.
134. Ibid., 223.
135. Ibid.
136. Interview, retired senior government official, Putra Jaya, Malaysia, February 2006; interview, Dr. Rosnani Hashim, February 2006; and interview, PAS official in the Ministry of Education, Feburary 2006.
137. Interview, Abdul Halim Bin Mohd Naam, February 2006.
138. Hamid, Ahmad Fauzi Abdul, "Islamic Doctrine and Violence: The Malaysian Case" (presented at the Conference on "Anatomy of Religious Conflict in South and Southeast Asia," organized by the Institute of Defense and Strategic Studies (IDSS), Nanyang Technological University (NTU), Singapore, May 3–4, 2005, 174).
139. Interview, Abdul Halim Bin Mohd Naam, February 2006.
140. Ibid Nik Adli Nik Aziz is the son of Kelantan's menteri besar, Nik Aziz Nik Mat. Many PAS officials whom I interviewed in Kelantan believed that the KMM was an antigovernment hoax to discredit PAS. However, scholars of Islamic radicalism and an ex-member of Jemmah Islamiyah refute this claim.
141. Abuza, Zachary, "Al Qaeda in Southeast Asia: Exploring the Linkages," in *After Bali: The Threat of Terrorism in SE Asia*," eds. Kumar Ramakrisna and See Seng Tan (Singapore: Institute of Defense and Strategic Studies, 2003), 143.
142. Interview, retired senior government official, February 2006.
143. Interview, Nasir Abas, former head of Mantiqi 3, Jemaah Islamiyah, Jakarta, Indonesia, March 2006.
144. Interview, PAS official, PAS headquarters, Kota Bahru, Kelantan, Malaysia, February 2006.
145. Amnesty International. "Malaysia: Amnesty International Human Rights Concerns," *Malaysia Report* (January–December 2005).

## Chapter 6

1. Byman, Daniel, and Green, Jerrold, *Political Violence and Stability in the States of the Northern Persian Gulf* (Arlington: Rand Institute, 1999a), 22.
2. Brown, Nathan, "What's at Stake in Kuwait's Parliamentary Elections." *Carnegie Endowment for International Peace Web Commentary*, May 2008, 1,

http://carnegieendowment.org/files/brown_kuwait_elections_FAQ_final.pdf (accessed on December 2, 2008).

3. Brown, Nathan. "Pushing toward Party Politics: Kuwait's Islamic Constitution Movement." *Carnegie Endowment for International Peace Paper* no. 79, January 2007, 8.

4. Ibid., 2.

5. Brown, "What's at Stake in Kuwait's Parliamentary Elections," 2.

6. Brown, "Pushing toward Party Politics: Kuwait's Islamic Constitution Movement," 11–12.

7. Byman and Green, *Political Violence and Stability*, 22.

8. Ibid.

9. Ibid., 73.

10. Whitlock, Craig, and Coll, Steve, "Terrorism Tempers Shifts to Openness," *Washington Post*, April 18, 2005, A01.

11. Rahman. B, "Jihadi Terrorism: From Iraq to Kuwait." *South Asia Analysis Group*, New Delhi (paper no. 1261, February 21, 2005).

12. Ibid.

13. Al-Dekhayel, Abdulkarim, *Kuwait: Oil, State and Political Legitimation* (Ithaca: Ithaca Press, 2000), 17.

14. Ibid., 57.

15. Ibid.

16. Zengin, Eyup, and Askerov, Ali, "State Formation and Oil: Kuwait and Qatar," *Journal of Qafqaz University* no. 6 (Fall 2000): 47.

17. Brown, "Pushing toward Party Politics," 8.

18. Ibid.

19. Baakalini, Abdoo, Denoeux, Guiliana, and Springborg, Robert, *Legislative Politics in the Arab World: The Resurgence of Democratic Institutions* (Boulder: Lynne Rienner, 1999), 180.

20. Barrett, Raymond, "Kuwait Walks a Tightrope on Iraq," *Daily Star*, December 14, 2004.

21. "Fierce Gun Battle in Kuwait City," *BBCNEWS*, January 30, 2005, and Smith, Craig, "Threats and Responses: Anti-Terror Arrest. Kuwait Says a Senior Qaeda Member Has Confessed to Planning 2 Attacks in Yemen," *New York Times*, November 17, 2002.

22. Byman and Green, "The Enigma of Political Stability in the Persian Gulf Monarchies," *Middle East Review of International Affairs* 3, no. 3 (September 1999b): 18, 32.

23. Bahry, Louay, "The Socioeconomic Foundations of Shiite Opposition in Bahrain," *Mediterranean Quarterly* (Summer 2000): 133.

24. Lancaster, John, "The Two Worlds of Bahrain; The Shiite Majority Wants its Share of Sunni-Ruled Island's Prosperity," *Washington Post*, June 13, 1995, A15.

25. Bahry, Louay, "The Opposition in Bahrain: A Bellweather for the Gulf," *Middle East Policy* 5, no. 2 (1997): 44–45.

26. Ibid., 45.

27. Ibid.
28. Ibid., 52.
29. Peterson, J.E., "Bahrain's First Steps toward Reform under Amir Hamad," *Asian Affair* 33, no.2. (2002): 219.
30. Ibid., 220.
31. Ibid., 219.
32. Kaye, Dalia Dassa, Wehrey, Frederick, Grant, Audra, and Stahl, Dale, *More Freedom, Less Terror? Liberalization and Political Violence in the Arab World* (Arlington: Rand, 2008), xviii.
33. Ibid.
34. Terhalle, Maximillian, "Are the Shia Rising," *Middle East Policy Council* (2007): 73, and Gause, Gregory, "Bahrain Parliamentary Election Results: 25 November and 2 December 2006," *International Journal of Middle East Studies* 39 (2007): 171.
35. Kaye, Wehrey, Grant, and Stahl, *More Freedom, Less Terror?*, xix.
36. Byman and Green 1999a, 89.
37. Lawson, Fred. "Repertoires of Contention in Contemporary Bahrain," in *Islamic Activism: A Social Movement Theory Approach* (Bloomington: Indiana University Press 2004), 98.
38. Ibid., 100–101.
39. Yaphe, Judith, "Islamic Radicalism in the Arabian Peninsula: Growing Risks," *National Defense University Strategic Forum* no. 67 (1996): 2, and Darwish, Adel, "Rebellion in Bahrain," *Middle East Review of International Affairs* 1 no. 3 (1999): 2.
40. Lawson, "Repertoires of Contention in Contemporary Bahrain," 101.
41. Bahry "The Opposition in Bahrain," 45.
42. Lawson, "Repertoires of Contention in Contemporary Bahrain," 103.
43. Ibid.
44. Ehteshami, Anoushiravan. "Reform from Above: The Politics of Participation in the Oil Monarchies," *International Affairs* 79 no. 1 (2003): 61.
45. Boustany, Nora, "In Bahrain, Doubts about Reform," *Washington Post,* June 24, 2005, A28.
46. Byman and Green, "The Enigma of Political Stability in the Persian Gulf Monarchies," 12
47. Ibid.
48. Bahry, "The Opposition in Bahrain," 50.
49. Ibid.
50. Ibid, 51.
51. Bahry, "The Socioeconomic Foundations of Shiite Opposition in Bahrain," 136.
52. Bahry, "The Opposition in Bahrain," 54.
53. Ibid., 49.
54. Byman and Green, *Political Violence and Stability,* 88.
55. Aneja, Atul, "Six al Qaeda Suspects Detained in Bahrain," *The Hindu,* January 23, 2004.

56. Jahan, Rounaq. "Bangladesh in 2002: Imperiled Democracy," *Asian Survey* 43, no.1 (2003): 223, and Ganguly, Sumit, "The Rise of Islamist Militancy in Bangladesh," *United States Institute of Peace Special Report,* no. 171, August 2006, 1.

57. Fair, Christine, and Ganguly, Sumit, "Bangladesh on the Brink," *United States Institute of Peace. Reprinted from the Wall Street Journal,* 2007, www.usip.org/newsmedia/op_eds/2007/fair_wsj.html (accessed on December 4, 2008).

58. Ahmed, Anis, "Nearly 2,500 Apply to Contest the Bangladesh Election," *Reuters,* December 1, 2008.

59. Riaz, Ali, *God Willing: The Politics of Islamism in Bangladesh* (Lanham: Rowman and Littlefield, 2004), 45.

60. Ibid., 16, and "Bangladesh Today," *International Crisis Group Asia Report,* no.121 (October 23, 2006): 15.

61. Riaz, *God Willing,* 15.

62. Ahsan, Aayadul, "Inside Militant Groups-1: Trained in Foreign Lands, They Spread Inland," *Daily Star,* 5, no. 440 (August 21, 2005), 1.

63. Ganguly, "The Rise of Islamist Militancy in Bangladesh," 5.

64. Ibid.

65. Jahan, "Bangladesh in 2002: Imperiled Democracy," 223.

66. Jahan, Rounaq, "Bangladesh in 2003: Vibrant Democracy or Destructive Politics," *Asian Survey* 44, no. 1 (2004): 56.

67. Ibid.

68. "Bangladesh Today," *International Crisis Group Asia Report,* 9.

69. Ganguly, "The Rise of Islamist Militancy in Bangladesh," 2.

70. Ibid., 6.

71. Riaz, *God Willing,* 89–90.

72. Lintner, Bertil, "Is Religious Extremism on the Rise in Bangladesh," *Jane's Intelligence Review,* May 2002.

73. Ibid., 2.

74. Ibid., 1.

75. Ahsan, "Inside Militant Groups-1: Trained in Foreign Lands, They Spread Inland," 1.

76. Ahsan, Aayadul, "Inside the Militant Groups-6 Agency Advice for Ban on Them Ignored Since 2003," *Daily Star,* 5, no. 445 (August 26, 2005), 1.

77. Ganguly, "The Rise of Islamist Militancy in Bangladesh," 7.

78. Riaz, Ali, "Bangladesh in 2004: The Politics of Vengeance and the Erosion of Democracy," *Asian Survey* 45, no.1 (2005): 113, and Griswold, Eliza, "The Next Islamist Revolution?" *New York Times,* January 23, 2005.

79. Jahan, Rounaq, "Bangladesh in 2003: Vibrant Democracy or Destructive Politics." p59.

80. Rashid, Harun ur, "The Rise of Islamic Extremism in Bangladesh," *Daily Star,* 5, no. 271 (March 2, 2005).

81. Riaz, Ali, *Islamist Militancy in Bangladesh: A Complex Web* (London: Routledge, 2008), 1.

82. Ganguly, "The Rise of Islamist Militancy in Bangladesh," 2.

83. Rashid, "The Rise of Islamic Extremism in Bangladesh." These are Harkatul Jihad, Jama'atul Mujihideen Bangladesh, Jagrata Muslim Janata Bangladesh, Islami Biplobi Parishad, Shahadat al Hiqma, Hizbut Towhid, Hizb-ut-Tahrir, Ahle Hadith Andolon, Towhidi Janata, Biswa Islami Front, Juma'atul Sadat, al Jomiatul Islamia, Iqra Islami Jote, Allahr Dal, Al Khidmat Bahini, al Muhihid, Jama'ati Yahi Al Turag, Jihadi Party, Al Harkat al Islamia, al Mahfuz al Islami, Jama'atul Faladia, Shahadat-e-Nabuwat, Joish-e-MOstafa, Tahfize Haramaine Parshad, Hizbul Mojahedeen, Duranta Kafela, and Muslim Guerilla.
84. Ibid.
85. "Bangladesh Today," *International Crisis Group Asia Report,* 6.
86. Rashid, "The Rise of Islamic Extremism in Bangladesh."
87. Riaz, *God Willing,* 36.
88. UN Human Development Report Statistics. Country sheet, http://hdr.undp.org/statistics/data/countries.cfm?c=IDN, July 24, 2006.
89. Khan, Zillur, "Bangladesh in 1992: Dilemmas of Democratization," *Asian Survey* 33, no.2 (1994): 150.
90. Shehabuddin, Elora, "Bangladesh in 1998: Democracy on the Ground," *Asian Survey* 39, no.1 (1999): 187.
91. Ganguly, "The Rise of Islamist Militancy in Bangladesh," 5–6.
92. "Bangladesh Today," *International Crisis Group Asia Report,* 12.
93. Ibid., 14.
94. Rashid, "The Rise of Islamic Extremism in Bangladesh."
95. Riaz, *God Willing,* 125.
96. Hossian, Gollam, "Bangladesh in 1994: Democracy at Risk," *Asian Survey* 35, no. 2 (1995): 175.
97. Ibid.
98. Lintner, Bertil, "Bangladesh: Breeding Ground for Muslim Terror," *Asia Times,* September 21, 2002c.
99. Lintner, "Bangladesh," and Ganguly, "The Rise of Islamist Militancy in Bangladesh," 7.
100. Ibid.
101. Schwedler, Jillian, "The Islah Party in Yemen: Political Opportunities and Coalition Building in a Transitional Polity," in *Islamic Activism: A Social Movement Theory Approach,* ed. Quintan Wiktorowicz (Indianapolis: Indiana University Press, 2004), 214.
102. International Crisis Group, "Yemen: Coping with Terrorism and Violence in a Fragile State," *International Crisis Group Middle East Report,* no. 8 (January 2003): 4.
103. Schwedler, "The Islah Party in Yemen: Political Opportunities and Coalition Building in a Transitional Polity," 214–215.
104. International Crisis Group, "Yemen," 9.
105. Browers, Michaelle, "The Origins and Architects of Yemen's Joint Meeting Parties," *International Journal of Middle East Studies* 39 (2007): 565, and Johnsen, Gregory, "The Election Yemen Was Supposed to Have," *Middle East*

*Report Online,* October 3, 2006, 4, www.merip.org/mero/mero100306.htm (accessed on November 19, 2008).

106. International Crisis Group, "Yemen," ii.
107. Ibid.
108. Ibid., 1–2, and Weir, Shelagh, "A Clash of Fundamentalisms: Wahhabism in Yemen," *Middle East Report Online,* no. 204, 1995.
109. Carapico, Sheila, "Yemen and the Aden-Abayan Islamic Army," *Middle East Report Online,* October 18, 2000, http://www.merip.org/mero/mero101800. html (accessed on April 20, 2005), 1, and "Yemen: Coping with Terrorism and Violence in a Fragile State," 11–12.
110. Phillips, Sarah, "Foreboding about the Future in Yemen," *Middle East Report Online,* April 3, 2006, 6, www.merip.org/mero.mero040306.html (accessed on November 19, 2008).
111. Ibid.
112. Phillips, Sarah, "Cracks in the Yemeni System," *Middle East Report Online,* July 28, 2005, 2, http://www.merip.org/mero/mero072805.htm (accessed on November 19, 2008).
113. Ibid.
114. Ibid.
115. Carapico, "Yemen and the Aden-Abayan Islamic Army," 1.
116. Carapico, *Civil Society in Yemen: The Political Economy of Activism in Modern Arabia* (London: Cambridge University Press, 1998), 206.
117. Phillips, "Cracks in the Yemeni System," 2.
118. Phillips, "Foreboding about the Future in Yemen," 4.
119. Carapico, *Civil Society in Yemen,* 124.
120. Ibid., 206.
121. Johnsen, Gregory, "The Election Yemen Was Supposed to Have," *Middle East Report Online,* October 3, 2006, 7, www.merip.org/mero/mero100306.html (accessed on November 19, 2008).
122. Carapico, *Civil Society in Yemen,* 124.
123. Ibid..
124. Weir, "A Clash of Fundamentalisms: Wahhabism in Yemen," and Phillips "Foreboding about the Future in Yemen," 5.
125. Phillips, Cracks in the Yemeni System, 5.
126. Carapico, *Civil Society in Yemen,* 156.
127. Ibid., 157.
128. Ibid., 206.
129. Ibid., 194, and International Crisis Group, "Yemen," 11.
130. International Crisis Group, "Yemen," 11.
131. Ibid.
132. Ibid., 1.
133. Ibid.
134. Carapico, "Yemen and the Aden-Abayan Islamic Army," 1.
135. International Crisis Group, "Yemen," 10.

## Chapter 7

1. "Survey Indonesia: Time to Deliver," *The Economist,* December 9, 2004, http://www.economist.com/surveys/displayStory.cfm?story_id=3444238.
2. Interview, Dr. Azyumardi Azra, Rektor-UIN Syarif Hidayatullah, Ciputat, Indonesia, March 2006.
3. One should not underestimate the contributions that NU and Muhammadiyah, with a combined total of 70 million members, have made to Indonesian education and welfare provision. In their efforts, however, they support the state rather than supplant it. In the unique Indonesian case, NU and Muhammadiyah do not attempt to undermine state legitimacy, but instead coexist alongside it.
4. Interview, Dr. Noraini Othman, professor of sociology at the Universiti Kebangsaan Malaysia, and Dr. Clive Kessler, professor emeritus of sociology at the University of New South Wales, Kuala Lumpur, Malaysia, February 2006.
5. Ibid.

## Epilogue

1. "AK Party Sweeps Polls for a Third Single Term in Power," *Today's Zaman,* June 19, 2011, *http://www.todayszaman.com/newsDetail_getNewsById.action?load= detay&newsId=247804&link=247804;* "Turkish Elections See Highest Voter Turnout in Years," *Today's Zaman,* June 13, 2011, *http://www.todayszaman. com/newsDetail_getNewsById.action?load=detay&newsId=247165&link= 247165.*
2. Discussion with Quinn Mecham, Assistant Professor in the Department of Political Science at Middlebury College, July 13, 2011.
3. Hwang, Julie Chernov, and Mecham, Quinn, "Institutional Incentives and the Electoral Success of Islamist Parties: Explaining the Divergent Trajectories of the PKS in Indonesia and the AKP in Turkey," under review at *Studies in Comparative International Development.*
4. *Kekuatan Elektoral Partai-Partai Islam Menjelang Pemilu 2009,* Lembaga Survei Indonesia. PowerPoint presentation, Jakarta. September 2008; Mujani, Saiful, "Macrocondition, Policy, and Electoral Attitudes on the Eve of the 2009 Election: Public Opinion Trends," Jakarta, March 2009.
5. Ibid.
6. Ibid.
7. Meitzner, Marcus, "Indonesia in 2009: Electoral Contestation and Economic Resilience," *Asian Survey* 50, no. 1: 187.
8. Noorhaidi Hasan, "Islamist Party, Electoral Politics, and Da'wa Mobilization Among Youth: The Prosperous Justice Party in Indonesia," *RSIS Working Paper,* no. 184, October 22, 2009, 22.

9. Fealy, Greg, "Indonesia's Islamic Parties in Decline," *Inside Story,* May 11, 2009.

10. Ibid.

11. Meitzner, "Indonesia in 2009," 13.

12. Platzdash, Bernhard, *Islamism in Indonesia,* Singapore: ISEAS (2009): 49.

13. Hamayotsu, Kikue, "Beyond Faith and Identity: Mobilizing Islamic Youth in a Democratic Indonesia," *Pacific Review* (March 31, 2010):19.

14. Fealy, Greg, "Indonesia's Islamic Parties in Decline," *Inside Story,* May 11, 2009.

15. "Gus Dur's PKB Loses Legal Battle," *Jakarta Post,* July 24, 2010; Bagus BT Saragih, "New Parties Aim Big, Despite Tougher Rules, Competition," *Jakarta Post,* May 11, 2011; PKBI Yenny Wahid Ganti Nama Jadi PKBN," *Republika,* July 20, 2011.

16. PKS internal party data, sent by e-mail by Mardani Ali Sera, Deputy Secretary General of the PKS party.

17. Hamayotsu, "Beyond Faith and Identity," 12.

18. Internal PKS data from Mardani Ali Sera, Deputy Secretary General, PKS, sent January 14, 2010.

19. Fieldwork notes on the campaign trail with PKS candidates Anis Matta, Sarah Handayani, Zulkieflimansyah, and Yoyoh Yusroh, March 2009, in Banten, West Java, and South Sulawesi.

20. Interview with Mohammed Razikun, Head of the Campaign Winning Team, March 2009, Jakarta, Indonesia.

21. Greg, "Indonesia's Islamic Parties in Decline," *Inside Story,* May 11, 2009.

22. Ibid.

23. Christianto, Dicky, "House, Gov't to Discuss Elections Bill," *Jakarta Post,* July 19, 2011.

24. "Islamist Parties Will Remain Divided Despite New Law," *Jakarta Post,* April 16, 2011.

25. Kimura, Ehito, "Indonesia in 2010," *Asian Survey* 51, No. 1 (January/February 2011): 190.

26. "International Religious Freedom Report," *Bureau of Democracy, Human Rights and Labor.* 2010.

27. Kimura, "Indonesia in 2010," 190.

28. "Indonesia, Monitor Trials of Deadly Attack on Religious Minority," *Human Rights Watch,* June 16, 2011.

29. Kimura, "Indonesia in 2010," 190.

30. International Crisis Group, "Indonesia: 'Christianization' and Intolerance," *Asia Briefing,* Jakarta/Brussels, November 20, 2010, 1.

31. Kimura, "Indonesia in 2010," 190.

32. International Crisis Group, "Indonesia 'Christianization' and Intolerance," 2010, 1.

33. Ibid.

34. Ibid.

35. "Indonesian Jihadism: Small Groups, Big Plans," *International Crisis Group Asia Report, #204*. April 19, 2011, 2
36. Ibid.
37. Arnaz, Farouk, Nirmala, Ronna, and Pasandaran, Camelia, "Arrests Point to New Face of Terrorism," *Jakarta Globe,* April 23, 2011.
38. Ba'asyir was sentenced to 15 years in prison in June of 2011 on charges of inciting terrorism.
39. In June 2011, Abu Bakar Ba'asyir was convicted by an Indonesian court of inciting and funding acts of terrorism and sentenced to 15 years in prison.
40. Arnaz, Farouk, "Police Say Anti-Terror Program is Faulty," *Jakarta Globe,* June 27, 2011.
41. "Indonesia: Jihadi Surprise in Aceh," *International Crisis Group Asia Report,* #189, April 20, 2010.
42. *Malaysia Star Online* (2008), "'Malaysia 2008 General Election—Malaysia Decides'," 19 August. Website: http://thestar.com.my/election.
43. Ibid.
44. Weiss, Meredith L., "Edging Toward a New Politics in Malaysia," *Asian Survey* 49, no. 5 (2009): 750
45. Ibid., 752
46. Ibid.
47. Ibid., 753
48. Ibid.
49. Conversation with Joseph Chinyong Liow, author of *Piety and Politics: Islamism in Contemporary Malaysia. July 15, 2011.*
50. It is important to note that Allah is the Arabic word for God, a term that actually predates Islam, and Christians throughout the Arab world commonly refer to God as Allah.
51. Ibid.
52. Liow, Joseph Chinyong, "No God but God. Malaysia's 'Allah'" Controversy," *Foreign Affairs,* February 10, 2010.
53. Wong Chin Huat, "No Compromise with Terrorism," *Malaysiakini,* January 11, 2010.
54. "Hadi Visits Church, Declares Arson Attacks 'Un-Islamic,'" *Malaysiakini,* January 9, 2010.
55. Ibid.
56. "PAS Backs Caning, Rejects Bar's Premise," *Malaysiakini,* August 26, 2009. For example, in August 2009, PAS leaders voiced their support for the Pahang Syariah High Court's decision to cane model, Kartika Sari Dewi Shukarno for consuming beer in a hotel lounge and in 2011, they called for the banning of entertainment during Ramadan in the Malay heartland state of Kedah.
57. Welsh, Bridget, "Five Promising Ideas from PAS' New Line-Up," *Malaysiakini,* June 4, 2011.
58. Aidila Razak, "Mat Sabu is PAS new deputy president," *Malaysiakini,* June 4, 2011.

59. Interview, Hatta Ramli, PAS Treasurer, August 2008, PAS Party Headquarters, Kuala Lumpur.
60. See www.bersih.org.
61. Conversation with Kian Ming Ong, scholar and observer of Malaysian politics. July 13, 2011.
62. See www.bersih.org.
63. "Joint Memorandum to Sukaham by BERSIH 2.0 and Suaram on Excessive Police Abuse of Powers During Perhimpunan BERSIH 2.0 on 9 July 2011," http://bersih.org/?p=4456#more-4456.
64. Kuek Ser Kuang Keng, "Bersih 2.0 Hails Rally as Success," *Malaysiakini,* July 9, 2011; Conversation with Kian Ming Ong, scholar and observer of Malaysian politics, July 13, 2011.
65. Krishnamoothy, "Marina ticks off gov't in its handling of Bersih," *Malaysiakini,* July 16, 2011.
66. Indonesia has no parties that self-define as multiethnic, although most parties in Indonesia are multiethnic. The reference to multiethnic parties is specific to Malaysia. PKS partners with Christian parties in majority Christian areas.

# Bibliography

Abas, Nasir. *Membongkar Jamaah Islamiyah: Pengakuan Mantan Anggota JI.* Jakarta: Grafindo, 2005.

Abdullah, Kamarulnizam. *The Politics of Islam in Contemporary Malaysia.* Bangi: Penerbit Universiti Kebangsaan Malaysia, 2003.

Abootalebi, Ali Reza. *Islam and Democracy: State-Society Relations in Developing Countries 1980–1994.* New York: Garland, 2000.

———. "Islam, Islamists and Democracy." *Middle East Review of International Affairs* 3i1 (1999).

———. "Civil Society, Democracy and the Middle East." *Middle East Review of International Affairs* 2il, no. 1 (1998).

Abou el Fadl, Khaled. *Islam and the Challenge of Democracy.* Princeton: Princeton University Press, 2004.

———. *The Place of Tolerance in Islam.* Boston: Beacon Press, 2002.

Abuza, Zachary. *Militant Islam in Southeast Asia: Crucible of Terror.* Boulder: Lynne Rienner, 2003.

Abu Bakar, Mohamad. "Islamic Revivalism and the Political Process in Malaysia." *Asian Survey* 21 (1981): 1040–1059.

"Ahmadiyah Can Worship, Kalla Says." *Jakarta Post,* June 11, 2008.

Ahmed, Anis. "Nearly 2,500 Apply to Contest the Bangladesh Election." *Reuters,* December 1, 2008.

Ahsan, Aayadul. "Inside the Militant Groups-6: Agency Advice for Ban on Them Ignored Since 2003." *Daily Star* (Bangladesh), August 26, 2005.

———. "Inside Militant Groups-1: Trained in Foreign Lands, They Spread Inland." *Daily Star* (Bangladesh), 5, no. 440, August 21, 2005.

"AK Party Sweeps Polls for a Third Single Term in Power." *Today's Zaman,* June 19, 2011.

Alagappa, Muthiah. *Political Legitimacy in Southeast Asia.* Stanford: Stanford University Press, 1995.

Al-Dekhayel, Abdulkarim. *Kuwait: Oil, State and Political Legitimation.* Ithaca: Ithaca Press, 2000.

"Aliran's ISA Watch." *Aliran Online.* http://www.aliran.com/oldsite/monthly/2001/3e.htm (accessed on March 15, 2009).

Amnesty International. "Malaysia: Amnesty International Human Rights Concerns." *Malaysia Report* (January–December 2005).

Ananta, Aris, and Evi Nurvidya Arifin. "Indonesia's Education Bill Opens Pandora's Box." *Straits Times*, October 6, 2003.

Aneja, Atul. "Six al Qaeda Suspects Detained in Bahrain." *The Hindu*, January 23, 2004.

"Another Killed in Poso Blast." *Jakarta Post*, September 10, 2006.

Ansari, Hamied. "The Islamic Militants in Egyptian Politics." *International Journal of Middle East Studies* 16 (1984): 123–144.

"Anti-Ahmadiyah Campaign Escalating." *Jakarta Post*, June 21, 2008.

Anwar, Zainah. "Islam: The Challenge of Extremist Interpretations." *Trends in Southeast Asia: Political and Security Outlook 2003*. Singapore: ISEAS, 2003.

Aragon, Lorraine. "Communal Violence in Poso, Central Sulawesi: Where People Eat Fish and Fish Eat People." *Indonesia* 72 (October 2001).

Aras, Bulent, and Gokhan Bacik. "The Mystery of Turkish Hizballah." *Middle East Policy* 9 (2002): 147–160.

Aras, Bulent, and Omer Caha. "*Fetullah Gulen* and His Liberal 'Turkish Islam' Movement." *Middle East Review of International Affairs* 4 (2000). http://meria.idc.ac.il/journal/2000/issue4/jv4n4a4.html.

Aris, Ananta, Evi Nurvidya Arifin, and Leo Suryadinata. *Emerging Democracy in Indonesia*. Singapore: ISEAS, 2005.

Arnaz, Farouk, Ronna Nirmala, and Camela Pasandaran. "Arrests Point to New Face of Terrorism." *Jakarta Globe*. April 23, 2011.

———. "Police Say Anti-Terror Program is Faulty." *Jakarta Globe*. June 27, 2011.

Aspinall, Edward. *Opposing Suharto: Compromise, Resistance, and Regime Change in Indonesia*. Stanford: Stanford University Press, 2005.

Atacan, Fulya. "Explaining Religious Politics at the Crossroad: AKP-SP." *Turkish Studies* 6 (2005): 187–199.

"Attacks Put Turkey in a Bind over Rebel Kurds. *International Herald Tribune*, May 24, 2007.

Ayubi, Nazih. *Political Islam: Religion and Politics in the Arab World*. London: Routledge, 1991.

Azam, Aziz, and Shamsul Amri Baharuddin. "The Religious, The Plural, the Secular and the Modern: A Brief Critical Survey on Islam in Malaysia." *Inter-Asia Cultural Studies* 5 (2004).

Azca, Muhammad Najib. "Security Forces in Ambon: From the National to the Local." In *Violence in Between: Conflict and Security in Archipelagic Southeast Asia*, edited by Damien Kingsbury, 231–254. Singapore: ISEAS, 2005.

Azra, Azyumardi. "Islam and Indonesian Transition to Democracy." In *Indonesia, Islam and Democracy: Dynamics in a World Context*. Jakarta: Equinox Forthcoming, 2006.

———. "The Islamic Factor in Post Suharto Indonesia." In *Indonesia, Islam and Democracy: Dynamics in a World Context*. Jakarta: Equinox Forthcoming, 2006.

———. "Communal Riots in Recent Indonesia." In *Indonesia, Islam and Democracy: Dynamics in a World Context*. Jakarta: Equinox Forthcoming, 2006.

Baakalini, Abdoo, Guiliana Denoeux, and Robert Springborg. *Legislative Politics in the Arab World: The Resurgence of Democratic Institutions.* Boulder: Lynne Rienner, 1999.

Bahar, Heymi. "The Real Winners and Losers of Turkey's July 2007 Elections." *Middle East Review of International Affairs* 11 (2007).

Bahry, Louay. "The Socioeconomic Foundations of Shiite Opposition in Bahrain." *Mediterranean Quarterly* (2000): 129–143.

————. "The Opposition in Bahrain: A Bellweather for the Gulf." *Middle East Policy* 5 (1997): 42–57.

Bardakoglu, Ali. "The Structure, Mission and Social Function of the Directorate of Religious Affairs." *Turkish Policy Quarterly* (2004): 29–36.

Barraclough, Simon. "The Dynamics of Coercion in the Malaysian Political Process." *Modern Asian Studies* 19 (1985): 797–822.

Barrett, Raymond. "Kuwait Walks a Tightrope on Iraq." *Daily Star,* December 14, 2004.

Barton, Greg. *Jemaah Islamiyah: Radical Islamism in Indonesia.* Singapore: Ridge Books, 2005.

————. "Theodicy, Theocracy and the Individual: The Challenge of Political and Jihadi Islamism to Pluralism and Liberal Democracy in Asia." Prepared for the Conference on Political Legitimacy in Islamic Asia, organized by Asia Research Institute. National University of Singapore, April 25–26, 2005.

————. "Islam, Islamism and Politics in Indonesia." In *Violence in Between: Conflict and Security in Archipelagic Southeast Asia,* edited by Damien Kingsbury, 75–103. Singapore: ISEAS, 2005.

————. *Abdurrahman Wahid Muslim Democrat, Indonesian President: A View from the Inside.* Honolulu: University of Hawaii Press, 2002.

Baswedan, Anies Rasyid. "Political Islam in Indonesia: Present and Future Trajectory." *Asian Survey* 44 (2004).

Bertrand, Jacques. *Nationalism and Ethnic Conflict in Indonesia.* Cambridge, UK: Cambridge University Press, 2004.

Boustany, Nora. "In Bahrain, Doubts about Reform." *Washington Post,* June 24, 2005, A28.

Bresnan John. *Managing Indonesia: The Modern Political Economy.* New York: Columbia University Press, 1993.

Browers, Michaelle. "The Origins and Architects of Yemen's Joint Meeting Parties." *International Journal of Middle East Studies* 39 (2007).

Brown, Nathan. "What's at Stake in Kuwait's Parliamentary Elections." *Carnegie Endowment for International Peace Web Commentary* (2008): 1. http://carnegieen-dowment.org/files/brown_kuwait_elections_FAQ_final.pdf (accessed on December 2, 2008).

————. "Pushing toward Party Politics: Kuwait's Islamic Constitution Movement." *Carnegie Endowment for International Peace Paper* 79 (2007).

Byman, Daniel, and Jerrold Green. *Political Violence and Stability in the States of the Northern Persian Gulf.* Arlington: Rand, 1999a.

————."The Enigma of Political Stability in the Persian Gulf Monarchy." *Middle East Review of International Affairs* 3 (1999b).

Cagaptay, Soner. "The November 2002 Elections and Turkey's New Political Era." *Middle East Review of International Affairs* 6 (2002): 42–48.

Camroux, David. "State Responses to Islamic Resurgence in Malaysia: Accommodation, Cooptation and Confrontation." *Asian Survey* 36 (1996): 852–868.

Carapico, Sheila. "Yemen and the Aden-Abyan Islamic Army." *Middle East Report Online* (October 11, 2000).

————. *Civil Society in Yemen.* Cambridge: Cambridge University Press, 1998.

————. "Introduction to Part One." In *Political Islam,* edited by Joel Beinin and Joe Stork, 29–33. Berkeley: University of California Press, 1997.

————. "Pluralism, Polarization, and Popular Politics in Yemen." In *Political Liberalization and Democratization in the Arab World: Volume 2, Comparative Experiences,* edited by Bahgat Korany, Rex Brynen, and Paul Noble, 241–266. Boulder: Lynne Rienner, 1995.

Chin, James Ung-Ho. "Malaysia: The Barisan Nasional Supremacy." In *How Asia Votes,* edited by John Fuh-Sheng Hsieh and David Newman. London: Chatham House Publishers, 2002.

Christianto, Dicky. "House, Gov't to Discuss Elections Bill." *Jakarta Post.* July 19, 2011.

"Cianjur 'Bans' Ahmadiyah." *The Jakarta Post,* September 29, 2005.

Collins, Elizabeth Fuller. "*Dakwah* and Democracy: The Significance of Partai Keadilan and Hizbut Tahrir." Volume 42, No 4 Forthcoming (2004). http://www.classics.ohiou.edu/faculty/collins.

————. "Partai Keadilan Sejahtera (PKS): Justice and Welfare Party or Prosperous Justice Party." Forthcoming (2002). http://www.classics.ohiou.edu/faculty/Collins.

————. "Indonesia: A Violent Culture." *Asian Survey* 42, No 4 (2002): 582–605.

Conboy, Ken. *The Second Front: Inside Asia's Most Dangerous Terrorist Network.* Jakarta: Equinox, 2006.

Crisp, Penny, and Santha Oorjitham. "How Can This Happen? Cults are Nothing New, but Raids on the Army Demand Some Answers." *Asiaweek* 26 (2000).

Crouch, Harold. *Government and Society in Malaysia.* New South Wales: Talisman, 1996.

Crystal, Jill, and Abdallah al-Shayeji. "The Pro-Democratic Agenda in Kuwait: Structures and Context." In *Political Liberalization and Democratization in the Arab World: Volume 2, Comparative Experiences,* edited by Bahgat Korany, Rex Brynen, and Paul Noble, 101–126. Boulder: Lynne Rienner, 1995.

Darwish, Adel. "Rebellion in Bahrain." *Middle East Review of International Affairs* 1 (1999).

Daud, Wan Mohd Nor Wan. *The Concept of Knowledge in Islam and its Implications for Education in a Developing Country.* London: Mansell, 1989.

Davidson, Lawrence. *Islamic Fundamentalism.* London: Greenwood Press, 1998.

Davidson, Roderic. *Turkey: A Short History.* England: Eothen Press, 1998.

"Death Penalty for Three Malaysians" *BBC News,* December 28, 2001. http://news. bbc.co.uk/2/hi/asia-pacific/1731503.stm.

Dekmejian, R. Hrair. *Islam in Revolution: Fundamentalism in the Arab World.* Syracuse: Syracuse University Press, 1995.

Dolmaci, Emine. "Turkish Elections See Highest Voter Turnout in Years." *Today's Zaman.* June 13, 2011.

"EFA Mid Decade Assessment Indonesia." EFA Secretariat, Ministry of National Education, Republic of Indonesia (2007).

Effendy, Bahtiar. *Jalan Tengah Politik Islam: Kaitan Islam, Demokrasi, dan Negara yang Tidak Mudah.* Jakarta: Ushul Press, 2005.

———. *Islam and the State in Indonesia.* Singapore: ISEAS, 2003.

Ehteshami, Anoushiravan. "Reform from Above: The Politics of Participation in the Oil Monarchies." *International Affairs* 79 (2003): 53–75.

Esmer, Yilmaz. "At the Ballot Box: Determinants of Voting Behavior." In *Politics, Parties and Elections in Turkey,* edited by Sabri Sayari and Yilmaz Esmer, 91–114. Boulder: Lynne Rienner, 2002.

Esposito, John. *Unholy War: Terror in the Name of Islam.* Oxford: Oxford University Press, 2002.

———. *The Islamic Threat: Myth or Reality.* Oxford: Oxford University Press, 1999.

Esposito, John, and James P Piscatori. "Democratization and Islam." *Middle East Journal* 45 (1991).

Esposito, John, and John Voll. *Islam and Democracy.* Oxford: Oxford University Press, 1996.

Fair, C. Christine. "Islam and Politics in Pakistan." In *The Muslim World After 9-11,* edited by Angel M. Rabasa, 247–296. Arlington: Rand, 2004.

Fair, C. Christine, and Sumit Ganguly. "Bangladesh on the Brink." *United States Institute of Peace. Reprinted from the Wall Street Journal* (2007). www.usip.org/ newsmedia/op_eds/2007/fair_wsj.html (accessed on December 4, 2008).

Faruqi, Shahad Saleem. "The Malaysian Constitution, the Islamic State and the Hudud Laws." In *Islam in Southeast Asia: Political, Social and Strategic Challenges for the 21st Century,* edited by K. S. Nathan and Mohammad Hashim Kamali, 256–277. Singapore: ISEAS, 2005.

Fealy, Greg. "A Conservative Turn: Liberal Islamic Groups have Prompted a Backlash." *Van Zorge Report* 10, no. 1 (2008).

———. "Indonesia's Islamic Parties in Decline." *Inside Story.* May 11, 2009.

———. "A Conservative Turn: Liberal Islamic Groups Have Prompted a Backlash." *Inside Indonesia,* no. 87 (2006).

———. "Parties and Parliament: Serving Whose Interests?" In *Indonesia Today: The Challenges of History,* edited by Grayson Lloyd and Shannon Smith. New York: Rowman and Littlefield, 2001.

———, and Bernhard Platzdasch. "The Masyumi Legacy: Between Islamist Idealism and Political Exigency." *Studia Islamika* 12 (2005): 77–99.

Feillard, Andree. "Traditionalist Islam and the State in Indonesia: The Road to Legitimacy and Renewal." In *Islam and the Era of Nation-States,* edited by Robert Hefner and Patricia Horavitch, 129–156. Honolulu: University of Hawaii Press, 1997.

"Fierce Gun Battle in Kuwait City." *BBCNEWS,* January 30, 2005.

"Four Arrested in Attack on Ahmadiyah." *Jakarta Post,* Jakarta, Malang, Semarang, February 7, 2006.

Friend, Theodore. *Indonesian Destinies.* Cambridge: Belknap Press, 2003.

Ganguly, Sumit. "The Rise of Islamist Militancy in Bangladesh." *United States Institute of Peace Special Report,* no. 171 (2006).

Gause, Gregory. "Bahrain Parliamentary Election Results: 25 November and 2 December 2006." *International Journal of Middle East Studies* 39 (2007): 170–171.

Ghadbian, Najib. "Political Islam and Violence." *New Political Science* 22 (2000): 77–88.

Ghannouchi, Rachid. "Participation in Non-Islamic Government." In *Liberal Islam,* edited by Charles Kurzman, 89–95. Oxford: Oxford University Press, 1998.

Goldstone, Jack. *States, Parties and Social Movements.* Cambridge: Cambridge University Press, 2005.

Goodwin, Jeff. *No Other Way Out: States and Revolutionary Movements, 1945–1991.* Cambridge: Cambridge University Press, 2001.

Guens-Ayata, Ayse, and Sencer Ayata. "Ethnic and Religious Bases of Voting." In *Politics, Parties and Elections in Turkey,* edited by Sabri Sayari and Yilmaz Esmer, 137–156. Boulder: Lynne Rienner, 2002.

"Gus Dur's PKB Loses Legal Battle." *Jakarta Post.* July 24, 2010.

"Hadi Visits Church, Declares Arson Attacks 'Un-Islamic,'" *Malaysiakini.* January 9, 2010.

Hafez, Mohammed. "From Marginalization to Massacres: A Political Process Explanation of GIA Violence in Algeria." In *Islamic Activism: A Social Movement Theory Approach,* edited by Quintan Wiktorowicz, 37–60. Bloomington: Indiana University Press, 2004.

———. *Why Muslims Rebel: Repression and Resistance in the Islamic World.* Boulder: Lynne Rienner Publishers, 2003.

Hafez, Mohammed, and Quintan Wiktorowicz. "Violence as Contention in the Egyptian Islamic Movement." In *Islamic Activism: A Social Movement Theory Approach,* edited by Quintan Wiktorowicz, 61–88. Bloomington: Indiana University Press, 2004.

Hamayotsu, Kikue. "Islam and Nation Building in Southeast Asia: Malaysia and Indonesia in Comparative Perspective." *Pacific Affairs* 75 (2002): 353–375.

———. "Beyond Faith and Identity: Mobilizing Islamic Youth in a Democratic Indonesia." *Pacific Review.* March 31, 2010.

Hamid, Ahmad Fauzi Abdul. "Islamic Doctrine and Violence: The Malaysian Case." Presented at the Conference on Anatomy of Religious Conflict in South and Southeast Asia, organized by the Institute of Defense and Strategic Studies (IDSS), Nanyang Technological University (NTU), Singapore, May 3–4, 2005.

————. "The Strategy of Islamic Education in Malaysia: An Islamic Movement's Experience." In *Islamic Education in South and Southeast Asia,* edited by S. Yunanto et al., 171–204. Jakarta: Ridep Institute, 2005.

Hari, Kurniawan. "House Passes Education Bill." *Jakarta Post,* June 12, 2003.

Harsanto, Damar. "Thousands Rally for Education Bill." *Jakarta Post,* June 11, 2003.

Hasan, Noorhaidi. "Islamist Party, Electoral Politics, and Da'wa Mobilization Among Youth: The Prosperous Justice Party in Indonesia." *RSIS Working Paper.* No. 184. October 22, 2009.

Hashim, Rosnani. *Educational Dualism in Malaysia: Implications for Theory and Practice* (South-East Asian Social Science Monographs). Oxford: Oxford University Press, 1996.

*Hasil-Hasil Muktamar XXX Nahdlatul Ulama.* November 21–26, 1999. At Pondok Pesantren Hidayatul Mubtadi'in Lirboyo Kediri, Jawa Timur.

*Hasil-Hasil Muktamar XXXI Nahdlatul Ulama.* November 28–December 2, 2004. At Asrama Haji Donohudan Boyoali, Java Timur.

Hefner, Robert. "Muslim Democrats and Islamist Violence." In *Rethinking Muslim Politics,* edited by Robert Hefner, 273–301. Princeton: Princeton University Press, 2005.

————. "Globalization, Governance and the Crisis of Indonesian Islam." Presented at the Conference on Globalization, State Capacity and Muslim Self-Determination, University of California-Santa Cruz, March 7–9, 2002.

————. *Civil Islam.* Princeton: Princeton University Press, 2000.

————. "Islamization and Democratization in Indonesia." In *Islam in the Era of Nation States,* edited by Robert Hefner and Patricia Horavitch, 75–128. Honolulu: University of Hawaii Press, 1997.

Hendytio, Medelina. "The State's Role in Social Development." *The Indonesian Quarterly* 32 (2004): 292–295.

Heper, Metin. "The Justice and Development Party Government and the Military in Turkey." *Turkish Studies* (2005): 215–231.

Hilley, John. *Malaysia: Mahathirism, Hegemony and the New Opposition.* London: Zed Books, 2001.

Hooker, Virginia Matheson. *A Short History of Malaysia.* New South Wales: Allen and Unwin, 2003.

Hossain, Golam. "Bangladesh in 1994: Democracy at Risk." *Asian Survey* 35 (1995): 171–178.

Howe, Marvine. *Turkey Today.* Boulder: Westview Press, 2000.

"Human Development Report 2007/2008: Fighting Climate Change: Human Solidarity in a Divided World." *United Nations Development Programme* (2008).

Human Development Report Statistics. Country sheet. http://hdr.undp.org/statistics/data/countries.cfm?c=IDN, July 24, 2006.

Human Rights Watch. "Breakdown: Four Years of Communal Conflict in Central Sulawesi." Report 14, December 2002.

Huntington, Samuel. "Clash of Civilizations." *Foreign Affairs* 72 (1993): 22–49.

———. *Political Order and Changing Societies.* New Haven: Yale University Press, 1969.

Hussein, Syed Ahmad. "Muslim Politics and the Discourse on Democracy." In *Democracy in Malaysia: Discourse and Practices,* edited by Francis Loh Kok Wah and Khoo Boo Tiek, 74–110. New South Wales: Curzon, 2002.

Hwang, Julie Chernov, and Mecham, Quinn. "Institutional Incentives and the Electoral Success of Islamist Parties: Explaining the Divergent Trajectories of the PKS in Indonesia and the AKP in Turkey," under review at *Studies in Comparative International Development.*

Ibrahim, Anwar. "Who Hijacked Islam." *Time Asia,* November 8, 2004.

"Indikator Pendidikan di Indonesia 2006/2007." *Departemen Pendidikan Nasional Badan Penelitian dan Pengembagan Pusat Statistik Pendidikan* (2007).

"Indonesia: Imprisonment of Usroh Activists in Central Java." *Amnesty International Report* (October 1988).

"Indonesia, Monitor Trials of Deadly Attack on Religious Minority." *Human Rights Watch.* June 16, 2011.

Inglehart, Ron, and Pippa Norris. "The True Clash of Civilizations." *Foreign Policy,* no. 135 (2003): 62–70.

International Crisis Group. "Indonesia: Implications of the Ahmadiyah Decree." *Asia Briefing* 78 (July 7, 2008).

———. "Indonesian Jihadism: Small Groups, Big Plans." *Asia Report.* #204. April 19, 2011.

———. "Indonesia: Jihadi Surprise in Aceh." *Asia Report.* #189. April 20, 2010.

———. "Indonesia: Christianization' and Intolerance." *Asia Briefing.* Jakarta/Brussels. November 20, 2010.

———. "Turkey and Europe: The Way Ahead." *Europe Report* 184 (August 17, 2007).

———. "Indonesia: Jemaah Islamiyah's Current Status." *International Crisis Group Asia Briefing* 63 (May 3, 2007).

———. "Bangladesh Today." *Asia Report* 121 (October 23, 2006).

———. "Yemen: Coping with Terrorism and Violence in a Fragile State." *Middle East Report,* no. 8 (January 8, 2003).

———. "Indonesia Backgrounder: How the Jemmah Islamiyah Terrorist Network Operates." *Asia Report* 43 (December 2002).

———. "Al-Qaeda in Southeast Asia: The Case of the 'Ngruki Network' in Indonesia." *Indonesia Briefing* Jakarta/Brussels (August 8, 2002).

———. "Indonesia Backgrounder: Jihad in Central Sulawesi." *ICG Asia Report.* No. 74. (February 3, 2004)

———. "Jihad di Indonesia: Poso di Ujung Tanduk." *Asia Report.* #127 (November 24, 2007)

———. "Indonesia: The Search for Peace in Maluku." *Asia Report* 31 (February 8, 2002).

"International Religious Freedom Report." *Bureau of Democracy, Human Rights and Labor.* 2010.

Iqbal, Allama Muhammed. *The Reconstruction of Religious Thought in Islam.* Lahore: Sh. Muhammad Ashraf, reprint, 1968.

"Islamist Parties Will Remain Divided Despite New Law." *Jakarta Post.* April 16, 2011.

Jahan, Rounaq. "Bangladesh in 2003: Vibrant Democracy or Destructive Politics." *Asian Survey* 44 (2004): 56–62.

———. "Bangladesh in 2002: Imperiled Democracy." *Asian Survey* 43 (2003): 222–229.

Jenkins, Gareth. "Muslim Democrats in Turkey." *Survival* 45 N (2003).

Johnsen, Gregory. "The Election Yemen Was Supposed to Have." *Middle East Report Online* (October 3, 2006).

"Joint Memorandum to Sukaham by BERSIH 2.0 and Suaram on Excessive Police Abuse of Powers During Perhimpunan BERSIH 2.0 on 9 July 2011." http://bersih.org/?p=4456#more-4456.

Juoro, Umar. "Indonesia." In *Political Party Systems and Democratic Development in East and Southeast Asia. Vol. 1. Southeast Asia,* edited by Wolfgang Sachsenroder and Ulrike Frings, 194–225. Aldershot: Ashgate, 1998.

Kamarudin, Raja Petra. "Someone Is Watching." *Malaysia Today,* March 6, 2006. *www.malaysia-today.net/loonyMY/2006/03/someone-is-watching.*

Karmon, Ely. "Radical Islamic Political Groups in Turkey." *Middle East Review of International Affairs* 1 (1997).

Kaye, Dalia Dassa, Frederick Wehrey, Audra Grant, and Dale Stahl. *More Freedom, Less Terror? Liberalization and Political Violence in the Arab World.* Arlington: Rand, 2008.

*Kekuatan Elektoral Partai-Partai Islam Menjelang Pemilu 2009.* Lembaga Survei Indonesia. Powerpoint presentation. Jakarta. September 2008, Mujani, Saiful, "Macrocondition, Policy, and Electoral Attitudes on the Eve of the 2009 Election: Public Opinion Trends." Jakarta, March 2009.

Kepel, Gilles. *Jihad: The Trail of Political Islam.* Cambridge: Belknap Press, 2002

———. *Muslim Extremism in Egypt: The Prophet and the Pharaoh.* Berkeley: University of California Press, 1985.

Khalik, Abdul. "State Still Fails to Provide Free Basic Education." *Jakarta Post,* July 17, 2005.

Khan, Zillur. "Bangladesh in 1992: Dilemmas of Democratization." *Asian Survey* 33 (1994): 150–156.

Khouw, Ida Indawati. "Guntur Refuses to Belong to the Silent Majority." *Jakarta Post* November 2, 2008.

Kimura, Ehito. "Indonesia in 2010." *Asian Survey.* Vol. 51. No. 1 (January/February 2011).

Kramer, Gudrun. "Islamist Notions of Democracy." In *Political Islam,* edited by Joel Beinin and Joe Stork, 71–82. Berkeley: University of California Press, 1997.

Krishnamoothy. "Marina ticks off gov't in its handling of Bersih." *Malaysiakini.* July 16, 2011.

Kuek Ser Kuang Keng. "Bersih 2.0 Hails Rally as Success." *Malaysiakini.* July 9, 2011.

Kurkcu, Ertugrul. "The Crisis of the Turkish State." *Middle East Report* (April–June 1999): 2–7.

Lancaster, John. "The Two Worlds of Bahrain; The Shiite Majority Wants Its Share of Sunni-Ruled Island's Prosperity. *Washington Post,* June 13, 1995, A15.

Lawson, Fred. "Repertoires of Contention in Contemporary Bahrain." In *Islamic Activism: A Social Movement Theory Approach,* edited by Quintan Wiktorowicz, 89–111. Bloomington: Indiana University Press, 2004.

Lee, Raymond. "Patterns of Religious Tension in Malaysia." *Asian Survey* 28 (1988): 400–418.

Lesser, Ian. "Turkey: 'Recessed' Islamic Politics and Convergence with the West." In *The Muslim World after 9/11,* edited by Angel Rabasa, Cheryl Benard, Peter Chalk, C. Christine Fair, Theodore Karasik, Rollie Lal, Ian Lesser, and David Thaler, 175–205. Arlington: Rand, 2004.

Lewis, Bernard. "What Went Wrong." *Atlantic Monthly* (January 2002). http://www.theatlantic.com/doc/200201/lewis (accessed on June 2, 2005).

———. "The Revolt of Islam." *New Yorker,* November 19, 2001, 50–62.

Liddle, R. William. "The Islamic Turn in Indonesia: A Political Explanation." *Journal of Asian Studies* 55 (1996): 613–634.

———. *Leadership and Culture in Indonesian Politics.* Sidney: ASAA Southeast Asia Publication Series of Allen and Unwin, 1996.

Liddle, R. William, and Saiful Mujani. "Indonesia in 2004: the Rise of Susilo Bambang Yudhoyono. *Asian Survey* 45 (2005): 119–126.

Lintner, Bertil. "Religious Extremism and Nationalism in Bangladesh." *Bangladesh Observer,* December 3, 2002.

———. "Bangladesh: Breeding Ground for Muslim Terror." *Asia Times,* September 21, 2002.

———. "Is Religious Extremism on the Rise in Bangladesh." *Jane's Intelligence Review* (May 2002).

Liow, Joseph. "Exigency or Expediency? Contextualizing Political Islam and the PAS challenge in Malaysian Politics." *Third World Quarterly* 25 (2004): 359–372.

Liow, Joseph Chinyong. "No God but God. Malaysia's 'Allah" Controversy." *Foreign Affairs.* February 10, 2010.

———. "Deconstructing Political Islam in Malaysia: UMNO's Response to PAS' Religio-Political Dialectic." Working Paper Series, Institute of Defense and Strategic Studies, Singapore, no. 45 (March 2003).

Loh, Francis. "Looking beyond the Pak Lah Factor." *Aliran Monthly* 3 (2004).

Machmudi, Yon. *Islamizing Indonesia.* PhD Dissertation. Australia National University. 2006

Madjid, Nurcholish. "The Necessity of Renewing Islamic Thought and Reinvigorating Religious Understanding." In *Liberal Islam,* edited by Charles Kurzman, 284–294. Oxford University Press: Oxford, 1998.

"Making the New Indonesia Work for the Poor." The World Bank. Jakarta. (2006).

"Malaysia." Amnesty International Human Rights Concerns Covering Events from January–December 2005.

*Malaysia Star Online.* "Malaysia 2008 General Election—Malaysia Decides," August 19, 2008. Web site: http://thestar.com.my/election.

Mango, Andrew. *The Turks Today.* New York: Overlook Press, 2004.

Manikas, Peter, and Dawn Emling. "Indonesia." In *Political Parties in Asia,* edited by Peter Manikas and Laura Thornton, 75–138. Washington, D.C.: National Democratic Institute for International Affairs, 2003.

Martinez, Patricia. "Mahathir, Islam and the New Malay Dilemma." In *Mahathir's Administration" Performance and Crisis in Governance,* edited by Ho Khai Leong and James Chin. Singapore: Times Books International, 2001.

Maulia, Erwide, and Andi Hajramurni. "Ahmadiyah Decree 'Bans Propagation, Not Private Prayer.'" *Jakarta Post,* June 14, 2008.

McAdam, Doug, Sidney Tarrow, and Charles Tilly. *Dynamics of Contention.* Cambridge: Cambridge University Press, 2001.

Meitzner, Marcus. "Indonesia in 2009: Electoral Contestation and Economic Resilience." *Asian Survey.* Vol 50/ 1.

"Mendagri: SKB Ahmadiyah di Tangan Menag." *Kompas,* June 9, 2008.

Miller, Judith. "God Has Ninety-Nine Names." New York: Touchstone Books, 1997.

Milne, RS, and Diane Mauzy. *Malaysian Politics under Mahathir.* London: Routledge, 1999.

———. "The Mahathir Administration in Malaysia: Discipline through Islam." *Pacific Affairs* 56 (1983–1984): 617–648.

Mohammad, Herry. "Rumah Baru Kaum Ahmadi." *Gatra,* July 9, 2008, 28–29.

Mujani, Saiful. "Macro Condition, Policy and Electoral Attitudes on the Eve of the 2009 Election: Public Opinion Trends." Powerpoint presentation for the World Bank, March 2009.

Munir, Lily. Comments as part of U.S.-Indonesia Society Conference, "In Search of a New Islamic Identity." http://www.usindo.org/Briefs/2003/In%20Search%20of%20Islamic%20Identity.htm, (Date accessed: November 11, 2003).

Mutalib, Hussin. *Islam and Ethnicity in Malay Politics.* Oxford: Oxford University Press, 1990.

Muzaffar, Chandra. *Islamic Resurgence in Malaysia.* Petaling Jaya: Penerbit Fajar Bakti SDN BhD, 1987.

Nair, Shanti. *Islam in Malaysia's Foreign Policy.* New York: Routledge, 1997.

Nakashima, Ellen. "Indonesian Islamic Party Reaps Rewards of Goodwill." *Washington Post,* July 14, 2005, A13.

Narli, Nilufer. "The Rise of the Islamist Movement in Turkey." *Middle East Review of International Affairs* 3 (1999). http://meria.idc.ac.il/journal/1999/issue3/jv3n3a4.html (accessed on November 2, 2005).

Nasr, Seyyed Vali Reza. *Islamic Leviathan: Islam and the Making of State Power.* Oxford: Oxford University Press, 2001.

———. "The Rise of Muslim Democracy." *Journal of Democracy* 16.2 (2005): 13–27.

Nathan, K. S. "Counter-Terror Cooperation in a Complex Security Environment." In *After Bali: The Threat of Terrorism in SE Asia,"* edited by Kumar Ramakrishna and See Seng Tan, 241–261. Singapore: Institute of Defense and Strategic Studies, 2003.

Noor, Farish. "Malaysia Boleh? PAS and the Malaysian Success Story." In *The Other Malaysia: Writings on Malaysia' Subaltern History,* 119–124. Kuala Lumpur: Silverfishbooks 2002.

Nugent, John Jr. "The Defeat of Turkish Hizballah as a Model for Counter-Terrorism Strategy." *Middle East Review of International Affairs* 8 (2004). http://meria.idc.ac.il/journal/2004/issue1/jv8n1a6.html (accessed on November 3, 2005).

Onis, Ziya. "The Political Economy of Islam and Democracy in Turkey: From the Welfare Party to the AKP." Unpublished revised draft (May 2005).

O'Rourke, Kevin. *Reformasi: The Struggle for Power in Post-Suharto Indonesia.* Crows Nest: Allen and Unwin, 2002.

Ozbudun, Ergun. *Contemporary Turkish Politics.* Boulder: Lynne Rienner, 2000.

Ozler, S. Iglu. "The Politics of the Gecekondu in Turkey: The Political Choices of Urban Squatters in National Elections." *Turkish Studies* (2000): 39–58.

"PAS Backs Caning, Rejects Bar's Premise." *Malaysiakini.* August 26, 2009.

Peletz, Michael. "Islam and the Cultural Politics of Legitimacy: Malaysia in the Aftermath of September 11." In *Remaking Muslim Politics: Pluralism, Contestation and Democratization,* edited by Robert Hefner, 240–272. Princeton: Princeton University Press, 2005.

"Pemerintah Tetap Akan Terbitkan SKB Soal Ahmadiyah." *Kompas,* June 2, 2008.

Perdana, Ari. "Poverty Alleviation and Social Insurance Policy: Past Lessons and Future Challenges." *Indonesian Quarterly* 32 (2004): 266–272.

Peterson, J.E. "Bahrain's First Steps towards Reform under Amir Hamad." *Asian Affairs* 33:2 (2002): 216–227.

Phillips, Sarah. "Foreboding about the Future in Yemen." *Middle East Report Online* (April 3, 2006).

———."Cracks in the Yemeni System." *Middle East Report Online* (July 28, 2005).

Piliang, Indra Jaya. "Manusia dan Politik PKS." *Media Indonesia,* July 27, 2005.

PKBI Yenny Wahid Ganti Nama Jadi PKBN," *Republika.* July 20, 2011

Platzdash, Bernhard. *Islamism in Indonesia.* Singapore: ISEAS (2009).

Pohl, Florian. 2006. "*Pesantren* and Global Integration." Paper presented at informal talk held at Center for Religion and Cross-Cultural Studies, Yogyakarta, Indonesia, May 6, 2006.

"Political Demonstration in Malaysia: Crackdown in KL." *Economist.* July 11, 2011.

Pope, Nicole, and Hugh Pope. *Turkey Unveiled.* New York: The Overlook Press, 1998.

Porter, Donald. *Managing Politics and Islam in Indonesia.* London: Routledge, 2002.

Rabasa, Angel. "Southeast Asia: Moderate Tradition and Radical Challenge." In *The Muslim World after 9-11,* edited by Angel Rabasa et.al, 367–412. Arlington: Rand, 2004.

———. "Overview." In *The Muslim World after 9-11,* edited by Angel M. Rabasa, 1–66. Arlington: Rand, 2002.

Rabasa, Angel, and John Haseman. *The Military and Democracy in Indonesia: Challenges, Politics and Power.* Arlington: Rand, 2002.

Rabi, Uzi. "The Kuwaiti Royal Family in the Postliberation Period: Reinstitutionalizing the 'First Among Equals' System in Kuwait." In *Middle East Monarchies: the Challenge of Modernity,* edited by Joseph Kostiner, 151–166. Boulder: Lynne Rienner, 2000.

Rahman. B. "Jihadi Terrorism: From Iraq to Kuwait." *South Asia Analysis Group,* New Delhi. Paper no. 1261 (February 21, 2005).

Ramage, Douglas. *Politics in Indonesia: Democracy, Islam and the Ideology of Tolerance.* London: Routledge. 1995.

Rashid, Harun ur. "The Rise of Islamic Extremism in Bangladesh." *Daily Star,* March 2, 2005.

Rashiduzzaman, M. "Bangladesh in 2001: The Election and a New Political Reality?" *Asian Survey* 42 (2002):183–191.

———. "Bangladesh in 2000: Searching for Better Governance." *Asian Survey* 41 (2001): 122–130.

Razak, Aidila. "Mat Sabu is PAS new deputy president. *Malaysiakini.* June 4, 2011.

Saragih, Bagus, BT "New Parties Aim Big, Despite Tougher Rules, Competition," *Jakarta Post.* May 11, 2011

"Repressive Laws." Human Rights Watch. http://www.hrw.org/campaigns/malaysia/2000/laws.htm (accessed on September 10, 2006).

Riaz, Ali. *Islamist Militancy in Bangladesh: A Complex Web.* London: Routledge, 2008.

———. "Bangladesh in 2004: The Politics of Vengeance and the Erosion of Democracy." *Asian Survey* 45 (2005): 112–118.

———. *God Willing: The Politics of Islamism in Bangladesh.* Lanham: Rowman and Littlefield, 2004.

Riddell, Peter. "Islamization, Civil Society and Religious Minorities in Malaysia." In *Islam in Southeast Asia: Political, Social and Strategic Challenges for the 21st Century,* edited by KS Nathan and Mohammad Hashim Kamali, 162–190. Singapore: ISEAS, 2005.

Robinson, Glenn. "Defensive Democratization in Jordan" *International Journal for Middle East Studies* 30 (1998).

Robinson, Richard, and Vedi R. Hadiz. *Reorganizing Power in Indonesia.* London: Routledge, 2004.

Roff, William. "Patterns of Islamization in Malaysia, 1890s–1990s: Exemplars, Institutions and Vectors." *Journal of Islamic Studies* 9 (1998): 210–228.

Roy, Oliver. *Failure of Political Islam.* Cambridge: Harvard University Press, 1994.

Rubin, Michael. "Green Money, Islamist Politics in Turkey." *Middle East Quarterly* (2005): 13–23.

Ryan, Curtis. "Reform Retreats amid Jordan's Political Storms." *Middle East Report Online* (June 10, 2005).

Said, Edward. "The Clash of Ignorance." *The Nation*, October 22, 2001. http://www.thenation.com/doc/20011022/said (accessed on May 3, 2005).

Sakallioglu, Umit Cizre. "Parameters and Strategies of Islam-State Interaction in Republican Turkey." *International Journal of Middle East Studies* 28 (1996): 231–251.

Sartori, Giovanni. *Parties and Party Systems: A Framework for Analysis.* New York: Cambridge University Press, 1976.

Sawitri, Adisti Sukma. "Government Told to Fix Health Care Scheme." *The Jakarta Post,* September 21, 2007.

Sayari, Sabri. "The Changing Party System." In *Politics, Parties and Elections in Turkey,* edited by Sabri Sayari and Yilmaz Esmer, 9–32. Boulder: Lynne Rienner, 2002.

Schulze, Kirsten. "Between Conflict and Peace: Tsunami Aid and Reconstruction in Aceh." London School of Economics Human Security Report, November 2005.

Schwarz, Adam. *A Nation in Waiting: Indonesia's Search for Stability.* NSW: Allen & Unwin, 2004.

Schwartz, Stephen. *The Two Faces of Islam.* New York: Anchor Books, 2003.

Schwedler, Jillian. *Faith in Moderation: Islamist Parties in Jordan and Yemen.* Cambridge: Cambridge University Press, 2007.

———. "The Islah Party in Yemen: Political Opportunities and Coalition Building in a Transitional Polity." In *Islamic Activism: A Social Movement Theory Approach,* edited by Quintan Wiktorowicz, 205–230. Indianapolis: Indiana University Press, 2004.

———. "Occupied Ma'an: Jordan's Closed Military Zone." *Middle East Report* (December 3, 2002).

———. "Don't Blink: Jordan's Democratic Opening and Closing." *Middle East Report* (July 3, 2002). http://www.merip.org/mero/mero070302.htm (accessed on November 20, 2008).

"Seorang Besar Dengan Banyak Teman." *Tempo Laporan Khusus 100 Tahun Mohammad Natsir. Edisi,* July 14–20, 2008, 83.

Shamsul, AB. "Identity Construction, Nation Formation and Islamic Revivalism in Malaysia." In *Islam in the Era of Nation States,* edited by Robert Hefner and Patricia Horavitch, 207–230. Honolulu: Hawaii University Press, 1997.

Shehabuddin, Elora. "Bangladesh in 1999: Desperately Seeking a Responsible Opposition." *Asian Survey* 40 (2000): 181–188.

———. "Bangladesh in 1998: Democracy on the Ground." *Asian Survey* 39 (1999): 148–154.

Shome, Anthony. *Malay Political Leadership.* New York: Routledge/Curzon, 2002.

Sidel, John. *Riots, Pogroms, Jihad: Religious Violence in Indonesia.* Ithaca: Cornell University Press, 2006.

Singer, Peter W. "Pakistan's Madrassahs: Ensuring a System of Education Not Jihad" *America's Response to Terrorism Analysis Paper* no. 14: Brookings Institution (2001).

Sivan, Emanuel. "Why Radical Muslims Aren't Taking over Governments. *Middle East Quarterly* 4, no.4 (December 1997).

———. *Radical Islam: Medieval Theology and Modern Politics.* New Haven: Yale University Press, 1985.

Smith, Anthony. "Indonesia: One State, Many States, Chaotic State?" *International Politics and Security Studies* 1 (2001).

Smith, Craig. "Threats and Responses: Anti-Terror Arrest. Kuwait Says a Senior Qaeda Member Has Confessed to Planning 2 Attacks in Yemen." *New York Times,* November 17, 2002.

Snyder, Jack. *From Voting to Violence.* New York: W.W Norton and Company, 2000.

*Social Safety New: Providing Hope to Indonesia's Underprivileged.* Jakarta: Badan Perencanaan Pembangunan Nasional (BAPPENAS), 2004.

Soroush, Abdolkarim, Mahmoud Sadri, and Ahmad Sadri. *Reason, Freedom and Democracy in Islam: Essential Writings of Abdolkarim Soroush.* Oxford: Oxford University Press, 2002.

Sufa, Theresia. "Bogor Disperses Ahmadiyah, Sends Followers Home. *Jakarta Post,* July 17, 2005.

———. "Thousands Besiege Ahmadiyah Complex." *Jakarta Post,* July 16, 2005.

Sukma, Rizal. "Ethnic Conflict in Indonesia: Causes and the Question for Solution." In *Ethnic Conflicts in Southeast Asia,* edited by Kusuma Snitwongse and W. Scott Thompson, 1–42. Singapore: ISEAS, 2005.

Sulaiman, Sadek. "Democracy and *Shura.*" In *Liberal Islam,* edited by Charles Kurzman, 96–100. Oxford University Press: Oxford, 1998.

Suparto. "Reforming *Pesantren:* While Reform of Islamic Education is Necessary, Secularization is Not." *Inside Indonesia* (January–March 2004).

"Survey Indonesia: Time to Deliver." *The Economist.* http://www.economist.com/surveys/displayStory.cfm?story_id=3444238 (accessed on December 9, 2004).

Suryadinata, Leo. *Elections and Politics in Indonesia.* Singapore: ISEAS, 2002.

Suryana, A'an. "Ahmadiyah Fights Back—In a Civilized Way." *Jakarta Post,* September 30, 2005.

Suwarni, Yuli Tri. "W. Java Police Back Closure of Churches." *Jakarta Post,* February 26, 2006.

Szyliowicz, Joseph. "Education and Political Development." In *Politics in the Third Turkish Republic,* edited by Metin Heper and Ahmet Evin, 147–160. Boulder: Westview Press, 1994.

Tan, See Seng, and Kumar Ramakrishna."Interstate and Intrastate Dynamics in Southeast Asia's War on Terror." *SAIS Review* XXIV (2004) 91–105.

Tank, Pinar. "Political Islam in Turkey: A State of Controlled Secularity. *Turkish Studies* 6 (2005): 3–19.

Tarrow, Sidney. *Power in Movement: Social Movements and Contentious Politics.* Cambridge: Cambridge University Press, 1998.

*Tempo Laporan Khusus 100 Tahun Mohammad Natsir. Edisi* 14–20 July 2008 [Tempo Magazine Special Issue: 1000 Years Mohammad Natsir]

Terhalle, Maximillian. "Are the Shia Rising." *Middle East Policy Council* (2007): 69–83.

Tessler, Mark. "The Origins of Popular Support for Islamist Movements: A Political Economy Analysis." In *Islam, Democracy and the State in North Africa,* edited by John P. Entelis, 93–126. Indianapolis: Indiana University Press, 1997.

Thaler, David. " The Middle East: The Cradle of the Muslim World." In *The Muslim World after 9-11,* edited by Angel M. Rabasa, 69–144. Arlington: Rand, 2004.

Thomas, Murray R. "The Islamic Revival and Indonesian Education." *Asian Survey* 28 (1998): 897–915.

Tiek, Khoo Boo. *Beyond Mahathir: Malaysian Politics and its Discontents.* London: Zed Books, 2003.

Tjhin, Christine, and Tommy Legowo. "Some Lessons of the Democratization Process: Post-Legislative and pre-Presidential Elections." *Indonesian Quarterly* 32 (2) (2004).

Toprak, Binnaz. "The State, Politics and Religion in Turkey." In *State, Democracy and the Military: Turkey in the 1980s,* edited by Metin Heper and Ahmet Evin, 119–136. Boulder: Westview Press, 1988.

Turan, Ilter. "Evolution of the Electoral Process." In *Politics in the Third Turkish Republic,* edited by Metin Heper and Ahmet Evin, 49–62. Boulder: Westview Press, 1994.

"Turkish Kurds in Iraq: We Want Peace, They Say." *The Economist,* August 31, 2006.

"Two Years of Party Performance: A Public Evaluation." Lembaga Survey Indonesia (LSI) National Survey Findings (March 2006).

Unidjaja, Fabiola Desy. "Megawati Eats Her Words, Signs Education Law." *Jakarta Post,* July 17, 2003.

United Nations Development Program-Bappenas-Indonesian Bureau of Statistics. "Towards a New Consensus: Democracy and Human Development in Indonesia." *Indonesia Human Development Report 2001* (2001).

Van Bruinessen, Martin. "Traditionalist and Islamist Pesantren in Contemporary Indonesia. Paper presented at the ISIM workshop on The Madrasa in Asia, Leiden, Netherlands, May 23–24, 2004.

———. "Genealogies of Islamic Radicalism in Post-Suharto Indonesia." *Southeast Asia Research* 10 (2002): 117–151.

———. "The Violent Fringes of Indonesia's Radical Islam." Background information after the Bali Bombing of October 2002. Extended version of article published in ISIM Newsletter11 (December 2002): 1–9. www.let.uu.nl/~martin. vanbruinessen/personal/publications/violent_fringe.htm.

———. "Islamic State or State Islam? Fifty Years of State-Islam Relations in Indonesia in: Ingrid Wessel (Hrsg.), *Indonesien am Ende des 20. Jahrhunderts.* Hamburg: Abera-Verlag, (1996), 19–34.

Van Klinken, Gerry. "The Maluku Wars: Bringing Society Back In." *Indonesia* 71 (2001).

Van Zorge, Heffernan, and Associates. "Clamping Down on Cults." X/1, January 2008.

————. "Grade Point Average" *Van Zorge Report on Indonesia* VIII/18, July 12, 2006.

————. "Creeping Sharia?" *Van Zorge Report on Indonesia* VIII/ 8, May 9, 2006.

————. "A Provincial Snapshot" *Van Zorge Report on Indonesia* VIII/8, May 9, 2006.

Vertigans, Stephen. *Islamic Roots and Resurgence in Turkey.* London: Praeger, 2003.

Voll, John. *Islam: Continuity and Change in the Modern World.* Boulder: Westview Press, 1982.

Weir, Shelagh. "A Clash of Fundamentalisms: Wahhabism in Yemen." *Middle East Report Online,* no. 204 (1995): 22–26.

Weiss, Meredith L. "Edging Toward a New Politics in Malaysia." *Asian Survey* Vol 49. Issue 5. (2009).

Welsh, Bridget. "Real Change? Elections in the Reformasi Era." In *The State of Malaysia: Ethnicity, Equity and Reform,* edited by Edmund Terence Gomez. New York: Routledge/Curzon, 2004.

Welsh, Bridget. "Five Promising Ideas from PAS' New Line-Up." *Malaysiakini,* June 4, 2011.

White, Jenny. B. *Islamist Mobilization in Turkey; A Study in Vernacular Politics.* Seattle: University of Washington Press, 2002.

Whitlock, Craig, and Steve Coll. "Terrorism Tempers Shifts to Openness." *Washington Post,* April 18, 2005, A01.

Wiktorowicz, Quintan. "Introduction: Islamic Activism and Social Movement Theory." In *Islamic Activism: A Social Movement Theory Approach,* edited by Quintan Wiktorowicz, 1–37. Bloomington: Indiana University Press, 2004.

————. *The Management of Islamic Activism: Salafis, the Muslim Brotherhood, and State Power in Jordan.* New York: State University of New York Press, 2001.

Williams, Clive. "The Question of 'Links' between Al Qaeda and Southeast Asia." In *After Bali: The Threat of Terrorism in SE Asia,"* edited by Kumar Ramakrishna and See Seng Tan, 83–96. Singapore: Institute of Defense and Strategic Studies, 2003.

Wong Chin Huat. "No Compromise with Terrorism." *Malaysiakini.* January 11, 2010.

Wright, Robin. "Islam and Democracy: Two Visions of Reformation." *Journal of Democracy* 7 (1996): 64–75.

————, and Michael Abramowitz. "US Warns Iraq to Halt Rebel Raids on Turkey." *Washington Post,* October 23, 2007, A01.

Yaphe, Judith. "Islamic Radicalism in the Arabian Peninsula: Growing Risks." *National Defense University Strategic Forum,* no. 67 (March 1996).

Yavuz, Hakan. *Islamic Political Identity in Turkey.* Oxford: Oxford University Press, 2003.

————. "Political Islam and the Welfare (Refah) Party in Turkey." *Comparative Politics* (1997): 63–81.

Yesilada, Birol. A. "The Virtue Party." *Turkish Politics* 10 (2002): 62–79.

————. "Realignment and Party Adaptation: The Case of the Refah and Fazilet Parties." In *Politics, Parties and Elections in Turkey,* edited by Sabri Sayari and Yilmaz Esmer, 157–178. Boulder: Lynne Rienner, 2002.

Yunanto, Sri. "The Logic behind the Growth of Militant Islamic Movements." In *Militant Islamic Movements in Indonesia and Southeast Asia,* edited by S. Yunanto et.al. Jakarta: Friedrich-Ebert Stiftung; Ridep Institute, 2003.

Yunanto, Sri, and Badrudin Harun. "Terminology, History and Categorization." In *Islamic Education in South and Southeast Asia: Diversity, Problems and Strategy,* edited by Sri Yunanto, 19–36. Jakarta: The Ridep Institute, 2006.

Zalkapli, Adib. "PAS Backs Use of Allah by Christians." *Malaysian Insider.* January 5, 2010. http://www.themalaysianinsider.com/index.php/malaysia/48498-pas-backs-use-of-allah-by-christians.

Zengin, Eyup, and Askerov, Ali. "State Formation and Oil: Kuwait and Qatar." *Journal of Qafqaz University* 6 (2000): 43–50.

Zubaida, Sami. "Turkish Islam and National Identity." *Middle East Report Online* (April–June 1996): 2–7.

# Index

CPSIA information can be obtained at www.ICGtesting.com
Printed in the USA
BVOW032346040112

279753BV00005B/3/P